ARTEM KUDELIA PHD

Hypnotherapy Fundamentals

Complete Guide

Access PSYCHOLOGY BOOKS FOR FREE!

Scan the QR code and subscribe to be the first to receive pre-releases of new psychology books with an applied, popular science, and medical focus.

Join our community of passionate readers and enjoy valuable insights, scientific breakthroughs, and thought-provoking academic works in exchange for your 5-star ratings and enthusiastic reviews.

YOUR FEEDBACK MATTERS!

First edition

ISBN: 9798853612082

This book was professionally typeset on Reedsy.
Find out more at reedsy.com

Hypnotic trance is a unique psychological state with specific physiological attributes that, at first glance, resemble sleep and are characterized by the individual's behavior under the control of a different state of consciousness, distinct from normal consciousness, defined for convenience as the unconscious or subconscious.

Milton Erickson

Contents

Foreword   iii

Preface   vi

Acknowledgement   viii

1   History of Trance Practices and Hypnotherapy   1

2   Psychopathological Profile of Hypnotizable Individuals   46

Psychoanalytic Profiling   52

Imprints of the Perinatal Sphere   55

Psychopathological Profiling   57

Hysteroid Personality Profile   60

Paranoid Personality Profile   65

Psychopathic Personality Profile   70

Obsessive-Compulsive Personality Profile   76

Schizoid Personality Profile   79

Epileptoid Personality Profile   83

Schizoid Personality Profile   86

Manic-Depressive Personality Profile   102

Psychopathological Personality Accents   106

3   Hypnotic Phenomena   108

4   The Use of Hypnotic Phenomena in Psychotherapeu-
tic Practice   146

5   Hypnotic Trance Depth Levels   151

Eugene Katkov's Model of Hypnotic Trance Levels   153

New Model of Hypnotic Trance Levels   155

6   Motives of Trance and Their Application in Psychotherapy   162

7   Styles and Vectors of Hypnotic Work   167

Hypnoanalytic Vector   170

Suggestive Vector   173

Provocative Vector   187

Humanistic Approach   195

Behavioral Vector   200

Transpersonal Vector   216

Cognitive Vector   226

Somatic Vector   239

8   Structural Elements of Hypnotic Work   245

9   Psychogeographical Direction in Hypnotic Work   250

10   Opponents of the Existence of Hypnosis   262

11   Hypnosis and Self-hypnosis in Oncology   266

12   Stage Hypnosis   268

13   Archetypal Sound Rhythms of Ancient Shamans and...   276

14   Neurotransmitters and Hypnotic Suggestion   282

15   Afterword   292

16   Bibliography   293

About the Author   304

Also by Artem Kudelia PhD   305

Foreword

The aim of the author of this book is twofold - to acquaint readers with the intricate and profound world of hypnosis and to showcase its "artistry." Until now, hypnosis has been relatively rarely associated with conscientious clinical practice in the eyes of the public and even within certain professional circles. When people hear the word "hypnosis," the first things that come to mind for the so-called "lay psychologist" (and not only for them but also for respectable and successful psychologists with professional education) are "tricks," "deception," "coding," "circus," "charlatanism," and the like. Many individuals are still ensnared by cultural myths about hypnosis that originated during the time of Mesmer.

Meanwhile, the number of psychotherapists, who confidently assert that hypnosis plays a vital role in their professional lives and is a key to success in their work is steadily growing. Numerous practitioners in the field of clinical psychology observe that incorporating suggestive influence as a primary component of intervention leads to profound transformations in clients' thinking, emotions, and behaviors. Some of the beneficial effects of hypnosis encompass "establishing a close collaboration with the client," the ability to "precisely target various motivational, cognitive, or behavioral mechanisms of mental disorders," achieving the "optimal combination of effective intervention strategies and methods," "aligning the client's attitude towards therapy as a whole," and inducing "profound, stable, and long-lasting changes" in personality and psyche, among others.

The presented book can prove highly valuable for both professionals and newcomers. Professionals have the opportunity to systematize and organize their existing knowledge about fundamental trance phenomena (the authors describe approximately forty phenomena), their manifestations, and their utilization in psychotherapeutic practice. Readers receive this invaluable information firsthand: the authors generously share their own experiences as well as examples from the practices of renowned international specialists (R. Bandler, S. Gilligan, L. Le Cron, B. Hellinger, M. Erickson, A. Danilov, V. Raikov, etc.). The authors are convinced that virtually any trance phenomenon can be utilized as a metaphor for transformation. To achieve this, they have developed a step-by-step model for utilizing hypnotic phenomena in psychotherapy.

For beginners, this book can serve as a guide to "getting started." The main reason that this guide can be beneficial for aspiring hypnotherapists is that it dispels their fear and concerns about "doing hypnosis incorrectly."

The book allows readers to obtain a comprehensive understanding of the history of hypnotherapy, the theoretical concepts underlying hypnosis, and the practical issues that arise when attempting to induce trance. By mastering this captivating text, the discerning reader, striving for excellence, can successfully acquire the essential skills of using hypnosis in psychotherapy. The authors have taken care of readers who aspire not only to know but also to be able to "move from words to action," to test the effectiveness of various hypnotic phenomena. For this purpose, step-by-step algorithms of trance work are provided, encompassing the procedural experience of both international and the authors' own extensive years of psychotherapeutic practice.

The system of beliefs and practices underlying the concept of "depth of hypnotic trance" has been significantly organized. Paying careful attention to the legacy of A. Forel and, unfortunately, the often-forgotten talented physiologist and hypnotist E. Katkov from Kharkiv, the authors have developed and substantiated a practical multi-level model (consisting of 12 levels) of the hypnotic trance.

Like any good and seemingly purely practical manual, this work stimulates the reader's reflections on scientific and research topics. Most of these topics revolve around three fundamental directions.

Firstly, there is the problem of seeking rigorous experimental evidence of the effectiveness of psychotherapy (i.e., ensuring the empirical basis of psychotherapy). Inducing trance (or, conversely, refraining from inducing it) can be used as a means of varying the independent variable, enabling confident statements about causal relationships in the process of psychotherapeutic interventions.

Secondly, it is the emergence of additional impetus in memory research (episodic, implicit, emotional, motor, etc.). The issue of memory has long been and still remains relevant for the Kharkov psychological school. It is worth mentioning that both authors are from Kharkov and are therefore representatives of this scientific school. Their perspective on the manifestations and resources of memory is analyzed in connection with the problem of repressed memories and providing elegant access to them in the process of trance work.

Thirdly, it is the interconnection between the authors' practical developments in the field of hypnotherapy and the achievements of cognitive neuroscience. These advancements have become possible in recent times due to the development of state-of-the-art brain activity visualization techniques, including functional magnetic resonance imaging (fMRI). The authors seek to answer not only the question of what hypnosis is from a psychological perspective but also the question of its physiological mechanisms.

While acquainting oneself with this guide, even the most skeptical reader of hypnosis becomes filled with optimism. The authors are highly persuasive in their arguments when they demonstrate that a psychotherapist can use any potential that a client possesses. Any response that the client provides in any specific situation, including their own symptoms, can be utilized. The book is filled with significant didactic material, making it an indispensable manual, especially for psychology and medical students interested in mastering not only the art of hypnotherapy but also achieving excellence in psychotherapy as a whole.

Preface

In the modern world, hypnotic suggestion has a multifaceted context of implementation. Hypnosis is familiar to many people who are not involved with it in a professional context and primarily understand it through social myths that abound in society. This book will be devoted to a comprehensive description of the process of hypnosis, with a particular focus on the psychotherapeutic context and working with trance in patients who require psychotherapeutic assistance. We will cover the psychological, physiological, cultural, and social aspects that provide an opportunity to view hypnosis as a mysterious and mystical process, a philosophy, and a neurochemical process in the human brain, as well as a socio-cultural phenomenon rooted in all psycho-spiritual traditions of the world.

Therefore, one of the emphases of this work will be an anthropological context, narrating the history of the formation of conceptions of hypnosis in various parts of the world and how this psycho-spiritual phenomenon became part of the practice of modern medicine in psychiatry, psychotherapy, and surgical anesthesia. What exactly is hypnosis from the perspective of psychology and physiology? What is the correct definition of such a process? Where can this phenomenon be applied in a social context? What personal characteristics of an individual will determine their ability to enter the state of hypnosis quickly or slowly, deeply or superficially? What can facilitate or hinder the induction of hypnosis? What knowledge and skills are necessary for a hypnotherapist to create hypnotic induction and interact with the patient in a trance state? We will seek answers to these questions in this book.

A part of the work will be devoted to general cognitive information, while another part will focus on the description of direct methods and techniques for inducing hypnosis. By mastering these techniques, you will be able to acquire a basic level of proficiency in the practice of hypnosis. It is better to practice other examples in training groups, as there are many nuances that are difficult to convey through text alone, and real demonstrations and trainer comments are necessary in the process of training work.

The communicative aspect of hypnosis can extend beyond the psychotherapeutic context, where we can discover that at a deeper level, hypnosis techniques are simply advanced forms of communication related to emotional intelligence, which is an integral part of the human experience and the ability to change one's own states and the states of others. To some extent, inducing trance is the ability to effectively convey information to another person. It is a tool that is not inherently moral, and depending on whose hands it falls into, it can heal or harm.

Therefore, a part of the work will be dedicated to discussing how people, even those unfamiliar with the phenomenon of hypnosis, regularly apply it in their communication, often creating non-ecological states in their interlocutors. Stage hypnosis, as one of the entertainment contexts, is highly controversial and also not very ecological, and it will also be part of our discussion, where we will touch upon the main strategies used by stage hypnotists. Essentially, their methods and the methods of psychotherapeutic hypnosis have a common root, but the techniques, practices, and phenomenology of trance can significantly differ.

Many individuals involved in mysticism and occultism apply a large number of hypnotic practices, where they perceive and define hypnotic phenomena as supernatural, magical manifestations. We will not discuss all of these situations in general, but a significant part of such phenomena can be recreated by an individual with hypnosis skills through fairly simple procedures. We will discuss and explore all of these topics throughout the book. For starters, let's begin with the history of the formation of conceptions of altered states of perception, hypnosis, trance, and various practices that have helped achieve them at different times.

Acknowledgement

I would like to express our gratitude to my teachers in the field of psychotherapy and hypnotherapy: Betty Erickson, Stephen Gilligan, Jean Becchio, and Claude Viro. I would also like to thank the students and patients who participated in scientific and psychotherapeutic research, as well as all the individuals who have contributed in various ways to the creation of this book.

1

History of Trance Practices and Hypnotherapy

At this very place, by the throne, resides the beautiful and youthful god of sleep, Hypnos. Noiselessly, he soars above the earth on his wings, holding poppy heads in his hands and pouring a soporific elixir from his horn. With his wondrous wand, he gently touches the eyes of humans, softly closing their lids and immersing mortals in a sweet slumber. Mighty is the god Hypnos, against whom neither mortals nor gods nor even the thunderer Zeus can resist. Hypnos closes his eyes as well, plunging him into a deep sleep.

   Myths of ancient Greece

If we consider the historical perspective, the phenomenon of trance induction and self-induced trance has existed throughout the entire existence of rational human beings. The presence of the social role of a shaman within a group, a person who assumed multifaceted functions as a philosopher, educator, and healer, has been consistent.

Modern anthropology indicates that the history of shamanism dates back 40,000 to 60,000 years, from the early stages of the shamanic role to its later manifestations in contemporary activities. Archaic shamanism played a multifaceted and socially significant role, complementing the role of a leader dominant in external social aspects of governance. The shaman took on the role of explaining, often, the inexplicable, the unseen, and the unknown, which could now be termed spiritual or numinous.

Mapping reality, giving names to the inexplicable, attempting to understand the structure of the universe and its governing principles—shamanism largely anticipated religion, being more of a pre-religion, a philosophy as an aspect of life wisdom, and an empirical criterion for understanding the world.

The shaman is a person standing on the border between the living and the dead, between the realm of the conscious and the realm of dreams, between the apparent and the unseen, between the comprehensible and the incomprehensible. The shaman serves as a connecting link between the concepts of duality within the human mind, accustomed to dividing everything into

2

good and bad, white and black, understandable and incomprehensible. This is precisely what defines the fundamental difference between humans and animals—their reasoning, which, in the overwhelming majority of cases, is unburdened by concepts of morality and duality.

Where there is morality, there is duality, and naturally, a latent sense arises to return to a feeling of wholeness and connection. Mapping reality primarily served as a natural psychotherapeutic function in ancient tribes because when you understand, or think you understand, the world, the level of anxious reactions naturally decreases. Every time we give something a name, we gain a sense of control. However, mapping is merely the first step, followed by the creation of a significant number of practices, patterns, and forms of activity with a specific goal: to interact with the unseen, the incomprehensible, and the unknown.

Creation of rituals whose essence was to induce altered states of consciousness aimed at solving pressing problems: emotional, physical, social, peaceful, military, agrarian, and so on. This is where we begin to recognize the fundamental roots of hypnotic influence and the fact that the intention behind modern clinical psychotherapeutic or anesthesiological hypnosis bears little difference from ancient archaic forms of shamanic chanting and dancing.

These traditions date back thousands or even tens of thousands of years, each with its own history, phenomenology, culture, and interpretation of reality. While there are differences in the details, the abstract cores of shamanic traditions are similar, possessing almost identical essences. The variations lie in the accents.

Without delving into a detailed historical exploration of shamanism, let us limit ourselves to understanding this form of activity as the origin, archetype, and primal form of the shaman—a transceiver capable of embodying multiple hypostases, external social roles, as well as internal numinous experiences accessible primarily to the individual rather than the crowd.

The ritualized process of altering states carries another crucial aspect—sublimation and ennoblement. In ancient Hinduism, the ability to perform ritual psychospiritual rites was a priority for the Brahmins, a caste of scholars and priests who considered this privilege one of the main criteria that defined a person's humanity. In other words, the ability to perform rituals aimed at altering consciousness, both in others and in oneself, and through these altered states, gain access to knowledge, skills, healing, and new conceptions of the world.

An important conclusion that can be drawn from these findings is that the primal prototype of the trans-like, hypnotic suggestor can play a crucial and prevailing role in the evolutionary process, both at the social group and intrapersonal levels. In subsequent chapters of our book, we will revisit how the trance process influences learning and the restoration of healthy mental and somatic homeostasis in individuals. For now, let us direct our attention to its more social and archaic aspects.

Beyond basic needs such as food, sex is also a fundamental aspect of human personality. If we carefully analyze various types of activities in ancient and modern humans, ranging from highly intellectual individuals to simpler ones, from young to elderly, we will discover that in every person's life, there are tools for altering states of consciousness that manifest in sublimated and non-sublimated forms. In other words, sex, sleep, and indulging in delicious food are natural instruments for altering states of consciousness.

However, the moment a person discovers substitutes for instinctual trance forms of activity, their personality undergoes radical changes, becoming more complex due to increased values and beliefs and the alteration of the value-motivational hierarchy. Aggression and excessive eroticism, which were more characteristic of ancient humans, gradually gave way to other forms of activity. Complete replacement only occurs in a few individuals, often those associated with shamanic or other psychospiritual orientations.

We can also observe that the abandonment of instinctual trance for specific periods of time in many spiritual cultures is primarily an initiatory act, where the adept renounces the animal in favor of the numinous to acquire personal strength, self-control, willpower, and the ability to face life's difficulties, undergoing significant social transformations.

The trans-like hypnotic process allows individuals to train their volitional qualities, such as volition, goal-setting, and decision-making, and it enhances the activity of the prefrontal lobes of the brain's cerebral hemispheres, as understood in modern neurophysiology. However, it is worth noting that it is the sublimating trance that leads to the latter.

In shamanism, the process of acquiring volitional qualities was equated with the process of gaining personal power, enabling individuals to live their lives, fulfill their social roles, and fulfill their destinies more effectively. The sacralization of trance as an evolutionary social and personal process can be traced as a structural element in all psycho-spiritual systems in the world.

Hypnosis, on the other hand, in a more contemporary sense, is merely a modern variation of shamanic rituals, oriented towards a more scientifically objective perception of the world, unlike the mythic worldview of ancient shamans. Naturally, we can see a wide range of differences when discussing pre-rational, rational, and post-rational ways of mapping reality.

Many modern scientists may not take shamanism and the psycho-practices of religion seriously, often dismissing them as unrealistic metaphorical descriptions of reality. However, once we begin to examine the structure of the experience, both ancient and modern, everything falls into place. The structure is almost identical, pursuing nearly identical goals and serving as the progenitor, the "genetic code," which determines the development of its "successor."

Religions can be viewed as the next stage of development in trance-hypnotic techniques, where the internal psychogeography of states is fundamentally transformed and ordered, which can be recreated through trance induction. A more consolidated and predominantly monotheistic form of perceiving archetypes of the unconscious is formed, naturally beginning to transform not only the maps of reality and the ritual practices of interaction with them but also the social fabric of human relationships in society.

The gradual transformation of shamanism into religious movements began to change the value-motivational structure of trance practices, tantric practices, psychospiritual visualizations, somatic practices, attentional fixations, and various types of meditations, leading to altered states of consciousness. However, the structure of the trance process itself remains unchanged from ancient shamanism to modern hypnotic psychotherapy. The social roles that utilize trance undergo transformation and modification. To some extent, it can be said that the type of trance induction within a social group largely determines an individual's social, ethnic, and moral orientation. For example, a Christian priest may disapprove of the work of a hypnotherapist, stating that "hypnosis steals the soul," an Islamic imam may criticize Hatha yoga as a practice of the infidels, and a scientific psychotherapist may skeptically regard transcendental meditation, considering it unscientific. Of course, it is an exaggeration to claim that all individuals with a particular psychospiritual orientation will necessarily avoid the trance-hypnotic methods of other schools. Nonetheless, there are integrative personalities that attempt to combine a multitude of different practices in their activities.

When examining the history of religion, we discover that various religious schools have been known to adopt certain practices from others throughout the centuries and present them as their own. However, currently, most canonized psychospiritual institutions, at a formal level, refrain from adopting practices from other schools. A psychotherapist in a clinic who treats patients through prayer and chanting mantras would likely be seen as overly eccentric. Similarly, a priest who attempts to conduct Ericksonian hypnotherapy during a church service may face suspension from their duties.

The preferred type of trance state determines the personal identity of an individual, along with the beliefs and values they embody. Consequently, the trance experience of one's own group is usually perceived as good and right, while the trance of another group is often seen as evil, until the individual reaches more integrative levels of identity development. Unfortunately, such occurrences are rare.

Trance-hypnotic practice has not always been exclusively associated with shamanic and religious contexts. Individuals involved in various other activities have, do, and will continue to enter hypnotic trance states that differ in quality from shamanic, religious, and psychotherapeutic trance states. These individuals may include hunters, athletes, warriors, and others.

It is enough to recall the hunter in archaic times who would draw an image of a bison on the ground or on a rock, symbolically slaying it with a spear to ensure a successful hunt.

The Scandinavian berserker warrior enters a state of combat trance, in which their physical strength significantly increases and their ability to feel pain diminishes.

The ancient Greek runner, capable of running over 200 kilometers without stopping from one city to another to deliver a message, did not feel fatigue; he was consumed by the rhythm of running.

While we can provide more historical examples, we only formally know about them through history. Let's focus on modern examples of trance masters recorded by contemporary scientists.

A living Dutchman, Wim Hof, demonstrated his ability to stay in icy water for over 2 hours thanks to a self-invented breathing technique. He did this in a laboratory under the supervision of scientists who monitored his body temperature with sensors. It turned out that his body maintained a temperature of 37 degrees Celsius throughout the entire period. Without self-induced trance, such a phenomenon would simply be impossible to replicate.

Ultramarathon runner Dean Karnazes covered 221 kilometers in 24 hours of continuous running. Without the ability to shift and maintain his consciousness in a trance state, this would be utterly unrealistic.

Dutchman Arnold Henske (known as Mirin Dajo) repeatedly demonstrated to doctors in a clinic how he could safely pierce his body with various types of cold weapons.

These are just three examples, and numerous others can be found. Some may appear quite realistic, while others may seem entirely unreal. We assert that all such phenomena are possible and can only be created through self-hypnotic induction.

At times, we encounter natural phenomena that arise spontaneously in individuals or due to specific stressful situations in life. Alternatively, we find that these individuals undergo specialized training to demonstrate such trance phenomena.

The formal starting point for clinical hypnosis can be considered the German physician and healer Franz Anton Mesmer, who developed the doctrine of "animal magnetism."

Franz Anton Mesmer (1734–1815)

Practicing magnet therapy, Mesmer wrote a treatise called "Introductio ad utilem usum Magnetis ex chalybe." Initially, his method involved applying magnets to the patient's body and creating iron-based preparations that were later given to the patients. In describing a case of his therapy, Mesmer writes that the disease left his patient within a few hours. From that moment on, he considers himself the discoverer of a new therapeutic method and continues his research. Later, Mesmer discovers that he himself is capable of "magnetizing" paper, glass, and water and declares that the use of magnets is optional. He sends messages about his discovery to major European universities but receives only doubts about the truthfulness of his discovery in the responses he receives. Mesmer faces an extremely cold reception from the scientific community. In anonymous correspondence from Vienna, he receives critical reviews and even ridicule for his method. After some time being pursued by the German scientific community, Mesmer moves to Paris in 1778.

According to historical accounts, Mesmer's group therapy appeared quite extravagant. Groups of patients were treated by immersing their feet in a fountain with magnetized water. They held onto wires connected to "magnetized" trees with their hands. Mesmer himself accompanied this process on the piano or glass harmonica.

Soon, the French medical community declares war on Mesmer, and he and his methods become the subject of examination by a scientific commission.

The scientific commission concludes that all therapeutic phenomena that could accompany his work method were nothing more than the vivid imagination of the patients. Despite the criticism from the scientific community, Mesmer managed to create his own community called the "Society of Universal Harmony," which had up to 430 members. Additionally, through his therapeutic and social activities, Mesmer manages to amass a considerable fortune, making him one of the wealthiest scientists in Europe.

Mesmer's theory states that disease in a person arises from the uneven distribution of magnetic fluid in the patient's body. He claimed that a doctor could transfer fluid to the patient through magnetic passes or touch.

Mesmer believed that in a state of magnetic trance, patients were capable of foreseeing the future or revealing distant past events, diagnosing diseases, and finding ways to treat them. Despite the highly psychospiritual connotations of his professional pursuits, he believed that the effects he achieved through his methods primarily had a physiological rather than psychological nature.

Despite the criticism of Mesmer's activities, his work continued to be of interest to some scientists, such as D. Braid, I. Bernheim, A. Liebeault, and J.-M. Charcot, for a significant period of time and largely shaped the initial understanding of hypnosis as a clinical practice method.

It was precisely after the establishment of Mesmer's theory in the early 19th century that the practitioners of hypnosis became divided into two key schools:

1. **Fluidists** - followers of Mesmer who believed that the basis of hypnotic suggestion lay in the transmission of magnetic fluids from the magnetizer to the magnetized subject.
2. **Animists** - opponents of Mesmer who believed that no such fluids

existed and that the basis of magnetization and hypnotization of the patient was suggestion or imagination.

Although Mesmer did not create the term "magnetism" himself but borrowed it from Paracelsus - Philippus Aureolus Theophrastus Bombastus von Hohenheim (1493–1541), who mainly dealt with medicine and alchemy and did not apply magnetic force as Mesmer did.

Paracelsus

Paracelsus, as far as we know, was the first physician to attempt to explain magnetic phenomena and, in fact, introduced the term itself from the Phoenician language, which meant "that which is transferred to another." Paracelsus hypothesized that magnets could attract not only metallic objects but also disease. He was also one of the first physicians to apply the future-discovered "placebo" effect in his practice. He believed that the power lay not so much in the magnet itself as in the deep belief that a miracle would occur. And it didn't matter what lay behind it.

Independent of Anton Mesmer, a variation of magnetic suggestion was developed in Portugal by Abbé Faria, who later became the prototype of one of the characters in the book "The Count of Monte Cristo." It is not possible to ascertain with certainty whether his method was independently created or borrowed from Mesmer or another person.

The fact is that Faria employed the techniques of fixed gaze, eye-to-eye contact, and verbal suggestion to induce a hypnotic state through repeated words like "you sleep, you fall asleep." Faria's technique shared similarities with the techniques employed by Mesmer and his followers. For example, Faria could take a Christian cross, raise it above another person's head, and ask them to gaze intently at its shining surface, expecting the mesmerized individual to fall asleep.

One of the most interesting successors of Anton Mesmer was the Scottish physician James Braid (1795–1860). While his primary specialization was surgery, at a certain stage of his professional journey, Braid made several discoveries that slightly diverted him from the path of an ordinary surgeon.

For instance, he made the intriguing discovery that prolonged fixation on shiny objects could induce a specific, cord-like state in a person.

James Braid (1795–1860)

Having read extensively about Anton Mesmer and the activities of mesmerists, James Braid developed a highly critical attitude towards their practices, considering the phenomenon of magnetism as deception, fraud, and trickery. History reveals interesting facts about James Braid's life. On November 13, 1841, Braid attended a performance by the mesmerist Lafontaine, further convincing himself that what was happening on stage was likely deceit and pretense. To definitively expose Lafontaine, six days later, Braid attended another performance but encountered a phenomenon that would later be termed "eyelid catalepsy." Lafontaine magnetized one of the spectators, suggesting that he was unable to raise his eyelids. And indeed, the "magnetized" subject was unable to lift his eyelids, no matter how hard he tried. This shocked Braid, prompting him to conduct experiments on the application of magnetism within his family and circle of friends.

During one such gathering, Braid asked his friend Walker to fix his gaze on the neck of an empty wine bottle. Braid then lifted the bottle above Walker's eyes to tire them, and after a few minutes, he observed that Walker's eyes closed, his head slightly leaned to the side, and his breathing deepened. Continuing his experiments, Braid focused on fixing the gaze of his subjects on various objects and discovered that he could almost always achieve a similar cord-like effect. He termed this state "nervous sleep." Based on his observations, he concluded that he was dealing not with magnetic force but rather with specific nervous processes occurring in individuals under certain conditions. After some time, Braid found a more suitable name for this phenomenon, in his opinion: "hypnosis," which later became established in the field of science.

One of the notable followers of James Braid's theories was the French physician Hippolyte Bernheim, a professor at the University of Strasbourg. After the Franco-Prussian War of 1871, he relocated to Nancy, where he assumed a position as a clinic professor. There, he established his psychoneurological clinic and began practicing hypnosis for therapeutic and research purposes.

Hippolyte Bernheim (1840–1919)

In many ways, Hippolyte Bernheim's theory related to comparing the hypnotic state to a cord-like phenomenon, viewing it as a kind of variation of sleep. It was Bernheim who first applied hypnosis as therapy in full clinical conditions. He conducted research on hysteria and its connection to hypnotic suggestion phenomena and discovered the phenomenon of hyper suggestibility in hysterical individuals within a clinical context. This led him to consider hysteria and hysterical behavior as manifestations of autosuggestion. Bernheim embarked on the path of a pioneer, unearthing invaluable information that would become key to the art of profiling individuals. Based on a patient's personality profile, he could predict the depth of the hypnotic state, the trance phenomena achievable during hypnosis, and the potential outcomes attainable using hypnotic methods.

One of Bernheim's scientific colleagues in the field of hypnosis research was the French physician Ambroise-Auguste Liébeault (1823–1904). Liébeault was the founder of the "Nancy School" of hypnosis, where he and his colleague Hippolyte Bernheim conducted psychotherapeutic hypnotherapy for patients in their clinic, primarily focusing on hysterical patients. Some sources even attribute him as the father of hypnotherapy, although this claim is somewhat debatable considering the work of figures such as Franz Mesmer, who simply did not use the term "hypnosis" to describe his practices. Naturally, James Braid, who extensively experimented with hypnosis but did not transform it into a widely adopted therapeutic method in clinical conditions, also influenced the field.

The fundamental idea of the Nancy School was that hypnosis itself had nothing to do with animal magnetism or the transmission of magnetic fluids to the patient. Instead, it was directly related to induced suggestion, which actualized the diverse range of hypnotic phenomena.

A. Liébeault had a friendship with Étienne Eugène Azam (1822–1899), the main French disciple of James Braid in France. This association significantly influenced Liébeault's hypnotic practice, aligning it with Braid's theory. Liébeault's primary work in the field of hypnosis was his book "Sleep and its Analogs, Mainly Considered from the Perspective of the Mind's Influence on the Body."

Additionally, Liébeault was greatly influenced by the ideas of Abbé Faria (1746–1819) and Alexandre Jacques François Bertrand (1795–1831).

Thanks to A. A. Liébeault, Sigmund Freud and Émile Coué were drawn to the Nancy School during their time there. Jean-Martin Charcot (1825–1893), the French physician, psychiatrist, and specialist in neurological diseases mentioned in the history of psychiatry as Sigmund Freud's teacher, was one of the most prominent clinical researchers of hypnosis in his clinical practice.

Jean-Martin Charcot (1825–1893)

Jean-Martin Charcot worked at the Salpêtrière Hospital, where he became the chief physician in 1862 and took charge of the department for "non-psychotic epileptics and hysterics." It is worth noting that at that time, hysteria was considered a neurological rather than a psychiatric disorder.

At the beginning of his clinical practice, J.M. Charcot focused primarily on the study and treatment of internal diseases such as tuberculosis, rheumatism, pneumonia, and others. Later, he redirected his interest towards diseases related to brain dysfunction, initiating studies on its structure and the localization of its functions.

While working with hysterical women in the clinic, J.M. Charcot initially believed that hysteria was exclusively a female condition associated with uterine dysfunction. However, during his work with hysterical patients, he discovered that they often suffered from somatic disorders such as blindness, paralysis, and convulsions without exhibiting the typical brain lesions associated with these conditions. Naturally, he also observed that hysterical patients were highly susceptible to hypnotic suggestion. J.-M. Charcot conducted numerous experiments involving the induction of paralysis in various body parts and achieved remarkable success both in creating these conditions and subsequently curing them.

As a result, J.-M. Charcot concluded that during hysteria, a person enters a state akin to hypnosis. It was Charcot who began to refer to hysterical disorder as a natural form of hypnosis since the phenomenology of hysteria and hypnosis were almost entirely identical, with the exception that hysterical patients did not require a hypnotist to induce an altered state of consciousness.

After J.-M. Charcot's death in 1899, his book "The Healing Faith" was published, emphasizing the role of faith as a key factor in the healing process. J.M. Charcot summarized various cases of miraculous healing associated with different spiritual symbols, connecting faith's influence to human neurophysiology. "The healing faith, whether religious or secular, cannot be dichotomous; it is the same cerebral process that produces identical effects," stated J.-M. Charcot. According to him, the patient's firm belief in the healing factor of therapeutic actions becomes a crucial element in the healing process, and the main task of the physician is to instill such conviction in the patient.

Doctors from Nancy adhered to the theory of understanding hypnosis as a general property of suggestibility that manifests in varying intensities. They emphasized its psychological nature, contrasting with J.-M. Charcot, who considered it organic.

Nowadays, it can be confidently stated that both schools were correct and that hypnosis involves both psychological and physiological factors.

Sigmund Freud's interaction with J.-M. Charcot predetermined his professional development and establishment. Freud interned under J.-M. Charcot for four months in 1885. Later, Freud wrote about J.-M. Charcot: "No man has had such an influence on me... I used to leave his lectures with a feeling as if I were leaving Notre-Dame de Paris, full of new insights into perfection."

In the late 19th and early 20th centuries, physicians increasingly sought physiological and scientific justifications for hypnotic processes. Active experimental investigations unfolded in Europe and Russia. For example, in 1881, doctors from Odessa, O.O. Mochutkovsky and B.A. Oks, conducted numerous hypnotic experiments with hysterical patients in the clinic, reproducing phenomena such as paresis, paralysis, catalepsy of the whole body, and multiple personality manifestations.

V.Ya. Danilevsky from Kharkov delivered a report at the International Congress of Physiological Psychology in 1889, discussing experiments on hypnotizing crustaceans, birds, rabbits, and other animals. He concluded that the phenomenon of hypnosis is not exclusive to human beings. It is worth noting that V.M. Bekhterev later conducted experiments on animal hypnosis.

Another psychiatrist, psychoneurologist, and hypnotherapist worth mentioning is Konstantin Ivanovich Platonov (1877–1969), who worked in Kharkov and was a student of V.M. Bekhterev.

Konstantin Ivanovich Platonov (1877–1969)

K.I. Platonov significantly interpreted the processes occurring in a patient during the state of hypnosis as specific neurophysiological mechanisms. He concluded that the depth of the hypnotic state and, at the same time, the phenomenon of suggestibility in individuals were not necessarily a result of deep hypnotization.

Platonov is also known for his original methodology for pain relief during childbirth and is the author of the 1930 monograph "Speech as a Physiological and Therapeutic Factor" (1930). As mentioned earlier, Sigmund Freud (1856–1939) studied hypnotic suggestion in the Salpêtrière and Nancy schools. At the beginning of his practice, he actively used hypnosis with his patients to recover lost memories of early childhood. In other words, he conducted hypnotic regression to access repressed emotions and facilitate their abreaction (emotional release).

Sigmund Freud (1856–1939)

Most often, he employed the methods of J.-M. Charcot, pressing his hand against the patient's forehead and inducing sleep, during which the patient was supposed to recall material necessary for therapy. He closely collaborated with his colleague, physician Josef Breuer, who also practiced hypnosis with his patients. Together with J. Breuer, he published the work "Studies on Hysteria." This work became the seminal text for future developments in hypnoanalysis and regression hypnotherapy.

One of J. Breuer's cases with one of his patients became a catalyst for S. Freud's creation of an alternative method of treatment apart from hypnosis. This case is mentioned in psychoanalytic literature under the name "the case of Anna O."

Anna O. was one of J. Breuer's young patients suffering from hysteria, manifested in symptoms such as hysterical paralysis, paresis of the right side of the face, and temporary dissociation of personality. It was revealed that the hysterical symptoms in Anna O. began after she had cared for her bedridden, debilitated father for over two years. J. Breuer worked with Anna for several months, almost every day, sometimes twice a day. He regularly recorded her delusions during her altered states of consciousness and conducted hypnotic sessions with her. He came up with the idea of transcribing what the patient said during her delusions and then reading the same text back to her while inducing her into a hypnotic state. Through this technique, he discovered that after the reading, the patient would start displaying a significant number of emotional ab-reactions. In other words, she would begin to experience intense emotions, cry, scream, and release suppressed emotions during the process of treating her father. J. Breuer continued his experiments with Anna, but after some time, he encountered a significant problem: the patient developed a rare phenomenon called phantom pregnancy, which sometimes occurs in women with hysterical symptoms. When asked about her condition, Anna claimed that she was carrying J. Breuer's baby in her abdomen. After this incident, J. Breuer discontinued the therapy and left with his wife for the Alps, presumably to save their marriage. Breuer named his form of therapy "cathartic therapy," which did not directly evolve into a separate approach but, as a concept and idea, became rooted in numerous future directions of psychotherapeutic practice.

After some time, S. Freud abandoned the practice of hypnosis, which, in his opinion, did not possess sufficient therapeutic depth, in favor of the psychoanalytic method he was developing, based on the technique of free association. Although much later, after the establishment of psychoanalysis, S. Freud hypothesized that pure psychoanalysis could be combined with hypnoanalysis to shorten the duration of therapeutic work, he believed that it might weaken the outcome. His opinion on this matter remains debatable, but unfortunately, his conclusions are unlikely to undergo thorough empirical analysis.

A notable opponent of S. Freud's theories but also a colleague in the practice of hypnotic suggestion, was French psychologist, neuropathologist, and psychiatrist Pierre Marie Félix Janet (1859–1947). Like Freud, he was a student of Jean-Martin Charcot. In his clinical practice, P. Janet developed the "psychological conception of neuroses" and considered neurotic disorders as processes that disrupt the balance between higher and lower mental functions. His theories shared similarities with those of American

21

behaviorists. He believed that consciousness should be regarded "as a special form of act, surpassing elementary behavior" and that psychology should be "objective in the sense that its subject matter should be directly observable." It is also worth noting that P. Janet considered the psychological factor to be the primary influential factor in hypnosis, rather than the physiological factor. According to his perspective, the psychological factor played a fundamental conditioning role in the process of hypnotization.

Pierre Marie Félix Janet (1859–1947)

There are intriguing examples of Pierre Janet's hypnotic work that are worth mentioning. One such case involved a twenty-year-old woman suffering from severe menstrual pain that would begin a few days before her period and continue for several days. Janet employed hypnoanalysis to uncover the cause of the woman's past pain. While in a hypnotic state, she recalled a situation when she was thirteen years old and had just started menstruating. Unaware of what was happening to her, she ventured out into the freezing cold and immersed herself in a barrel of icy water in an attempt to stop the bleeding. Afterward, her menstrual cycle ceased and did not resume until she turned fifteen, but when it returned, it was accompanied by excruciating pain. It should be noted that the reduction or temporary cessation of menstruation can indeed be achieved if a woman immerses herself in icy water during her period. In our own practice, we have encountered several similar cases. However, in our observations, this did not lead to their prolonged cessation as it did in Janet's patient.

After obtaining the analytical material, Janet decided to embark on an unusual experiment with his patient, which he would later refer to as "lying therapy." Janet regressed the patient back to the age of thirteen using hypnoanalysis and suggested to her that on the day her menstrual cycle began, she went outside but did not immerse herself in the cold water barrel; instead, she simply stood near it. He then brought her out of hypnosis and observed her until her next period. Miraculously, her menstrual cycle no longer accompanied the typical intense pain. This experiment led Janet to realize that he was touching upon some new, unexplored processes of our consciousness. To confirm his suspicions, he dared to conduct another experiment with the same patient, who had almost lost vision in her left eye at the age of six. Using a similar method of hypnoanalysis, Janet regressed the patient to the age of six and discovered that her symptoms began after an incident where her sick cousin, who had a skin condition, came to her home. Contrary to hygiene rules, her parents allowed her brother to sleep in the same bed with her, to her left. She described the intense negative feelings she experienced while lying in bed. Following this event, her vision in the left eye deteriorated almost to zero. In a hypnotic state, Janet suggested to the patient that her brother was completely healthy and that she was happy to see him. Over the next few months, he observed the restoration of her vision in the left eye.

In the future, Janet's findings were implemented by other hypnologists, who achieved similar successes at times, but often the restoration of vision through hypnosis was only temporary. We will delve further into this topic in subsequent chapters when discussing methods of vision therapy using hypnosis.

A notable student of the Nancy School and Hippolyte Bernheim was the

French psychologist and pharmacist Émile Coué (1857–1926), who developed a system of psychotherapy based on self-hypnosis and autosuggestion.

Emile Coué's self-suggestion method involved the repeated recitation of healing phrases and affirmations aimed at improving or alleviating the patient's condition. An example of a phrase could be as follows: "Every day, in every way, I am getting better and better," "My health improves every day, regardless of what I do," "My intellect and physical strength constantly increase; I feel motivated to exercise, and I am full of energy." Coué tailored affirmations specifically for each patient or, if necessary, provided pre-prepared ones. The recommendation for the self-suggestion process was to regularly repeat the affirmation at least twenty times a day—in the morning, afternoon, and evening.

The duration could vary depending on the need and requirement, with the primary criterion being the patient's recovery. Therefore, the use of affirmations often continued for one to several weeks. Occasionally, Coué would recommend the continued use of affirmations as a preventive measure against illness. Naturally, affirmations could be utilized not only for the purpose of psychotherapy but also for personal growth.

Emile Coué (1857–1926)

Coué believed that the key to therapy lay in changing the patient's uncon-scious thinking. He emphasized that he himself is not a healer but merely teaches others to heal themselves. One of Coué's fundamental beliefs was that any person who suggests to themselves the phrase "I will succeed!" will inevitably achieve their desired outcome, despite criticism from the conscious mind and apparent external obstacles.

Another interesting belief held by Coué was that imagination triumphs over willpower, and whatever we envision as reality and affirm as reality through affirmation will eventually be realized.

Working as a pharmacist from 1882 to 1910, Coué made a remarkable dis-covery regarding the increased effectiveness of medication when presented to the patient as highly potent and reliable, compared to medications about which nothing was said. This finding anticipated the discovery of the placebo effect, which we will discuss in our book later on. This discovery marked the beginning of Coué's research in the fields of hypnosis and autosuggestion.

Coué also made the intriguing observation that a person cannot be hypnotized against their will, thus introducing a significant theoretical element to the theory of hypnosis. It is worth mentioning that other researchers of hypnosis were more inclined to talk about the individuals they successfully hypnotized than those with whom the phenomenon of hypnosis failed. Jean-Martin Charcot, Hippolyte Bernheim, and Auguste Liébeault, who predominantly worked with hysterical patients known for their exceptional hypnotic susceptibility, are often mentioned in the literature on hypnosis. However, the fact remains that individuals with different personality profiles sometimes encounter substantial difficulties in entering a trance state or are almost entirely incapable of doing so due to specific internal psychological processes. We will extensively discuss this topic in the chapter dedicated to personality profiling and its significance in the practice of hypnosis. This topic is highly significant but has been largely ignored and not discussed in the literature on hypnosis.

While offering tools for hypnotization, it is important to acknowledge that they may not work at all for individuals with certain profiles.

It is also worth mentioning that Emile Coué had a significant influence on Johann Heinrich Schultz (1884–1970), a German psychiatrist and psychotherapist who developed autogenic training. Schultz began practicing clinical hypnosis in 1909 and conducted various pathophysiological studies alongside it. Besides Emile Coué, he was greatly influenced by the works of Oscar Vogt and Sigmund Freud.

Johann Heinrich Schultz (1884–1970)

One of his major works was the book "Autogenic Training," published in 1932. It is noteworthy that the methods of autosuggestion and their application in psychotherapeutic practice were subsequently adopted worldwide.

One of his fundamental psychotherapeutic positions was the belief that therapy should take into account the "dynamic nature of the past" and the "current life situation of the individual patient."

The primary basic exercises in the autogenic training method involve the targeted creation of specific sensations in the body, such as warmth, cold, heaviness, and lightness, through self-suggestion, similar to the affirmations of Emile Coué. For example: "My hand is warm," "My hand is heavy," and so on. As the student developed the skill of inducing specific states through regular self-suggestion, more complex exercises were introduced.

One of the most intriguing personalities in the field of practical hypnotic suggestion was Dave Elman (1900–1967), an American radio host, comedian, and singer. He taught numerous doctors the practice of hypnosis and wrote the book "Findings in Hypnosis" in 1964, later renamed "Hypnotherapy." D. Elman was famous for developing various forms of rapid hypnotic induction and adapting them for medical practice. It often took about three minutes to induce a hypnotic state using his methods.

It is also mentioned that the first heart surgery performed under hypnosis instead of anesthesia was conducted by one of D. Elman's students under his guidance. Further detailed information about this surgery is not available to us, but it is likely that the operation was carried out without general anesthesia, relying on local anesthesia, as this form of hypnotic work is now one of the most popular in clinics in France, Germany, England, and Italy.

Dave Elman (1900–1967)

Surgeries performed exclusively under local anesthesia using hypnosis on the heart are rare, as they require specific professional skills from the hypnotherapist and cannot be standardized. In less complex procedures, the use of hypnosis is very common nowadays because the hypnotization process is highly standardized and can be reproduced as a pattern even at lower levels of hypnotic practice competency. It should be noted that Dave Elman himself was neither a physician nor a psychologist; initially, his hypnotic techniques were aimed at creating a theatrical and demonstrative effect. Stage hypnosis is not considered a form of psychotherapy, as it emphasizes the creation of vivid hypnotic phenomena rather than therapeutic effects.

We should also mention the work of Swiss neurologist and psychiatrist Auguste Henri Forel in the field of hypnosis. Many of Forel's scientific research studies focused on topics such as the structure of the human central nervous system, hypnosis in psychotherapeutic practice, and other psychic phenomena. He worked as a professor of psychiatry in Zurich and was an honorary doctor of the University of Zurich. Some of his works were dedicated to combating alcohol addiction.

Auguste Henri Forel (1848–1931)

28

In this work, I would like to illustrate his use of hypnotherapy with a female patient suffering from severe menstrual pain, similar to the case of Pierre Janet. However, Forel employed a different approach compared to the intricate practice involving hypnotic regression and the implantation of false memories. He favored direct directive suggestion, wherein the symptom was alleviated through the direct suggestion of the desired state. According to the patient's description, her menstruation typically lasted over a week and was accompanied by intense pain. Over the course of several weeks, Forel conducted a series of hypnosis sessions with her, repeatedly suggesting that her menstruation would be reduced to three days, become moderate in intensity, and be nearly painless. As he later reported, the patient's subsequent menstrual cycles corresponded to the suggestions he had given her.

It is worth noting that when examining the works of early hypnotherapists, one can find numerous examples of successful practices in both hypnosis and symptom elimination, with very few descriptions of unsuccessful attempts. It is reasonable to assume that some challenges in practice were simply left undocumented. While hypnosis can yield astonishing results in the short term, it frequently leads to the regression of "rapid healing," with the reemergence of old symptoms. Understanding such regression phenomena often lies in the concept of the positive intention underlying the symptom.

To further illustrate this point, allow me to share a case from my own practice involving a 60-year-old male patient, a high-ranking military officer, who was grappling with severe alcoholism. This patient demon-strated a high level of hypnotizability, readily entering into a deep hypnotic state. The induction of a simple trance state alone had a positive therapeutic effect, resulting in a significant reduction in his alcohol consumption over several months of weekly hypnotherapy sessions. It is important to note that the patient, while conscious, was resistant to the complete elimination of his addiction, asserting his strong willpower and attributing hypnosis as a tool only for the weak-minded. Consequently, we opted for a strategy that avoided direct interventions aimed at countering the addiction, such as suggestions like "you do not want to drink alcohol" or "alcohol repulses you."

During the hypnosis sessions, we focused on motivational interventions, emphasizing the healing of his mind and body. We provided suggestions such as "your body and mind are undergoing a process of healing," "you no longer have the desire to harm your body," and "your consciousness is becoming more integrated and healthy." After several successful hypnotherapy sessions, we cautiously attempted to suggest to the patient, while he was in a deep hypnotic trance, the phrase "vodka is poison to you." To our surprise, he immediately emerged from the trance and expressed a strong desire to terminate the session. It became evident that the patient, perhaps unconsciously, was fiercely protecting his addiction.

In a subsequent hypnosis session, we explored the patient's memories of early breastfeeding by his mother, uncovering a significant psychological factor underlying his alcohol dependency. It is worth digressing and commenting that some alcoholics unconsciously associate alcohol with the comforting experience of maternal milk, attempting to recreate the sense of well-being from their childhood. Alcohol, like maternal milk, triggers the release of neurotransmitters such as GABA, oxytocin, and dopamine in the brain, which can serve as an "adult" substitute for the emotional nourishment they seek. Attempting to directly eliminate alcohol dependence without providing alternative psychological resources deprives the individual of the opportunity for psychological balance. Without appropriate substitutes, the symptom is likely to resurface.

Let's take a simple example from our practice with a 60-year-old male patient, a professional general, who suffered from severe alcoholism. The man was capable of consuming up to three bottles of vodka per night, coming home after work. He was referred for treatment by his family members. During the hypnotic work, he exhibited a high level of hypnotizability and easily entered a hypnotic state. Simple immersion in a hypnotic trance had a healing effect. Over the course of several months, conducting weekly hypnotherapy sessions, we observed a significant reduction in the amount of alcohol the patient consumed.

It is worth noting that in his conscious state, he did not want to completely rid himself of his addiction, justifying it by claiming that he was a strong-willed individual and capable of overcoming the dependency on his own. He believed that only weak-willed people resorted to "coding" through hypnosis. Due to this, we chose a strategy of avoiding direct interventions that curbed the addiction, such as suggesting statements like "you don't want to drink alcohol," "alcohol disgusts you," "you feel nauseous at the smell of alcohol," and so on. For a while, we provided motivational interventions during the hypnotic state, such as "your body and mind are healing," "you have no desire to harm your body," "your consciousness becomes more whole and healthy."

When several successful hypnotherapy sessions were established, we attempted to implant the phrase "vodka is poison to you" while the patient was in a deep hypnotic trance. We witnessed the instant emergence of the patient from the trance and his desire to leave. It was evident that the patient, seemingly unconsciously, was "protecting his addiction." In one of the subsequent hypnotherapy sessions, we discovered the patient's memories of early breastfeeding, a process underlying the need to consume alcohol. At this point, it is worth making a brief digression and commenting that, indeed, some alcoholics unconsciously project the qualities of maternal milk onto alcohol, attempting to recreate the sense of well-being experienced during infancy. Alcohol, like maternal milk, can stimulate the production of neurotransmitters such as GABA, oxytocin, and dopamine in the brain, easily becoming an "adult" substitute for the latter in emotionally challenging situations for an individual.

Attempting to directly eliminate a person's alcohol dependency merely deprives them of alternative psychological balancing, and if no substitutes are provided, the symptom will resurface or manifest in another, sometimes more destructive, form. The same applied to our patient when we asked him how it happened that he frequently consumed alcohol. He mentioned that his life consisted of a constant circulation between work-related stress and conflicts in the domestic sphere. Alcohol dependency had become the only means of relaxation for an extended period. In this case, we observe the conscious inclination to protect one's addiction. In numerous other similar patients, we discover similar, often unconscious processes that cannot be corrected without additional verbal psychotherapy. In this regard, hypnosis appears as a tool that can facilitate change only when the patient's unconscious is ready to accept it. If the hypnotic suggestion does not resonate with the hidden beliefs and values of the patient, we often witness a regression to the previous symptom after a certain period of time. Although, based on our observations, there are many hypnosis specialists claiming to be able to cure alcoholism without analytical correction, we question such beliefs, considering the impossibility of directly resolving the underlying situation that led to the dependent behavior. In the practical part of the book, we will delve deeper into the specifics of hypnotic psychotherapeutic work and the factors contributing to the emergence of addictive behavior.

Milton Erickson (1901–1988)

One of the most renowned psychiatrists and hypnotherapists of the 20th century was the American physician Milton Erickson (1901–1988), the creator of the non-directive form of hypnosis and an entire direction of psychotherapy named after him.

A particularly interesting aspect of his biography was his childhood illness, poliomyelitis. At that time, this disease had no known cure, and its presence often implied a fatal outcome. He overheard a doctor commenting to his mother that he would not survive until the next day. However, contrary to the doctor's expectations, he continued to live, paralyzed and only capable of thinking and moving his eyes. His mother placed his bed in the kitchen of their home so she could attend to her duties while keeping an eye on her son. Milton, lying in bed, exerted his willpower and imagination to suggest to himself that he could move his fingers. After some time, he succeeded. Then he managed to convince himself that he could move all his limbs and eventually his entire body. Against all odds, he gradually recovered, although he remained in considerable pain. Milton faced several physical challenges. In addition to poliomyelitis, which appeared when he was 17, he suffered from color blindness and difficulty distinguishing sounds by pitch. As Milton grew up and entered medical school, where he later specialized in psychiatry, one of his professors told him that he would be an excellent psychiatrist. Milton inquired about the reason for such a statement, and the professor replied that Milton was small, sickly, and unattractive. Therefore, he would not arouse a desire to compete among men, and women would feel sympathy for him, making them more likely to collaborate with him. Despite the absurdity of this assumption, his mentor turned out to be right in many respects. It is worth adding that Milton's fame and success did not come early in his life.

Milton Erickson first encountered clinical hypnosis while serving as a medical intern and observing the work of the American psychologist and hypnotherapist Clark Hull. It is difficult to assess the influence of C. Hull on Milton Erickson's work since Milton never mentioned him in his writings or acknowledged using his methods. Perhaps at the beginning of his professional journey, Milton did utilize directive suggestion methods borrowed from C. Hull. However, most of what we know about Milton Erickson's hypnotherapy is that he developed the majority of his methods independently within the context of his psychotherapeutic practice.

A very interesting experiment was conducted by M. Erickson in 1936, where he observed how a person creates associations with a stimulus word that directly describes their problem. For example, one of his patients associated the word "stomach" with words like pain, worry, baby, fear, surgery, illness, and forgotten. These associations reflected information about her unwanted pregnancy, which she had forgotten.

After his research, M. Erickson hypothesized that it is possible to interact with the patient's unconscious from a different "riverbank" by giving them hinting words related to a specific process or command. Thus, through indirect suggestion rather than direct and directive means, the patient's resistance is bypassed. This study laid the foundation for his exploration and development of his own method of hypnotherapy, which significantly differed from the methods previously known in psychotherapy. His approach prioritized indirect suggestions and metaphors. M. Erickson referred to his technique as "hypnotic trance" rather than "hypnosis," verbally distinguishing his method of hypnotic suggestion, which went beyond ordinary suggestion. However, it would be incorrect to say that M. Erickson exclusively used nondirective methods. Rather, he elegantly combined his working styles based on their appropriateness. M. Erickson believed that the state of hypnotic trance is a natural tool of consciousness necessary for processing internal experience. The act of entering a hypnotic state itself can have a healing effect. Despite this, he developed numerous procedures that could be performed in a trance state to accelerate the healing process.

Erickson specialized in creating various hypnotic phenomena that could be utilized either to demonstrate trance phenomenology or to act as triggers for entering a trance state and directing the healing process. His favorite trance phenomena included catalepsy of the hand, which allowed flexibility in positioning the hand and maintaining that position for a period of time without the patient's conscious effort, and levitation of the hand, an unconscious movement of the hand in the air characterized by autonomous lifting and a certain duration of movement. M. Erickson conducted many experiments in creating anesthesia and analgesia phenomena, both on himself due to his own illness and on his patients, especially those suffering from cancer. While he could not cure cancer through hypnosis, he could alleviate some of the patients' suffering. He also actively practiced the creation of other trance phenomena, such as positive and negative visual hallucinations, hypnotic hypermnesia and amnesia, nonverbal analog body signals, and so on. We will discuss them in more detail in the section of the book dedicated to the phenomenology of hypnotic trance.

Erickson became famous only in the last 20 years of his professional career. He never sought fame but diligently worked with patients, often doing remarkable things that genuinely helped them. In the modern world, M. Erickson is primarily known for his methods of hypnotic induction, but hypnosis was just one of the many tools he used in psychotherapy. He didn't use hypnosis with many of his patients, instead employing direct and behavioral metaphors to correct their behavior. It is worth providing examples of some of these techniques, which are not direct hypnosis but reflect the essence of his therapeutic work.

Once upon a time, a man came to M. Erickson and complained that he was an alcoholic and couldn't quit drinking. He mentioned that many members of his family were heavy drinkers, as were his colleagues at work. He constantly found himself in contexts where alcohol was present, which led to him being drawn back into the "alcohol pit" even when he tried to abstain. M. Erickson pondered for a while and then said he could help him, but first, the man had to promise to carry out an assignment despite its outward strangeness and peculiarity. The man agreed immediately. M. Erickson instructed him to go to the city's botanical garden and find the section dedicated to cacti. He was to walk through that section, look at the cacti, examine these plants closely, and contemplate how they could survive for up to two years without water. He was to walk, observe, and think, think, think... The patient agreed to fulfill M. Erickson's directive and left his office. After that, M. Erickson didn't hear from him for six years.

Six years later, a young woman knocked on M. Erickson's office door and asked where she could find Dr. M. Erickson. He asked her why she wanted to see him, and she replied that she had long wanted to meet the doctor who had advised an alcoholic patient to go to the botanical garden, look at the cacti, and then quit drinking.

In this case, we observe that M. Erickson created a behavioral metaphor for the patient that was embedded with images and profound meanings that were most likely not consciously understood by the patient. However, his unconscious mind found interpretations for them and manifested the effect at the level of neurophysiological reactions. The alcoholic himself served as an analogy to the cactus, and alcohol served as an analogy to water. Two years without water symbolized the ability to exert willpower to overcome addiction. This work by M. Erickson, if we think about it, carries even more meaning than we can imagine. Initially, we discover the rule that metaphors encode our subconscious and enable us to do one thing and not do another. M. Erickson believed that what the patient did not consciously grasp influenced him much more than conscious realizations. He substantiated his theory through his practice and examples, although he also believed that psychotherapy could not afford the luxury of having rigid theoretical frameworks regarding personality theory and psychotherapeutic methods.

Many psychotherapists believe that M. Erickson contributed as much to the practice of psychotherapy as Sigmund Freud contributed to its theory. In many ways, this statement holds true. We can learn a lot about patients from both Freud's and Erickson's psychotherapeutic sources. With Freud, we do not find descriptions of patients' recovery but mostly theorizing and constructing models of personality. M. Erickson rarely engaged in theoretical discussions. However, his work often resulted in the actual healing of the patient.

Another question that arises after considering the case of working with an alcoholic is whether the metaphor, whose meaning is not consciously grasped, can help a person exert willpower. In that case, what is primary?

It turns out that the unconscious metaphorical experience of a person completely determines their ability to exercise will, life motivation, behavioral reactions, and the meanings we attribute to the world. Does freedom of choice exist in such a scenario, or does the overwhelming majority of a person's reactions relate to the reproduction of unconscious metaphorical experience? On one hand, the answer may seem philosophical, but on the other hand, it constructs an entirely new map for describing the hierarchy of neurophysiological processes in the human brain. Metaphors, as complete programs living in a person's consciousness, acting as algorithms for both psychological and neurophysiological processes, seem capable of encoding processes of volition and many other behavioral processes in humans.

As another interesting example of M. Erickson's non-hypnotic work, which vividly illustrates our concept of the primacy of unconscious metaphorical experience in relation to the process of volition, let's consider his work with a high jumper who needed to learn how to jump half a meter farther than he believed he was capable of. M. Erickson discovered that the athlete had developed a belief in his inability to overcome this barrier during training and competitions. Whenever the athlete thought about the need to jump half a meter farther than his best performance to win a competition, he would become discouraged and lose motivation, and naturally, his athletic performance would not improve.

Erickson attempted to shake his limiting beliefs about his abilities in the following way. The first question he would ask him was, "Do you think you can jump one centimeter farther than your record? Can you overcome this barrier?" The athlete confidently replied that he saw nothing impossible about it. M. Erickson then assigned him the task of trying to add that one centimeter to his record over the next week. And miraculously, after a week of training, the athlete achieved a new record with an additional centimeter. M. Erickson then asked him to try adding one or two centimeters to his new record every week. The athlete successfully completed the tasks, and in six months, he finally jumped half a meter farther than his initial limit. In this situation, we observe how M. Erickson worked on reshaping the patient's belief about his inability to overcome the barrier, demonstrating that it resided more in the individual's mind and was not directly linked to his true abilities. Here we can recall the old psychotherapeutic metaphor: "How do you eat an elephant? One bite at a time." It is an elegant alternative approach to working with the patient's consciousness, not relying on literal hypnotic suggestion but nonetheless reprogramming the patient's mind as effectively, and possibly even better, than direct directive suggestion that a clinical directive hypnotist might employ. These cases primarily serve as examples of a psychotherapist's ability to work with the patient's resistance, a process that often poses a significant stumbling block for many psychotherapists.

In our experience, we have witnessed hypnotic triumphs and "fails" by highly successful hypnotherapists. If the structure of resistance is not understood and acknowledged by the hypnotherapist and the patient's personality profile is not taken into account, the process of hypnotherapy becomes akin to playing "Russian roulette," with the thought, "What if it backfires?" After all, clear and fixed hypnotic methods, both directive and non-directive, can have varying effects on patients' consciousness. Here are a few vivid examples from our practice.

One patient who underwent psychotherapy with us requested to be hypnotized in order to assess her hypnotizability. In the hypnotic work with her, we initially adopted the style of a gentle, non-directive Ericksonian approach, where the process of hypnotization is carried out with a slow, gentle, and calm voice. After ten minutes of work, we observed that such delivery of suggestions did not work on the patient; she constantly experienced anxious reactions that disrupted her hypnotic state. Intrigued by her resistance, we engaged in a conversation to understand what was happening in her consciousness when anxiety arose. It turned out that the patient, who had conflicting relationships with her mother, had an interesting association related to her mother's voice. Her mother always used a soft and calm voice to tell her what to do and what not to do. This always frustrated her, and in her mind, this type of voice became associated with her mother's attempts to give her advice or commands that were unpleasant to her.

This is an example of how even the most comfortable and non-intrusive form of hypnotic work can encounter "hidden reefs" of resistance associated with the patient's personal experience.

Another example comes from a seminar on Ericksonian hypnotic work that we conducted. During the seminar, one of our hypnotherapist colleagues participated in a demonstration of trance induction for the group of participants. When we asked him for feedback on the effectiveness of the hypnotic induction, we encountered a situation where certain hypnotic phrases from the non-directive Ericksonian hypnosis, which we used abundantly, unconsciously irritated our colleague. He commented that he was quite familiar with the examples of hypnotic interventions used in the Ericksonian style, and when he heard them being applied to him, he began to resist the hypnotic induction, explaining that he felt manipulated. In a subsequent personal conversation with him, we discovered that throughout his life, he had been subjected to various manipulations from his mother, manipulations that he was well aware of. There were many emotions involved, and he needed to redirect them somewhere. Verbal, non-directive Ericksonian interventions became the victim. According to his personal comments, when direct imperative hypnosis was applied to him, where the suggestion was always evident on the surface, it symbolized sincerity and a lack of desire to manipulate him. In this case, he entered the hypnotic trance easily and effortlessly.

Erickson often utilized behavioral metaphors to alter patients perceptions. It is important to emphasize that he achieved success not only with neurotic patients but also with severely psychotic individuals. One such case involved a thirteen-year-old girl who was admitted to the clinic due to intense, aggressive outbursts, making it nearly impossible for the medical staff to interact with her. She would lunge at doctors and nurses, attempting to bite them and pull their hair. When left alone in her room, she would tear apart the bedding and break furniture.

Erickson aimed to develop a therapeutic approach and establish a connection with her based on three fundamental principles that guided both his hypnotic and behavioral therapy. These principles were: joining the patient's behavior, leading them through its expression, and therapeutic utilization.

Erickson coordinated with the clinic director to shut off the hot water supply to the radiator in the girl's room and enlisted the help of a specific nurse to assist him in a particular form of behavioral therapy for the patient. He then entered the girl's room and initiated a conversation with her. Sitting on the bed, she glared at him with hostility, ready to attack. Sensing her readiness to express aggression, Erickson grabbed the bed sheets and tore them apart in front of her with ferocious intensity. She was taken aback by this display. He then seized a pillow, ripped it open, and scattered feathers throughout the room. The girl was astounded by what she witnessed. She had never seen herself from an external perspective while engaging in similar destructive behavior. Seizing the opportunity, Erickson invited her to participate in the "destruction" of the bedding. After a while, the girl joined him in this destructive tandem. Thirty minutes later, they celebrated their accomplishment as the bedding was completely destroyed. Erickson then suggested dismantling the radiator from the wall, and after another half hour of struggling, they successfully achieved this as well. By that point, the girl saw Erickson as a close friend. Urging her to take a walk in the corridor, Erickson hurried to the door, and she eagerly followed him. Waiting outside the door was the "prepared" nurse, who had willingly agreed to participate in this eccentric form of psychotherapy. Erickson rushed toward her, grabbing her by the sleeves of her coat and abruptly tearing them off. The patient observed her therapist's destructive behavior without actively participating, feeling a mild sense of fear. After a brief moment of confusion, she asked him, "Dr. Erickson, are you sure it's okay to do this?"

Numerous stories like this can be found in Milton Erickson's books, where he successfully aligned himself with the behavior of even the most irrational patients, bringing them back to an appropriate state of mind. Erickson recognized in his psychotherapeutic practice that patients truly started to listen and hear him only when he shared their reality, no matter how outrageous it may have been. To be understood, one must learn to speak the language of the other person. If one desires others to follow, they must first lead by following someone else. If one wants someone to share their cousin's story, they should share their own story first. A similar analogy was applied during trance interactions with patients: "If you want to induce someone into trance, first enter into trance yourself." These beliefs significantly differentiated Erickson's therapy and hypnosis methods from those of other therapists, who rarely employed such principles.

It is important to note that in Ericksonian hypnosis, rapport primarily focuses on aligning with the patient, contrasting with classical directive hypnosis, where the concepts of rapport and trust could be interpreted differently. It is worth mentioning that Anton Mesmer initially regarded rapport as the process of transmitting magnetic fluid from the hypnotist to the patient through physical contact. According to Erickson, rapport primarily involves sharing the patient's reality. It represents an entirely different level of working with resistance and the therapeutic process.

The therapeutic approach of M. Erickson's philosophy shares similarities with the philosophy of the ancient Chinese philosopher Lao Tzu. However, it is doubtful that Lao Tzu's works directly influenced M. Erickson's professional development. In this case, an appropriate aphorism by Lao Tzu would be as follows:

"Many mountain rivers flow into the deep sea. The reason is that the seas are lower than the mountains. Therefore, they can govern all the streams. Similarly, a wise person, desiring to be above others, becomes lower than them. Wanting to be in front, they position themselves behind. Thus, although their place is above others, they do not feel burdened by it. Although their place is in front, others do not perceive it as unfair."

In addition to the use of the key concepts of joining, leading, and utilization, M. Erickson was an advocate of the antipsychiatric philosophy in psychotherapeutic practice. This philosophy takes a softer approach to the understanding of pathological behavior and places the primary goal of therapy not in conforming the patient to traditional standards of health, but in their social adaptation within society. It matters little whether a person thinks they are Napoleon or sees things that aren't there; what is important is their ability to be socially adapted and derive pleasure from life.

An example of M. Erickson's antipsychiatric psychotherapeutic work is as follows: On one occasion, M. Erickson had the opportunity to work with a patient who believed he was Jesus Christ. M. Erickson asked him, "Are you Jesus?" The patient replied, "Yes, of course!" M. Erickson then said, "Listen, I have a job for you. They're building an extension next to the clinic, and they need a carpenter. Can you help?" What do you think Jesus replied to? Of course, he said "Yes."

"But I will ask one thing of you: please do not tell people that you are Jesus. It will frighten them, as they are not yet ready to comprehend exactly who is before them. Can you do this for them?" posed another question by M. Erickson. The patient agreed joyfully. For six months, he worked as a carpenter, concealing his "true" identity. During this time, the patient behaved normally, and his claims of involvement in events from the New Testament were no longer heard from him.

Psychiatrists decided to form a commission to interview the patient and inquire about how his perception of the world had changed in order to determine whether to release him from the clinic or keep him further. M. Erickson persuaded the patient not to disclose his "true" name to the doctors and instead use only the name from his passport. It was for their own good, of course, as this way he would be able to leave the clinic and spread goodness in the world. And, of course, if they were to release him, he was not to tell others but simply act as Jesus. To do good and help others. The patient went through the commission, left the clinic, moved to another city, and eventually established a community to aid and support those in need, becoming highly successful and sought-after in this field. Every year, on Christmas, he would write a lengthy greeting card to Milton H. Erickson, expressing gratitude for his assistance. At the bottom of the letter, he would sign his name as it appeared on his passport but would always add the initials "J.C" (Jesus Christ) in lowercase.

We won't claim that such a therapeutic approach could be effective in many other cases of schizophrenic personality disorder. Each case of illness can be highly individual and require an individualized approach to treating the symptoms. The depth of the psychiatric symptom and the patient's intellectual level will naturally have a significant influence. However, M. Erickson's work demonstrated at times that even a patient who initially seemed resistant to therapy could, with proper assistance, find their path to healing.

Naturally, M. Erickson effectively applied the technique of joining the patient's state during direct hypnotization. Through this method, he was occasionally able to hypnotize patients who exhibited strong resistance, even those who consciously resisted. Contrary to Emil Coué's belief that if a patient intentionally resists, it would likely be impossible to induce a hypnotic state. However, M. Erickson was truly a master of hypnotic tricks. Here's an example of one of the most amusing ones. One day, a man entered M. Erickson's office and asked him to try to hypnotize him. He was curious whether M. Erickson could succeed. Accepting the challenge, M. Erickson fully understood that the man would consciously resist. He attempted to hypnotize him using several standard methods that were typical for him, and he became convinced that the man was a tough nut to crack and the usual hypnotization methods would not work. Then he told the man that he would step out for a couple of minutes, left the office, and went to the reception area where his secretary was sitting. He quickly induced her into a deep trance state and suggested that she go into his office, sit across from the man, and gaze intently into his eyes until he entered a state of deep hypnotic trance. She left. M. Erickson refrained from entering his office for a while and drank tea. When he finally entered, he saw two people sitting on chairs in a very deep trance state.

Resistance to trance induction is always directed towards something. It could be towards the person themselves—their gender, hair color, social hierarchy, body position, and so on.

In this case, M. Erickson simply assumed that all the resistance was directed towards him personally. The patient came to him specifically to demonstrate their ability to resist him, not the young female secretary who unexpectedly became his hypnotist.

We could provide numerous examples of such fixed resistance. Let us share an interesting one from our experience.

A few years ago, we conducted a hypnotic laboratory where we experimented with the ability to memorize large amounts of information in a hypnotic state. We invited a large number of our students to participate in the experiment. Some of the students who had previously participated in the experiment had experienced hypnotic states, while others came to try trance for the first time.

When we worked with a novice female student, we found that the first few minutes of hypnotic speech had no effect on her state at all. She continued to sit, look at us, and blink, showing no signs of a hypnotic trance. We continued our hypnotic work, fully confident in our abilities.

The next five minutes showed that our efforts still had no desired effect. The student clearly resisted trance induction strongly. We continued the hypnotic speech as if she were already in a trance, despite her reactions. None of the tricks we tried worked on her. This situation persisted even after fifteen minutes.

The audience became nervous, but we continued our work as if there were no resistance. Finally, as our last attempt at hypnotic work, we set a verbal frame, saying that we would count from ten to one, and when we reached one, the girl would exit the trance state (even though she was still awake). When we uttered the word "one," her eyes closed and her head slightly tilted forward. She entered a hypnotic trance.

We continued to work with her for another fifteen minutes, accomplishing our research goal. This is an example of paradoxical induction. The girl's resistance persisted until the hypnotic frame was established. As soon as she heard that she could exit the trance, it signaled her to stop resisting hypnotic induction.

While such examples are not common in practice, they vividly illustrate M. Erickson's concepts for working with patient resistance.

Ericksonian hypnotic style is focused on finding an adequate method of hypnotic induction. If one approach doesn't work, another one might. The key is to understand what the client's resistance is directed towards and to select an appropriate method of hypnotic work. However, it is worth admitting that even for M. Erickson himself, the search for a method sometimes took more than a day.

When we talk about the key techniques of rapport-building with the patient during hypnosis in the works of M. Erickson, it is worth mentioning the practices he developed for matching the patient's postures, movements, and breathing. These techniques became particularly popular thanks to the work of M. Erickson's students, R. Bandler and J. Grinder, who later created Neuro-Linguistic Programming (NLP) and made these techniques a fundamental tool in their methodology.

If we covertly mimic the patient's movements and postures for an ex-tended period, a sense of identity between themselves and us may begin to arise in their consciousness. What is in a similar rhythm to me—either I myself or someone close to me whom I can trust. Any shared rhythms inspire trust, and the more there are, the greater the trust grows. Matching the depth and rhythm of breathing has a similar effect. A vivid example that illustrates matching body posture and breathing is a case of psychotherapeutic work by one of Milton Erickson's students, John Grinder, who once tried to use these techniques to bring a catatonic schizophrenic out of a stupor in a psychiatric clinic.

During catatonia, a schizophrenic can sit in one place for many hours without reacting to the world, words, or actions of others. In the over-whelming majority of cases, any attempts to rouse them have no effect. If you place them in a different posture, they will maintain it without exiting the stuporous state. John Grinder decided to match the patient's posture and breathing—the only criteria that could be mirrored in his behavior. For forty minutes, he simply sat next to the schizophrenic, adopting his posture and breathing in rhythm with him. Then he lightly tapped him on the shoulder and said, "Give me a cigarette." The schizophrenic came out of the stupor, turned towards him, and replied that he didn't smoke. Prior to this, any direct attempts by doctors to bring him out of the stuporous state had not yielded any constructive results. It is worth commenting a bit on this case, as we believe that John Grinder took some risks, as not all catatonic schizophrenics behave peacefully when they come out of the catatonic stupor. There is always a high probability of aggressive actions towards others when their catatonia is interrupted. However, this does not imply the ineffectiveness of the "awakening" method for patients. It rather emphasizes the importance of precautionary methods that need to be observed when reproducing such practices with severely psychotic patients.

2

Psychopathological Profile of Hypnotizable Individuals

Since the times of Anton Mesmer, James Braid, Jean-Martin Charcot, Hippolyte Bernheim, and Ambroise-Auguste Liebeault, doctors have noticed that some patients exhibit extremely high hypnotizability, entering a state of deep hypnotic trance either instantly or within a few minutes. With other patients, it takes some effort to induce a hypnotic trance, and there have always been individuals who show such strong unconscious resistance that the best methods, which worked on others, fail when attempting to hypnotize them. Initially, practitioners of hypnosis were perplexed by the reasons behind these vastly different effects.

The initial models of hypnotizability and non-hypnotizability were limited to elementary attempts at classifying individuals as either neurologically predisposed or not predisposed to the process of hypnosis. In contemporary literature, remnants of such notions can still be found, where readers are presented with "clinical" data stating, for example, that 15% of people are highly hypnotizable, 70% are moderately hypnotizable, and the remaining 15% are weakly hypnotizable or non-hypnotizable altogether. While these figures may vary in different sources, you will generally find similar data. However, such data is absurd considering that these studies did not take into account a multitude of factors that could be crucial in the creation of such clinical data.

What are these factors? For example, what was the composition of the individuals involved in these studies? Were they male or female? Were they physically healthy or ill? Similarly, were they mentally healthy or not? If some of them were ill, what were their illnesses, and to what extent did they affect them? What were their cultural and national backgrounds? What social class did they belong to? What were their ages? Were they religious or atheists? What kind of upbringing did they have in their childhood, and what was their relationship with parental figures in the family? Did they experience any aggressive physical or sexual abuse during their lifetime?

Furthermore, a key omission in compiling such statistics was the question of who exactly hypnotized the people included in the aforementioned statistics. Was it one specialist? Two? Ten? What was the level of their competence? What methods did they use during hypnosis? Was there a single method employed for everyone, or did it vary? Did some of them utilize different styles of hypnotic work? What were the gender and age of the hypnotists themselves? We assert that depending on these factors, the level of hypnotizability would vary significantly. As you can understand, creating a comprehensive statistical database that could yield meaningful correlations among these criteria is very challenging, if not impossible.

Our research data indicates that understanding the key characteristics of psychoanalytic, psychopathological, cultural-ethnic, and socio-cultural profiles can provide highly accurate predictions regarding the majority of hypnotizability and non-hypnotizability criteria in individuals. In this book, we aim to present a comprehensive integrative model of conceptualizations concerning the key predisposing factors for entering the hypnotic trance.

Let's begin with an elementary discussion of the aforementioned criteria and initially focus on the clinical data obtained by the earliest researchers in the field of hypnosis in clinical practice. Physicians observed that women are much more susceptible to hypnotic suggestion than men, with deeper and more intense trance states. Unfortunately, we did not find logical explanations for this phenomenon in the literature. To evaluate this phenomenon, it is necessary to turn to contemporary findings in the field of neurophysiology and pay attention to the connection between the hypnotic state and the activities of various brain regions. In the 1940s, a model of the brain emerged in neurophysiology that divided our brain into three main sectors:

1. **Archicortex**
2. **Limbic system**
3. **Neocortex** (or simply the cortex)

This model was named the triune brain model. The archicortical region is predominantly associated with our instinctive activities, processing basic elementary movements and actions, and actualizing needs for food, water, sleep, and sexual relationships. This brain region was also referred to as the "reptilian brain" since scientists believe it originated in reptiles and then passed on to primates and eventually to humans through evolution. The activity of this brain region is inherited through the evolutionary process. Reptiles experience almost no emotions and are primarily oriented towards instinctual behavior (previously we would have said they experience no emotions at all, but in the context of modern research, we can say they do not experience them as higher animals and humans do, although some signs of emotional processes can still be traced at the neurochemical level in reptiles). Emotional activity emerges in animals with the development of a new brain region, the limbic system, which gives rise to various emotional processes. Animals are capable of experiencing anger, fear, joy, etc., which naturally influences their activities and is not solely based on the instinctual processes of the archicortex. At the level of activity in the limbic system and the beginnings of the neocortex, animals are already capable of performing certain types of activities that can be evaluated as forms of thinking. Modern ethology suggests that the intelligence of higher primates is sometimes comparable to that of 4-6-year-old children. These animals are capable of receiving feedback from the external world and performing activities not typical of their species in order to solve a given task. Although we could provide numerous examples of intellectual activities in animals and birds, we will refrain from delving into this topic as it would deviate from the essence of our research. Let us focus on the fact that the emergence of the neocortex, that is, the full development of the cerebral hemispheres, enables humans to enhance the intellectual capabilities inherent in animals and make verbal thinking possible.

Research on the neurophysiology of hypnotic states and other altered states of consciousness shows that when a person is able to immerse themselves in a state of hypnotic trance, the activity of the cerebral cortex of the brain's hemispheres dampens to some extent, while greater activity is observed in the subcortex. The less active the cerebral cortex, the deeper and more uncontrollable the trance state we can achieve. The higher its activity, the more superficial and controllable the trance becomes.

This information allows for numerous conclusions to be drawn. For example, one might assume that the more verbal and cognitive activity a person exhibits, the less susceptible they are to hypnosis. However, this is not entirely true. The verbal and cognitive domains and their level of development do not directly determine the possible depth of hypnotic induction.

But if we consider individuals whose line of work or life experiences require them to focus their thinking around the theme of self-preservation, we will find that attempting to hypnotize such individuals presents certain challenges. The activity of the cerebral cortex in these individuals has become part of their survival strategy, and ceasing to think about danger or relinquishing conscious control over the situation is synonymous with death or something similar. This process is almost always evident in people suffering from paranoid personality disorder. Paranoid individuals are among the worst subjects for hypnosis.

In contrast, schizoid personalities, who also predominantly live in their "heads" and exhibit heightened activity in the cerebral cortex, can display very deep trance states with properly constructed hypnotic suggestions, temporarily releasing the activity of the cerebral cortex.

Let's return to the topic of men and women and provide data from a highly specific neurophysiological study in the field of sexology. Scientists

49

became interested in understanding what happens in the human brain when experiencing an orgasm and how these processes differ between men and women. We will not delve into the specifics of this study, but we will comment on the fact that brain activity during orgasm does indeed differ between men and women.

What is the main difference? During orgasm, the cerebral cortex in the vast majority of cases is only partially deactivated in men. On the contrary, in women, the cortex's activity is more often completely deactivated during orgasm, allowing them to experience more sensations (particularly pleasure) from sex and, naturally, be less aware of them due to the absence of control.

A philosophical question arises: what is better or worse? To experience more pleasure but not be fully aware of what one is experiencing, or to experience less pleasure but be conscious of what is happening.

There was a Greek legend about whether men or women derive more pleasure from sex. Once, a Greek hero was walking through the forest when he came across two mating snakes. He threw a stick at them, interrupting their sexual act. The gods witnessed his act and punished him by transforming him into a woman for nine years (apparently, becoming a woman was considered a punishment in ancient Greece). Our hero lived as a woman for nine years and then transformed back into a man.

Afterward, he was asked, "Having been both a man and a woman and having engaged in lovemaking in these roles, tell us, who derives more pleasure from sex?" He replied, "A woman derives nine times more pleasure." The legend might have seemed like a beautiful story if it weren't for modern neurophysiological studies, which partly seem to confirm its veracity.

Naturally, if we observe similar neurophysiological effects in the majority of women, it indicates a genetic factor predisposing them to this. We can make an assumption as to why such a division occurs. In the context of evolution, men, being hunters, warriors, and protectors, often died if they lost control of their primary sphere of activity. Even during lovemaking, ancient men had to remain vigilant to ensure their own safety and the safety of their wives. More vigilant men survived more often than inattentive ones.

Thus, through natural selection, the careless were eliminated. Women, on the other hand, did not have the need to be overly vigilant since they relied on men beside them to fulfill this function.

Based on the given information, we can assert that the behavior of the brain during orgasm, specifically whether self-control is inhibited during sex, provides us with a comprehensive understanding of an individual's capacity to immerse themselves in a hypnotic trance or other altered states of consciousness and the depth they can reach.

In our practice, while working with a significant number of men, we have made intriguing findings when encountering highly hypnotizable individuals. Almost all of them had some involvement with cult religious organizations at some point in their lives. These men were capable of delving into the deepest levels of hypnotic trance, performing various phenomena, and being unaware of what was happening to them. On the one hand, they were intellectually developed, indicating a high level of development in the cerebral cortex of the brain's hemispheres. On the other hand, it appears that their cerebral cortex could be deactivated, similar to women with hysterical disorders. We hypothesized that trance-inducing rituals in religions train the human brain to engage in trance-like processes. Whether it involves chanting, mantra recitation, prayers, and so on, the human mind is capable of learning to disable self-control (meta-self-control). When such individuals participate in a hypnotic session, even if it is their first experience of being hypnotized, their brains are already accustomed to this form of activity. In our opinion, in ancient communities, particularly shamans, individuals who practiced trance rituals learned to deeply deactivate the activity of the cerebral cortex, enabling them to access numinous revelations during trance states, which subsequently formed the foundation of religious beliefs. By the way, some contemporary psychiatrists perceive the activities of shamans as manifestations of hysteria and epilepsy, disorders that often provide fertile ground for hypnotic suggestion and the reproduction of various hypnotic phenomena. This serves as an example of the differentiation between male and female profiles.

It is worth noting that the resistance of some men to the process of hypnotization is at times linked to particular beliefs about the correlation between susceptibility to hypnosis and personal strength. This rigidity can be especially noticeable in men with wounded masculine egos, where feelings of inadequacy are profound. If a man is hypnotized by another man, it can become another confirmation of his perceived inadequacy. However, this rule is not absolute, and variations and nuances can be observed. This will be particularly evident when discussing the hypnotizability of alcoholics and drug addicts.

Once again, let's list the four main categories for profiling an individual's hypnotizability:

1. **Psychoanalytic profiling.**
2. **Psychopathological profiling.**
3. **Cultural-ethnic profiling.**
4. **Socio-cultural profiling.**

We will place the greatest emphasis on the first two points, as they are the most significant in our opinion.

Psychoanalytic Profiling

In psychoanalytic profiling, it is worth noting the four main profiles of a person's relationships with their parents.

1. **Daddy's and mommy's child**:
   This is a person who loves and accepts both the father and the mother.

2. **Daddy's child, but not mommy's child**:
   This person loves and accepts the father but not the mother.

3. **Mommy's child, but not daddy's child**:
   This person loves and accepts the mother but not the father.

4. **Neither daddy's nor mommy's child**:
   This person, in essence, does not love or accept either the father or the mother.

Daddy's and mommy's child

Individuals with this profile are often highly hypnotizable, at average to high levels, depending on the gender of the hypnotherapist. Trust and love for parental figures become not only psychological but also neurological processes, involving the ability to produce the neurotransmitter oxytocin in the brain, which implies the potential for rapport-building. All patients who underwent therapy with us and corresponded to this profile were hypnotizable and capable of reproducing various trance phenomena.

Daddy's child, but not mommy's child

While working with individuals in this profile, we have found that their ability to enter a hypnotic state is significantly related to their trust in the mother figure. Presumably, this is because the mother is the individual's very first "hypnotherapist," lulling the child to sleep, comforting them during infancy, and being one of the most significant figures from whom the child draws security and peace. When this connection is disrupted, the ability to find an alternative source of balance in the world is also disrupted. We have often observed examples where individuals of this profile initially enter a trance state, but then something seems to interrupt it within them. Deep levels of hypnotic trance are typically less accessible to representatives of this profile. Overall, it should be noted that individuals who are primarily daddy's children do not particularly favor the hypnotic trance; they tend to ignore it, not actively participate in the hypnotic process, and observe others being hypnotized.

Mommy's child, but not daddy's child

On the other hand, mommy's children enjoy the trance state, and quite strongly at that. They are the most hypnotizable subjects among all four psychoanalytic profiles. The vast majority of mommy's children are more willing to surrender control over their consciousness and, at a subconscious level, have a greater desire for the experience of trance. The trance state they experience is usually even deeper than that of Daddy's and Mommy's children. Here, we have made the assumption that the figure of the father in a person's consciousness represents control in various senses of the word. Individuals who love and accept their fathers are generally more willful subjects, which leads us to speculate that the activity of the left prefrontal cortex, associated with a person's volitional qualities and abilities to make independent decisions, may directly relate to the child's psychological relationship with the father figure. Similarly, the activity of the amygdala, anterior and posterior cingulate cortex, brain regions associated with the capacity for empathy and compassion, may be connected to the child's relationship with the mother.

Neither daddy's nor mommy's child

This is the most problematic profile. Subjects with this profile are often only mildly hypnotizable. The lack of emotional connection with the mother greatly hampers their ability to experience the trance state. Moreover, the absence of a connection with the father denies them any opportunities to build their life according to their own desires. Furthermore, it should be added that this profile is the most stagnant and problematic for undergoing psychotherapy. While approaches can eventually be found for other profiles, in this case, any psychotherapeutic interventions are rendered ineffective. The situation changes if it is possible to transform the client's profile into another one, which, in reality, occurs extremely rarely.

Imprints of the Perinatal Sphere

The following model of psychoanalytic profiling will be the model proposed by **Stanislav Grof** to describe the psychomotional imprints of the perinatal sphere. This model consists of four **basic perinatal matrices** (**BPM**s) that are analyzed by Grof in terms of their content. However, the analysis of fixations on any perinatal matrices as a capacity for entering into a hypnotic trance has not been conducted, as far as our observations indicate. We will fill this gap by briefly describing these matrices and how their content determines the quality of immersion into a hypnotic state.

BPM-1

The first perinatal matrix, describes almost the entire experience of being in the womb for the infant until the onset of contractions. It is usually associated with a subconscious sense of oceanic bliss, tranquility, and the happiness of unity with the larger world. If the mother did not experience significant stress or emotional turmoil during the entire period of pregnancy, which influences the emotional life of the child, it becomes imprinted on the infant as a favorable state of altered perception. This imprint acts as a beneficial foundation for the ability to enter a hypnotic state. However, experiencing traumatic events during this period does not necessarily imply the opposite effect. Nonetheless, the overall image of an "anxious womb" is likely to disturb profound trust in the world and, specifically, the work of a hypnotherapist.

BPM-2

This perinatal matrix is associated with the experience of the onset of labor, placental rupture, and the initial contractions before cervical dilation. In this matrix, we often encounter the darkest and gloomiest imprints on our psyche. Several factors determine the level of negativity in this matrix. These factors include the level of maternal anxiety at the onset of labor, the duration of the period from the start of contractions to the opening of the cervix, and the general physiological state of the mother during labor. Strong fixation on this matrix can lead to the development of psychopathic or paranoid states in adults, hindering their ability to comfortably experience altered states in general and hypnotic states in particular.

BPM-3

The third perinatal matrix is associated with the process of birth from the beginning of cervical dilation until the moment the baby exits the womb. The passage through the birth canal always leaves a painful imprint on the child. The emotional states experienced by the mother largely determine the child's state, regardless of the difficulties encountered during the process of entering the world. Intense fear, anxiety, and anger in the mother can create the worst imprints, damaging the child's trust in the world throughout childhood and adulthood. Through our analysis of this matrix, we have discovered an interesting correlation: difficult births can sometimes serve as a basis for the child's ability to enter very deep trance states. We explain this phenomenon by speculating that prolonged and painful labors may provoke bursts of activity in an excessive number of opioid receptors in the mother's brain to alleviate the pain of childbirth. This activation may also lead to a deeper suppression of the cerebral cortex, which naturally becomes imprinted on the child. It is worth noting that we have observed this correlation primarily in female hypnotic subjects who have experienced severe physical abuse during childhood. If the abuse did not shape a paranoid personality structure, these subjects often exhibit a high level of hypnotizability. This dependency was not observed as frequently in male hypnotic subjects, possibly because attacks on them from the external world more often result in a need for hyper-control and activation of the cerebral cortex rather than a deep trance state. It should be added that any unexpressed aggression is much easier and more natural to sublimate in an altered state of consciousness. If, for some reason, an individual does not want or cannot express aggression in their normal state of consciousness, one of the optimal outlets for them is immersion into an altered state of consciousness, specifically a hypnotic state. Unfortunately, many individuals resort to alcohol and drugs for self-therapy purposes in order to express hidden aggressive feelings.

BPM-4

According to Stanislav Grof, the fourth perinatal matrix is associated with the period from complete emergence from the mother's womb until approximately five hours after birth. The key element for the harmonious passage of this matrix is the ability of the child to establish physical contact with the mother during this period. This physical contact will play a significant role in the child's ability to establish a psycho-emotional connection with the external world, trust it, and maintain contact. Of course, this factor is just one among many others that influence such states, so we should not attribute absolute influence to this factor. Another significant criterion that requires comment is that if the child does not receive contact with the mother during this time frame, feelings of resentment and aggression can become key imprints within this matrix, negatively affecting a person's ability to enter a hypnotic trance or experience favorable states within it.

Psychopathological Profiling

This form of personality profiling provides one of the most detailed maps, enabling us to assess the hypnotizability of individuals. In our work, we will discuss eight fundamental psychopathological profiles and describe how their characteristics influence the level of hypnotizability in a person.

1. **Hysteroid Personality Profile**
   The hysteroid personality profile refers to individuals who exhibit excessive emotionality, attention-seeking behavior, and a tendency to dramatize situations. Such individuals may display high suggestibility

and possess a strong need for approval and recognition.

2. **Paranoid Personality Profile**

The paranoid personality profile is characterized by a pervasive distrust and suspicion of others. These individuals tend to interpret innocent actions as malicious and may struggle to establish rapport and trust with the hypnotist.

3. **Psychopathic Personality Profile**

The psychopathic personality profile refers to individuals who lack empathy, display impulsivity, and engage in manipulative behavior. Due to their resistance to external influences and a tendency to exert control, individuals with this profile may exhibit low hypnotizability.

4. **Obsessive-Compulsive Personality Profile**

The obsessive-compulsive personality profile is associated with perfectionism, rigidity, and a need for control. Individuals with this profile may find it challenging to relax and relinquish control, impacting their ability to enter a hypnotic state.

5. **Schizoid Personality Profile**

The schizoid personality profile describes individuals characterized by social withdrawal, emotional detachment, and introspection. These individuals may encounter difficulties establishing rapport with the hypnotist and may exhibit low hypnotizability.

6. **Epileptoid Personality Profile**

The epileptoid personality profile is linked to emotional instability, impulsivity, and intense emotional reactions. Individuals with this profile may demonstrate heightened hypnotizability due to their susceptibility to emotional states.

7. **Schizophrenic Personality Profile**

The schizophrenic personality profile involves disturbances in perception, thought processes, and social functioning. The level of hypnotizability may vary among individuals with this profile, depending on the severity of their symptoms and their ability to maintain focus.

8. **Manic-Depressive Personality Profile** (Bipolar)
   The manic-depressive personality profile is characterized by extreme mood swings, ranging from manic episodes of high energy to depressive episodes of low mood. The hypnotizability of individuals with this profile may fluctuate depending on their current mood state.

All the manifestations of these psychopathological profiles can be differentiated into **three levels of intensity**:

1. **Accentuated Level**:
   Pathology is in its incipient stage and does not significantly impact social adequacy. It merely gives the personality a specific direction.

2. **Neurotic Level**:
   Pathology significantly impairs social adaptation.

3. **Psychotic Level**:
   The ability for social adaptation is almost completely disrupted by various forms of symptom manifestation.

By understanding these profiles and their intensity levels, we gain insights into an individual's susceptibility to hypnosis, enabling us to tailor therapeutic approaches accordingly.

Hysteroid Personality Profile

As the starting point for developing this profiling model, we took the illness of hysteria and its less pathological form of expression, known as hysteroid (demonstrative) accentuation. As we mentioned, early hypnotherapists discovered that women suffering from hysteria were extremely hypnotizable. Hysteria was initially considered a predominantly female disorder. Hippocrates believed that hysteria was a manifestation of the "wandering womb." Plato stated that hysteria afflicts women who are unable to conceive. Ancient Greeks often recommended marrying young girls as a quick remedy for hysteria. It is also mentioned that in Ancient Greece, methods involving Dionysian practices, such as wine and orgies, were sometimes used to treat hysteria. We will not assert the correctness of the ancient Greeks, but we can assume that these methods may have provided temporary improvement while likely worsening the condition in the long term. In medieval Europe, women suffering from hysteria were often accused of witchcraft by the Inquisition and burned at the stake. It is worth noting that hysterics are highly hypnotizable, and we are convinced that if a hysteric woman is suggested to be possessed by an evil force, she will eventually "play out" this possession. Early psychiatrists considered hysteria the mother of imitation since they noticed that hysterical individuals were capable of displaying almost all the symptoms characteristic of other illnesses in their behavior. Even in the 19th century, the treatment of hysteria did not differ significantly from the Dionysian methods of the ancient Greeks. Physicians in Britain, France, and some other European countries could suggest clitoral massage as a therapy for hysterical patients.

In the late 19th century, sets for "self-massage" even started being sold in British pharmacies. As some contemporary psychiatrists write, these are the milestones in the history of medicine that today's medical professionals might feel ashamed of. We don't know about shame, but when we share this historical information with our students during courses on psychopathology and psychotherapy, we mainly observe laughter.

Here we can clearly trace a peculiar dependence. Early psychiatrists primarily treated hysteroid women with massages and hypnosis. They witnessed the complete compliance of their patients with their suggestions. Orgasm and deep hypnotic states share similarities in their neurophysiological processes. The deeper the trance state, the lower the activity in the cerebral cortex of the brain.

Understanding the hysteroid personality profile is essential in the context of psychopathological profiling. Individuals with this profile tend to exhibit attention-seeking behavior, dramatic expressions of emotions, and a strong desire for recognition. They may display high hypnotizability due to their inclination toward suggestibility. It is important to note that the term "hysteroid" is used here to describe a specific accentuation or emphasis within the personality structure rather than a clinical diagnosis of hysteria. By studying this profile and its influence on hypnotizability, we gain valuable insights into therapeutic approaches that can be tailored to individuals with such characteristics.

It is crucial to approach the historical treatment methods mentioned with critical analysis and acknowledge the progress made in medical ethics and evidence-based practices. Contemporary understanding and treatment of psychopathology, including the hysteroid personality profile, emphasize the importance of comprehensive assessment, evidence-based interventions, and a compassionate therapeutic relationship. By integrating psychological theories, clinical expertise, and ethical considerations, we strive to provide effective and ethical care to individuals with various psychopathological profiles.

Working with patients who exhibited prominent symptoms of hysteria or hysteric accentuation, we have confirmed that this symptom provides an ideal foundation for hypnosis. Hysteroid patients not only more frequently enter very deep altered states of consciousness, but their style of entering a hypnotic state is often extravagant, vivid, and memorable. These are truly the moments that are easily remembered and stay with us for years.

Let us provide some vivid examples from our practice. One of our students, clearly possessing hysteroid accentuation, had the ability to enter a state of hypnosis simply by touching her forehead and giving the command, "Sleep!"

Within a couple of seconds of this, her body would completely relax and become "gelatinous." If she was seated in this state, she would eventually attempt to fall to the floor.

Once, she participated in an evening hypnosis class that lasted from 5:00 PM to 9:00 PM. At the end of the class, we took her for a hypnotic session and easily and quickly induced her into a hypnotic state. We suggested to her that she would forget the past four hours and that upon awakening from the hypnotic trance, she would firmly believe that she had just arrived for the evening session. We also suggested that she fully remember the forgotten time by the next morning.

Then we commanded her to awaken from her hypnotic sleep. She looked at us in surprise, then at the other participants in the group, and finally out of the window, where it was already dark. She was shocked by the sudden change in lighting outside and then commented with surprise, "I have a strange feeling as if everything has already happened." For several hours after the group session, fragments of the lost time would emerge for her. By the following morning, all the memories had returned. This was one of the most vivid examples in our practice of selective hypnotic amnesia.

It was impossible to reproduce the phenomena of catalepsy and levitation of the hands in her case, as her body in trance was always "gelatinous." Suggestions did not help in this case. In the hypnotic trance state, she perfectly executed suggestions to open her eyes and see things that were not there, meaning she experienced positive hallucinations.

In one of the seminars on Ericksonian hypnosis, while in a hypnotic trance, we suggested to her that she would easily enter a hypnotic trance upon hearing the key phrase "Stormy Petrel." Then we induced amnesia regarding the suggestion, brought her out of trance, placed her in the center of the auditorium (with a young man standing behind her to catch her if she fell), and said the suggested word. Her eyes began to close, and her body started to slump downward. When we repeated the key phrase, she collapsed to the ground. The young man caught her just in time. This example clearly demonstrates the phenomenal level of her hypnotic susceptibility.

Another student, also possessing hysteroid accentuation, was highly suggestible, just like the previous one. It only took a couple of words, sometimes just a touch to her forehead, and she would already be deep in a hypnotic trance.

Her main difference from the previous student was her motor disinhibition during the process of trance induction. A single touch to her hand and lifting it upwards would create a stable catalepsy of the hand. Moreover, it was possible to quickly induce this form of hypnotic catalepsy even when she was not in a typical hypnotic trance state. We could induce catalepsy in both her hands and legs simultaneously during the trance. Furthermore, the catalepsy of the hands would frequently transition naturally into levitation. In other words, the hands would smoothly move in the air and live their own peculiar life.

It was with her that we easily and naturally created the phenomenon of catalepsy of the entire body, where the body acquires wax-like flexibility and pliability, assumes a stable standing position, and then, with the help of an assistant, the hypnotized body is placed on the backs of chairs. The upper part of the back on one chair and the lower part of the legs on another chair. We could place up to five metal office chairs on her abdomen during this procedure, and her body remained stable.

Additionally, she exhibited excellent positive and negative hallucination phenomena during hypnosis sessions. The phenomena of hypermnesia, amnesia, anesthesia, analgesia, taste illusions, and other phenomena were easily achieved. It is worth noting an interesting aspect of her profile. She almost completely denied her own sexuality and had no desire to engage in any sexual relationships. This persisted until she turned 25. We do not possess information about what happened after the age of 25.

It would be logical to assume that her hyper-hypnotizability was somehow related to sexual repression. However, it is not that simple. The previous hypnotic subject we described, who was highly suggestible, did not exhibit sexual abstinence at all.

All the clients with hysteroid accentuation who participated in our hypnosis sessions frequently and effortlessly achieved a somnambulistic trance state, and the manifestations of trance were particularly vivid and remarkable.

By employing elementary behavior analysis, it was possible to identify manifestations of hysteroid accentuation in clients, thereby suggesting a higher level of hypnotizability.

Key characteristics of hysteroid behavior:

1. Constant attention-seeking behavior.
2. Desire to actively participate in discussions.
3. Willingness to publicly discuss personal aspects of their life and the lives of others.
4. If the hysteroid individual is female, their behavior is often sexualized, especially around men.
5. Display of intense emotions.
6. Problems with self-control, willpower, and goal-setting.
7. Occasional tactlessness and unethical behavior.
8. Hysteroid men have a high likelihood of substance abuse and alcohol dependence.
9. Frequent lying.
10. Inclination towards fantasy.
11. Desire for public engagement and exposure.
12. Strong craving for public approval.
13. High probability of infidelity towards their sexual partner.
14. Often characterized by an attention-grabbing appearance and clothing.
15. Tendency to engage in unexpected, sometimes shocking actions.

By observing a person for just a couple of hours, many of these criteria will begin to manifest in their behavior. In our opinion, individuals fitting this profile are ideal for demonstrating various phenomena of hypnotic trance.

Assessment of Hypnotic Susceptibility Profile Characteristics:

1. Very high hypnotic susceptibility
2. Rapid induction into a hypnotic state
3. Almost complete absence of resistance to the hypnotherapist
4. Exaggeration of hypnotic effects
5. Exaggeration of therapeutic effects
6. Deeper and faster immersion into a hypnotic state in public settings
7. High risk of erotic transference onto the psychotherapist
8. Strong short-term and weak long-term therapeutic effect

Paranoid Personality Profile

Paranoid personalities are no less intriguing in hypnotherapy than hysteric ones, as they represent the diametrical opposite in their ability to enter a state of hypnotic trance. The paranoid profile is one of the least hypnotizable profiles in our model. Paranoid individuals have existed throughout the history of humanity. A paranoid personality organizes their thinking in a way that constantly seeks to perceive threats to themselves, their family, their city, their country, and so on. To some extent, a paranoid individual lives in their own world, where they believe that their surroundings intend to make them victims. In our opinion, there are six main types of paranoia that can actively develop in a person's mind.

1. **Paranoia of rumors:**
   The person believes that others speak negatively about them, insult them behind their backs, consider them bad, insignificant, immoral, and so on.

2. **Physical harm paranoia:**
   The person believes that they may be beaten, maimed, injured, or subjected to any other form of physical harm.

3. **Sexual harm paranoia**:

   This type of paranoia is predominantly found in women. They believe that they are in danger of being raped, seduced, or sexually exploited. They develop a conviction that men are only interested in one thing.

4. **Theft paranoia**:

   These individuals have persistent thoughts that their apartment will be burglarized, their personal belongings will be stolen, or that someone will deceive them in order to gain material benefits. They develop a worldview in which financially motivated people surround them, willing to do anything for a penny, and so on.

5. **Social harm paranoia**:

   The main focus here is on conspiracies aimed at demoting them from a position, firing them from work, blocking their career advancement, and so on.

6. **Betrayal by friends and infidelity paranoia**:

   Intrusive thoughts about being abandoned by loved ones.

These are the primary manifestations of paranoia, which can actively occur within an individual's mind.

From our experience, the majority of different cases of paranoia in individuals can be classified into one of these six categories. Sometimes paranoia remains in a passive form, where a person contemplates the world but refrains from taking any significant actions based on their thoughts. However, the stronger the paranoia,

the greater the desire to transition into an active form, where the paranoid individual, instead of waiting for an attack, becomes the attacker themselves. They inflict harm upon people they suspect of conspiracy and betray their partners after inventing the belief that the partner has already betrayed them.

The main distinction from paranoid schizophrenia is that a paranoid individual does not experience hallucinations or sensory illusions. Everything happens within the framework of an ordinary cognitive process that remains confined to their mind.

Naturally, the constant fixation of one's thoughts on potential danger keeps the individual in a state of both emotional and muscular tension. The cortex of the cerebral hemispheres is constantly hyperactive, causing significant difficulties for the person to naturally enter altered states of consciousness, particularly hypnosis. Over the years, we have observed how individuals with a paranoid personality accent or suffering from full-blown paranoia are capable of reacting to the process of inducing a hypnotic trance.

Trust issues typically arise at the beginning of hypnotic work, where the patient expresses numerous negative assumptions and concerns about what they may expect in the trance state. Men may often worry about whether the hypnotic trance will negatively affect them. Women, on the other hand, are more frequently plagued by sexual paranoia, fearing that they will be helpless with a hypnotherapist who may do whatever they desire. Such fantasies can sometimes be found in the imaginations of female clients.

Regarding the impact on states in the context of hypnotic induction, paranoia can be divided into deep, true paranoia and superficial, hysterical paranoia. Deep, true paranoia primarily affects neurophysiological processes, interrupting any attempts to enter a trance state with active cognitive processes and physical tension. The client may already be consciously convinced that nothing threatens them, but old paranoid defense mechanisms will hinder the entry into an altered state of consciousness in any attempts by the hypnotherapist. Let me provide an example.

About five years ago, we conducted a workshop dedicated to hypnotic suggestion in an anti-café in the city. The owner of the establishment, who provided the venue for the event, participated in the class. In the final part of the seminar, we demonstrated a session of group induction into a hypnotic trance, during which anyone in the group could immerse themselves in an altered state. At the end of the trance session, participants provided feedback regarding the states they experienced during the hypnotic induction. When it was the turn of the establishment owner, she commented the following:

"I sat with my eyes closed, and thoughts kept racing through my head that while we were sitting like this, you were rummaging through our bags." In this case, we clearly observe paranoia related to theft and causing material harm.

Analyzing the causes of such states in clients, we found either situations where the person had been repeatedly robbed in the past, resulting in a significantly increased level of anxiety regarding the safety of their belongings, or the person themselves had once been a thief and is now simply projecting their past actions onto others, unwilling to remember and acknowledge their own deeds. When it comes to sexual paranoia among women, the situation differs slightly.

If the first criterion remains similar to the previous one, and if a woman has experienced sexual violence, attempted sexual violence, or aggressive sexual harassment, then the main second criterion will be paranoia induced by suggestion. For example, it could stem from the mother or grandmother in the woman's childhood, where constant ideas were instilled in the family that the image of a man is that of a lustful animal who only wants "one thing." Sometimes we can observe combinations of both the first and second criteria.

We made another very interesting observation regarding the process of hypnotization as well as other practices of altered states of consciousness. It is inherent for people to project those feelings that they usually repress or wish to repress in their everyday lives. During the anticipation of hypnosis and often during the first hypnosis session, these repressed products begin to actively enter the conscious sphere. As a result, individuals may experience aggressive, anxious, phobic, sexualized emotions, feelings of helplessness, sadness, and so on. However, if a person does not possess a paranoid personality accent, these symptoms usually subside after the first hypnosis session and do not return. In contrast, individuals with a paranoid personality accent may remain fixated on negative experiences for an indefinite amount of time. Sometimes, suppressed negative emotions may somatize during the first hypnosis session. For example, a strong headache may arise, which can persist for several hours after the hypnosis session. In all cases we observed, the initial somatization never recurred during subsequent trance sessions.

Superficial hysterical paranoia often manifests as exaggerated anxiety regarding what to expect during the hypnotic state. Clients express their concerns, display hesitancy, and approach everything with caution. However, if the trance session can be initiated, these anxieties usually transform into a passive background form, allowing the client to enter a light or even moderate level of hypnotic trance.

In the vast majority of cases, a paranoid personality accent makes hypnotherapy minimally productive or unproductive altogether. Occasionally, prolonged verbal therapy can reduce paranoid reactions, enabling the utilization of hypnotic practices during later stages of psychotherapy.

Key characteristics of the paranoid type:

- Distrust
- Suspiciousness
- Fixation on negative outcomes of events
- Inability to acknowledge one's own mistakes
- Interpreting all life events according to a paranoid worldview
- Anxiety
- Unconscious provocation by the environment to engage in negative actions
- Hypochondria
- Pessimism
- Persecutory delusions
- Paranoid fantasies

Assessment of the hypnability profile:

- Low or minimal level of hypnotizability
- Almost complete inability to engage in the hypnotic process, particularly during initial attempts

- If trance does occur, it is often superficial and not deep
- Underestimation of the power of hypnotic effects by the patient
- Underestimation of the therapeutic effects
- Public induction of trance may increase patient discomfort
- Risk of aggressive transference onto the psychotherapist.

Psychopathic Personality Profile

There are a wide variety of manifestations of psychopathic behavior. Behind psychopathic behavior, certain **key personality characteristics** are often present. Let's list them:

1. Inability to experience guilt, shame, or embarrassment.
2. Disregard for morality in various forms.
3. Almost complete absence of fear.
4. Almost complete inability to sympathize, empathize, or show empathy.
5. Almost complete absence of depressive and anxious symptoms.
6. Living day by day without significant future planning.
7. Narcissism, selfishness, and self-centeredness.
8. High level of Machiavellianism (life principle: "the ends justify the means").
9. Often, high levels of communication skills.
10. Often, a high level of personal charm.
11. Pleasure derived from causing suffering to others in various forms.

Naturally, the intensity of these manifestations can vary greatly, ranging from microscopic expressions where the psychopath simply derives pleasure from causing relatively minor emotional pain to severe forms of physical and sexual violence.

Separate from typical true psychopathy is sexual psychopathy, where an individual simply has a need to engage in deviant sexual acts, sometimes involving violence and harm to others and sometimes without it. This can include fetishes, BDSM, voyeurism, exhibitionism, pedophilia, necrophilia, and more. Various forms of sexual psychopathy may not necessarily be sadistic in nature, where an individual derives sexual pleasure specifically from the process of strangling a sexual partner, but masochistic, where there is a strong desire for certain ritual forms of violence to be performed on the individual themselves, resulting in sexual gratification. In our work, we will not delve deeply into the topic of sexual psychopathy, as it deserves separate and detailed attention. For now, we will simply outline its general contours to link it to the theme of the patient's hypnotizability in the process of hypnosis.

Sometimes psychopathy takes on a hysteroid, demonstrative accent when a person seeks to appear unfeeling, narcissistic, and walking over corpses— a "genius of our time." But in reality, we will see that beneath the mask hides a frightened individual.

Based on our experience, **true psychopaths are almost entirely unhypnotizable**. Problems with hypnotizing individuals of this profile can be even more pronounced than with individuals of the paranoid profile. Sexual psychopaths, without extreme forms of manifestation, can vary in their response to hypnotic suggestion, ranging from strong resistance to complete compliance, similar to hysteroid personalities. These changes, in our opinion, vary according to the psychoanalytic profile of the individual.

Based on our observations, demonstrative psychopaths are more often hypnotizable at a low or moderate level. Let us provide examples to further analyze representatives of this profile and its variations.

We will not describe severe forms of psychopathy, only those that we interpret as accentuated forms.

A 38-year-old female patient came with a very interesting request related to her husband and several lovers in different countries who are competing for her hand. She sleeps with each of them in turn, and she enjoys it, but she is troubled by the fact that she enjoys it. It is worth mentioning that her request was extremely original.

During the conversation, it became clear that she completely lacks a sense of guilt for her relationships with men. As she said, she constantly has 2-3 men in her life, and these are not just lovers but full-fledged relationships.

Fortunately, they are all scattered across different countries. In most of these relationships, she does not experience complete sexual satisfaction, which often leads her to engage in autoeroticism. She does not feel the need to choose one particular man. This displays a symptom closely resembling nymphomania.

She mentioned that she collects rings from men who have asked her to marry them. She often brings these relationships to the point of marriage and then runs away. When she was 18 years old, she started a relationship with a 26-year-old college director where she was studying. The man was in love with her and, as she said, carried her in his hands. They planned their wedding. However, she did not show up for the wedding and instead went to another man, with whose help she had an abortion. She got pregnant by the next man and had an abortion with him as well. She then met a man who became her husband and the father of her child.

Her attitude towards men is devoid of sentimentality and is seen as a means to satisfy her sexual needs. She denies feeling guilt for any of her actions. She regards psychotherapy as an interesting game, much like any psychopath. In this case, we observe a combination of true and sexual psychopathy. On the one hand, true psychopathy blocks almost all natural entry points into a hypnotic state. On the other hand, sexual uninhibitedness can significantly contribute to the presence of a need for deep unconscious states. In this case, true psychopathic accentuation predominated.

The patient became interested in hypnosis practice. She was very nervous before the session, as if she couldn't find her place. During attempts to hypnotize her, her body experienced spasms, and almost every muscle tensed, even though she did not make any conscious effort to do so. Her reactions to the hypnotherapist somewhat resembled those of paranoid personalities, but without any explicit expectation of harm to herself. After intentionally closing her eyes at the request of the hypnotherapist, she began to think that the hypnotherapist was looking at her face very intently. The tension in her body increased, and she abruptly opened her eyes. This happened several times during the session.

The psychopath's ego faced a direct attack on its defense mechanisms.

Psychopaths constantly suppress the sense of guilt for their actions, but the process of suppression requires constant energy expenditure, manifested in the body as fixed muscle tension. If a psychopath tries hypnotic influence, it relaxes their muscular framework, connecting them to a sense of guilt, which is painful for them. The only way to prevent this is to do anything to avoid it. We have discovered similar reactions in true psychopaths to Stanislav Grof's holotropic breathwork. Most other profiles can immerse themselves in interesting and vivid states of consciousness using this method in psychotherapeutic work, but true psychopaths often experience intense suffering and usually terminate the session as unbearable.

It should be noted that psychopathic personalities often replace natural trance states with substances like heroin, cocaine, and marijuana. However, not all of them do so.

So let's summarize true psychopathy. Patients in this category are among the most unhypnotizable individuals. However, such patients rarely seek therapy, and if they do, they perceive it as an interesting pastime rather than a psychotherapeutic process. When you tell these people directly to their faces that they don't want to change their way of life, they sincerely confirm this belief and continue attending psychotherapy sessions. A natural question arises: why? The answer here is almost unequivocal. The world of a psychopath is a world of aggressor and victim, and it is vital for them to continue playing the role of the aggressor with all their might. At the first opportunity, a psychopath will try to assume the role of the victim towards the therapist, if successful. If they realize that they are unlikely to succeed, they leave psychotherapy and return to their usual activities.

The situation may be somewhat different with pure sexual psychopaths. Sexual psychopathy manifests itself in various forms, and we have not had the opportunity to work with many of them using hypnotic suggestion. Our observations indicate that certain sexual perversions performed in privacy or with mutually agreed-upon partners can significantly influence the depth of hypnotizability, sometimes enabling individuals to reach ultra-deep trance states.

Unfortunately, in our opinion, the overwhelming majority of psychopaths and sexual deviants do not voluntarily seek psychotherapists, making it genuinely challenging to assemble a comprehensive clinical picture in such cases. Let's provide an example of a case of sexual psychopathy.

A 27-year-old female patient during the course of therapy. From childhood until the age of 18, she regularly experienced aggressive violence. Her father would regularly beat her, grab her by the hair, slam her head against the tiles, and humiliate her. She always assumed a passive victim position towards her father. Menstruation began at the age of 15. Her sexuality remained inactive until the age of 21. At 21, she encountered a young man with whom she had a relationship for a while. Then, in the woods, according to her comments, she had sexual intercourse coerced by him. After that, she broke up with him, and for the following 3 years, she displayed strong sexual uninhibitedness in her behavior. She engaged in relationships with dozens of men, whom she could simply find on the street and bring home for one-time sexual encounters. She doesn't remember the names of most of these people. During this period and subsequently, she exhibited a strong attraction to BDSM in her sexual relationships, assuming a passive position. After these three years, her sexuality somewhat calmed down, and she found a somewhat regular sexual partner with whom she had sex several times a year. She also found a married man whom she fell in love with and continuously attempted to win over from his wife, a pursuit she continued for many years. At times, she felt the need to find a BDSM "dominator" who could engage in perverted forms of intercourse with her. As she commented, she experienced special pleasure when performing fellatio with such men, "until tears, pain, and vomiting." This particular form of sex provided her with intense sexual and psychoemotional release. During psychotherapy sessions, she directly referred to herself as a sexual psychopath, expressing her enjoyment and eagerly describing her sexual exploits in detail. At the same time, she claimed to love only one man, who happened to be married. She wanted to marry him and have a child with him.

Her reactions to hypnotic trance were some of the deepest we have seen. Any form of hypnotic induction quickly and easily induced an altered state of consciousness in her. She was capable of delving into deep, unconscious levels of hypnotic trance. She could generate many, but not all, hypnotic phenomena. For example, she experienced difficulties reproducing the cataleptic arm phenomenon since her body relaxed at the deepest level of hypnosis, becoming jelly-like. Encountering similar bodily reactions in some patients on multiple occasions, we named this phenomenon the "limp body syndrome" and the "limp arm syndrome," in which any form given to the body or its parts is lost and dissolves. During trance sessions, she generated a multitude of meaningful associations, which distinguished her from other hypnotic subjects.

During the process of working with holotropic breathwork, she also displayed phenomenal results. While other participants sometimes required at least 15–20 minutes to experience initial changes in their state of consciousness through intensive breathing, it only took her about five minutes for a true "psychedelic" revolution to unfold within her. She had visions of her past incarnations, associations with animals, and so on. During a holotropic breathwork session, she would frequently pause every 5 minutes, grab a pen and notebook, and record fragments of her journey into the depths of the unconscious. We rarely witnessed such extraordinary abilities to recreate the depth and intensity of trance states in anyone else.

It is worth adding some other elements to her profile. In all other areas of life, she is a very kind and compassionate person, capable of empathy towards others. She adores pets and enjoys participating in volunteer movements that aid others during challenging periods of their lives.

Based on our observations, individuals with a sexual psychopathy profile similar to the example described above tend to have a significant predisposition to immerse themselves in very deep trance states. We explain this phenomenon by the fact that this category of individuals extensively trains the cortex of their cerebral hemispheres to temporarily disconnect, allowing more ancient archaic brain structures to become active for a certain period of time. By the way, the situation with hypnotizability among alcoholics is similar to that of accentuated sexual psychopaths.

Assessment of hypnotizability characteristics within the profile:

- Minimal, weak, and moderate levels of hypnotizability are possible, depending on the orientation of psychopathy.
- Hyper-hypnotizability is possible in cases of sexual psychopathy.
- The trance state is never truly deep.
- There is a risk of deception in the patient's feedback regarding the hypnotic process.
- The ability to manifest only certain minor hypnotic phenomena.
- Almost complete absence of psychotherapeutic effect.

Obsessive-Compulsive Personality Profile

Obsessive-compulsive personality disorder manifests in various forms of obsessive thinking and subsequent ritualistic behavior. The thinking triggers personal anxiety, which can only be reduced or alleviated by performing a specific sequence of actions. For example, a person leaves home and then has the obsessive thought that they didn't lock the door. They return to the door, check the lock, confirm that it's locked, move away from the house, and once again experience the same worry that the door might not be securely closed, prompting them to return to the lock. In mild cases of OCD, the number of repetitions may be 2-3, while in severe cases, it can reach dozens. We knew a patient who had such obsessiveness and attempted to cope with it in a unique way by recording the process of closing the door on their mobile phone. When they experienced anxiety upon leaving the house, they simply played the video on their phone, watched the recording, and temporarily calmed down.

The ritualistic form of OCD can take various forms, such as arranging objects symmetrically in a room, tidying up the space, checking electrical appliances to ensure they are unplugged, or verifying that the gas on the stove is turned off, among others. The unfulfilled need for compulsive action always leads to an increase in anxiety levels, and sooner or later, the patient "breaks down." Attempts to exert voluntary control over the behavior often yield no results. Moreover, the patient is fully aware of the absurdity and genuine uselessness of such actions. Sometimes, the ritualistic behavior takes on a mythological character as the patient tries to attribute special meanings to their actions. They may invent their own signs or follow popular beliefs.

One of our patients with OCD, when he entered our office and saw that the books on the shelf were not arranged thematically, asked us for permission to rearrange them. Then, as his gaze fell upon the certificates hanging on the wall, he noticed that some of them were not perfectly level and expressed the desire to adjust them.

The key emotion for individuals with OCD is guilt. The compulsion to align, correct, and check everything reflects an experience where something was not done well enough. Symbolically, the compulsion brings the person back to the traumatic experience and attempts to complete or redo its content.

From a psychoanalytic perspective, we have found that the severity of the disorder is closely related to the patient's relationship with the father figure. OCD patients often view the father figure as flawed and unworthy of emulation. The aforementioned patient, who obsessively wanted to adjust the books and certificates in our office, was a former priest. He was a very kind and balanced individual with a vast knowledge base. His father was a highly aggressive and unpredictable person.

OCD patients approach any form of psychotherapy very cautiously, some-times perceiving it as a ritual to relieve their sense of guilt, which is not always fully recognized. This applies to hypnotic practice as well. Their need for everything to be correct and harmonious is so great that it influences neurological processes in the context of hypnotic induction.

Trans-states usually have a moderate-to-deep level of depth. Processes of understanding and reevaluation unfold actively during trance. As for hypnotic phenomena, what we have observed is that catalepsy of the hand, levitation, anesthesia, and analgesia are excellently formed. More complex phenomena, such as positive and negative hallucinations, are less effectively formed.

Another significant value of trance for individuals with OCD tendencies is that, unlike hysteroids and sexual psychopaths, they possess a special sense of moderation in reproducing trance phenomena, never exaggerating their effects, in our opinion. In many ways, in terms of the experience of hypnotic trance, they resemble epileptoid-accentuated personalities, which we will discuss briefly later.

Additionally, it is worth noting that when applying the method of holotropic breathing developed by Stanislav Grof, we observe a relatively rapid and deep immersion into an altered state. Simply participating regularly in the process of trance induction can significantly alleviate anxiety states and reduce the intensity of compulsive actions.

Key characteristics of the paranoid OCD type include:

- Obsessive thoughts, actions, and reminiscences (visual memories).
- Perfectionism.
- Tendency toward closure of gestalt.
- Inability to stop obsessions.
- Increased anxiety when unable to complete tasks.
- Ritualization of actions.
- Conscious or hidden feelings of guilt.

Assessment of hypnability profile characteristics:

- Strong or maximum level of hypnotizability.
- Very high need for trance states. Unlike hysteroid profiles, the phenomena are more 'realistic'.
- Working with trance without exaggeration or understatement of the trance effect.
- Working with trance without exaggeration or understatement of the psychotherapeutic effect.
- Strong short-term and long-term psychotherapeutic effects.

Schizoid Personality Profile

A person with a schizoid personality profile is emotionally cold and absorbed in their thoughts about the world and their fantasies. They avoid emotional relationships with others. Ernst Kretschmer, a German psychiatrist, referred to schizoids as 'Friends of Books and Nature.' Schizoids lack affective resonance with other people. They are unable to effectively express their own emotions and understand the emotions of others. They may not attach much importance to social norms and live by their own rules, but they do not disrupt social order and are often perceived by others as 'not of this world.'

The main characteristics of schizoid disorder may include the following:

- Emotional coldness.
- Difficulties in expressing emotions.
- Difficulties in understanding the emotions of others.
- Need for solitary activities.
- Stiff and robotic gait.
- Monotonous and cold voice.
- Almost complete lack of eye contact during communication.
- Inclination towards highly intellectual activities.
- Wearing peculiar clothing.
- Ignoring other people's problems (the 'tree and glass' symptom).
- Narcissism.
- Self-sufficiency.
- Either no friends or very few (often just one close friend for schizoids).
- Strong emotional vulnerability that schizoids try not to show to anyone.
- Dislike of sports and physical practices in general.

Naturally, all the mentioned symptoms can occur at different levels of intensity. However, they most often form a cohesive and comprehensive profile.

Based on our observations, individuals with a schizoid personality are often resentful towards the maternal figure in their family, and less frequently towards the father, especially if the mother assumes a more masculine role in the family. The inability to establish a meaningful emotional connection with a significant figure in the family deeply wounds the schizoid, causing them to withdraw into themselves.

In childhood or adolescence, the schizoid learns that they can mostly rely only on themselves and that, essentially, they do not need anyone else. As schizoids tend to become self-sufficient much earlier than others, thanks to their considerable cognitive abilities, their self-esteem develops and they display it in extravagant ways, further complicating their already challenging emotional relationships with others.

In childhood, schizoids are often rejected by their peers and become outcasts. However, as they mature and develop their personalities, schizoids become sought after in various groups due to their professional qualities, thoughtfulness, perseverance, and original creative ideas. It is during this time that they gradually gain more and more opportunities for emotional contact with other people. If circumstances align favorably, they can gradually emerge from their cocoon. However, strong stress and negative emotions in relationships can easily pull them back in.

On the surface, it may seem that a schizoid personality is resistant to hypnosis, but that is not the case at all. Hypnotic work can reveal surprising possibilities for psychotherapy, especially when the schizoid profile is combined with a paranoid aspect. If the paranoid aspect is not involved, hypnotic work can be quite effective in therapy.

Empathy toward the surrounding world is greatly blocked in schizoids due to their past emotional traumas. Their inability to empathize with others is a form of aggression. The more aggression they harbor towards the world, the greater their need for dissociation and detachment. This is how the schizoid seeks revenge against the world, to some extent destroying themselves in the process. Furthermore, the stronger their aggression, the more peculiar their world of illusions and fantasies becomes.

However, if a person capable of sharing their often strange reality appears and consistently demonstrates loyalty to their world through actions, a 'miracle' can occur, and the schizoid may accept that person as their own.

This person doesn't necessarily have to be another schizoid, although that is possible. Cooperation can also occur with individuals of other profiles. A similar structure of relationships can emerge in an alliance with a psychotherapist. Through the therapeutic process and their professional skills, the therapist establishes rapport with the patient. With increasing trust, the therapist can become the schizoid's 'sole friend.' This is beneficial as the schizoid gains the opportunity to relearn trust in the world, to speak about their feelings, and to express them freely. However, this often requires time—sometimes months.

During the initial stages of psychotherapy, patients with this profile avoid eye contact, may appear peculiar, and often complain about difficulties in forming friendly and intimate relationships. The sexual sphere is almost always problematic for schizoids. They either completely deny its existence or sometimes settle for autoeroticism. Some of them engage in sexual relationships not because they desire them but, as they say, 'to not stand out too much from others.' However, this is rare. In this case, the depth of the schizoid accent in their personality plays a significant role. Naturally, the deeper the symptomatology, the poorer the prognosis. Sexual connections may be absent until the ages of 25, 30, 35, or even longer. The first sexual experience for a schizoid can end in both emotional and sexual failure and can completely close them off from intimacy for many years.

With a psychotherapist, a schizoid can eventually open up and engage effectively, participating in hypnotherapy sessions that yield significant results in terms of change and transformation. However, the schizoid often desires to turn the psychotherapist into a friend and almost a family member, attempting to replace key social roles. The dynamics of this process can vary greatly and are highly individual.

When discussing the schizoid's ability to participate in hypnotherapy sessions, it is important to mention that initially, the schizoid may exhibit reactions similar to those of a highly ungainable individual. Their tendency towards hyper-rationalization and criticism, resulting in hyperactivity of the cerebral cortex, does not dissipate quickly. However, with each session, deeper levels can be reached, and over time, an individual who initially seemed almost entirely ungainable may begin to exhibit phenomena accessible to highly hypnotizable individuals. Naturally, as hypnotizability improves, we have observed numerous enhancements in social communication skills. The unveiling in hypnotic trance could become a metaphor for the unveiling in social communication.

For instance, one patient with a schizoid profile initially complained about not being able to grasp social rhythms, constantly saying inappropriate things that irritated colleagues at work. Throughout a year of regular therapy, he participated in multiple hypnotherapy sessions, continuously discovering something new while in trance. Over this period, his social communication with colleagues and friends underwent slow but steady changes. More emotions emerged in his communication, and he became less afraid of being rejected, becoming more socially active. By the end of the year, he could already recount instances where he became the life of the party at work, easily engaging in humor and philosophical discussions on various topics. Of course, therapy was not without its challenges, but the overall trajectory was positive.

We have observed a fascinating phenomenon regarding how schizoid individuals can integrate trance experiences into their behavior. Some of them, after a series of hypnosis sessions, may begin to attempt to recreate the state of trance and certain hypnotic phenomena themselves. For example, one young man, after experiencing catalepsy of the entire body several times (a phenomenon where the subject's body is placed between the backs of chairs after catalepsy is induced), started asking us, "Can I achieve this on my own at home?" Another patient began sharing that deep trance states with vivid and colorful sensory presentations started occurring to him at home while he was engaged in various activities. This same patient started integrating the phenomenon of analog body signaling, which we had repeatedly created in our hypnosis sessions (more details about this phenomenon will be provided in the chapter dedicated to hypnotic phenomena), into his everyday life. Another patient started attempting to induce hypnotic states by himself at home. Here we see that the overall strategy towards the world, where the schizoid attempts to do everything independently, disregarding social connections, is sometimes nearly unshakeable.

Evaluation of hypnotizability characteristics within the profile:

- At the beginning of therapy, a minimal level of hypnotizability may be present, but as rapport develops, experiences of heightened hypnotic responses become possible.
- Initial attempts at inducing a trance may be unsuccessful.
- With each hypnotic induction, a positive trend and deeper level of hypnotic trance can be observed.
- The hypnotic trance itself teaches the schizoid individual a sense of connection with the world.
- The act of inducing the hypnotic state itself is more therapeutic than the specific suggestions given during the trance state.

Epileptoid Personality Profile

The epileptoid personality is emotionally "hot" in contrast to the cold schizoid personality. It is characterized by emotional outbursts, often accompanied by motor activity. While working with epileptoids, we have found an adequate metaphor in the strategy of relating to the world: the "guilty criminal." On the surface, the epileptoid is often highly moral and even religious. However, as soon as someone provokes them, they can instantly forget about their morality and cause significant harm or even kill. Later, when the emotions are discharged, the epileptoid regains composure and begins to reproach themselves, feeling strong guilt and remorse. They seek forgiveness, attempt to atone for their guilt, and promise that they will never behave that way again. And most importantly, they sincerely believe it. In reality, however, after some time passes and another irritating stimulus arises, there is a high probability that they will repeat what they did before. And the cycle repeats itself.

Once, one of our epileptoid patients came home, where he lived with his lover. As he later recounted, she kept provoking him for about three hours, and then he couldn't take it anymore and punched her in the jaw, causing significant physical injuries. The next morning, he took her to the hospital and then came to us for a consultation. He appeared crushed by feelings of guilt and shame, saying that he himself didn't understand how it happened, as if he fell into a trance where something else was controlling him. Similar situations occurred in his life from time to time, regardless of his attempts at volitional control, which is an extremely rare occurrence among individuals with an epileptoid profile. They most often follow their emotions and instincts, although they can be highly intellectual. This tendency often predisposes them to fights, promiscuous sexual relationships, alcohol and drug abuse.

If we are dealing not only with an epileptoid personality profile but with epilepsy as a disease, the influence of hypnosis and other practices altering the state of consciousness can trigger epileptoid seizures.

These seizures range from minor absences, where the patient seems to disconnect from consciousness while maintaining the same bodily position for several minutes, to a grand epileptoid seizure involving falling to the floor, rolling back the eyes, foaming at the mouth, and convulsions.

Therefore, some specialists do not recommend using hypnosis with epilepsy patients due to the high likelihood of such an outcome.

During a lecture on psychotherapy where we conducted and demonstrated group hypnosis techniques, a student suffering from epilepsy, after emerging from trance, remained frozen with her eyes open and stayed in a similar state for a few minutes, barely breathing, before spontaneously returning to a normal waking state.

However, when she participated in holotropic breathwork group therapy, the epileptoid phenomenon of absence recurred. For a few minutes, it was as if she disconnected, stopped breathing, and then abruptly returned to her usual state of consciousness. She did not experience a major epileptic seizure.

Nevertheless, it is worth noting that she was highly hypnotizable. The hyperactive areas of the brain that could potentially trigger an epileptoid seizure during hypnosis can explosively discharge their tension.

On the one hand, this makes the trance healing for the patient, but on the other hand, it increases the likelihood of experiencing an epileptoid seizure.

Let us discuss how both individuals with epilepsy and those with an epileptoid profile have a very strong inner need to experience trance states and intuitively grasp such an opportunity as it provides them with psychoemotional relief.

It is precisely for this reason that epileptoid personalities often become hostages to alcohol, drugs, and various unpleasant emotional situations where excessive aggression is exhibited.

Speaking generally about the hypnotizability of epileptoid personalities, they are one of the most hypnotizable profiles. The trance emerges in the initial minutes of the hypnotic process, and the suggestee quickly reaches a high level of trance depth with numerous sensory and motor representations.

The influence of a typical relaxing and positive trance is not necessary for epileptoids. One trance session helps achieve high therapeutic indicators.

It is also worth noting that in trance, epileptoids tend to focus on experiencing bodily sensations, almost completely disregarding visual experiences. Therefore, the experience of visual hallucinations and illusions is nearly closed off to them.

At the same time, catalepsy of the hands and body, as well as hand levitation, can be relatively easily reproduced.

Among individuals with an epileptoid profile, we have discovered a very interesting common psychodynamic pattern. Almost all of them are "mother's children" and have limited or no significant connection with their father figure.

There is also another intriguing characteristic. They are not just "mother's children"; deep down in their souls, they fear their mothers. We often observed situations where the future epileptoid's mother did not want the child during pregnancy, either attempting to abort or contemplating it.

In our opinion, during the perinatal phase of their development, the child internalizes the aggression from the mother, and epileptoid seizures or simply epileptoid behavior serve as a form of catharsis, expressing the perinatal fear of the mother.

However, at this point, we merely propose this as a hypothesis that still requires repeated confirmation.

Key characteristics of the epileptoid type:

- Excitability
- Emotional uninhibition
- Aggressiveness, predominantly motor
- Lack of behavioral control during an affective outburst
- Feelings of guilt after the manifestation of an affect
- Hedonism
- Proneness to alcoholism and drug addiction
- Uninhibited sexuality
- Tendency to impulsively engage in socially disapproved actions
- Love for sports

Assessing the hypnotizability characteristics of the profile:

- Maximum level of hypnotizability
- Unlike the hysteroid profile, the external phenomenology of trance is relatively limited, but the internal manifestation of phenomena is highly extensive and diverse
- Both the induction of trance itself and the experiences within it have a strong psychogenic effect on the individual.

Schizoid Personality Profile

In our opinion, there is a fine line between the actual illness of schizophrenia and its personality accentuation. The ability for basic social adaptation serves as a key characteristic. If a person, due to specific symptoms indicating the presence of schizophrenia, can maintain socialization skills and derive pleasure from life, we refer to it as a schizoid accentuation. However, let us first describe the main forms of schizophrenia that can be observed in the clinical picture, and only then discuss the simple schizoid personality profile, which can differ significantly from a full-fledged disorder. In contemporary psychiatry, five primary subtypes of schizophrenia are most commonly recognized:

- **Paranoid schizophrenia**
- **Catatonic schizophrenia**
- **Hebephrenic schizophrenia**
- **Undifferentiated schizophrenia**
- **Residual schizophrenia**

Paranoid schizophrenia manifests through the emergence of various sensory illusions and hallucinations, most of which elicit a negative emotional response in the patient. Different personality distortions may arise, including absurd narcissism - megalomania, where a person begins to ascribe grandiose and peculiar identifications, such as Napoleon, Stalin, Director of the Universe, Chief Architect of Communism, Chairman of Planetary Forces, or even naming themselves after angels or demons, and so on. Patients may even create artificial credentials describing their "titles" and "accomplishments."

Naturally, absurd narcissism can be accompanied by hallucinatory processes and a strange worldview where the individual believes they are being pursued and tormented. In paranoid schizophrenia, the Kandinsky-Clérambault syndrome is manifested precisely in the hallucinatory delusion of persecution and influence on the subject. Such delusions of persecution can be conditionally divided into technical and magiphrenic types.

In the case of technical delusions, the patient may have fantasies that they are being irradiated with radiation, influenced by radio waves, laser beams, remotely hypnotized, implanted with "bugs" in their body, and so on. In magiphrenic delusions, the patient creates a picture of magical influence on themselves. They believe they are being bewitched, subjected to magical rituals, having enchanted objects thrown at them, having demons possess them, and so on. Naturally, the manifestation of symptoms is accompanied by vivid sensory experiences.

In the case of the reverse Kandinsky-Clérambault syndrome, the patient begins to believe that they themselves are the influencing subject. For example, they may think that they have the power to control the weather through their thoughts or that someone may die due to their bad mood. They believe they can command and control a country, and so on.

Once, our former student brought her friend to us for a consultation. She had been diagnosed with paranoid schizophrenia two years ago, when she was 28 years old. The patient was actively taking antipsychotic medications, which caused behavioral and emotional suppression.

She recounted that when she was 28, she worked at a canteen in a local theater studio, and the symptoms began unexpectedly, appearing as strange paranoid fantasies telling her that the actors in the studio were gathering in the neighboring room to influence her through remote hypnosis, implant thoughts in her mind, and control her actions. Over the course of several weeks, the symptoms intensified, and then full-fledged kinesthetic hallucinations of certain entities emerged. These entities initially crawled on her skin and then began to crawl under her skin. One such spherical creature, twice the size of a tennis ball, settled beneath her right shoulder blade and occasionally moved, driving her to madness.

She sought help from psychiatrists, who prescribed neuroleptic therapy, which had little effect on her. Later, as she mentioned, she was given some experimental American medications, which also did not significantly reduce her symptom complex. Several months passed; orthodox medicine failed to help her, and she decided to seek unconventional healers, sorcerers, psychics, and exorcists. Sorcerers recited spells over her, all in vain. Psychics tried to cleanse her "aura," also with no success.

Interestingly, her unconventional treatment achieved some effect when she worked with Christian exorcists, who ritually performed prayers to expel demons from her. During each exorcism session, her symptoms took on new qualities. She would fall to the ground, crawl on all fours, hiss, grimace, and spit. After some time, the demon would "leave" her body, only to return again. Priests conducted this ritual several times, always with the same dramatic effect. There would be an outpouring of emotions, followed by a return to her previous state.

Our student, who was studying psychotherapy at our university, brought her to us to try hypnosis with her, hoping it might help. We knew that hypnotic practices with such patients rarely yielded any results. Nevertheless, we decided to give it a try for experimental purposes.

During our conversation and attempts to inquire about her childhood, she mostly responded in a monotonous and brief manner, clearly showing no attempts to remember anything. This could be due to strong resistance or the inability to engage in introspection due to neuroleptic intoxication. In essence, she was completely unresponsive to verbal analytic therapy, although she maintained relative social adequacy in communication. We attempted traditional Ericksonian hypnotic induction with her, and within five minutes, it became evident that it was ineffective for her. She displayed no signs of trance.

After some consideration, we decided to explore a hypnotic practice involving communication with different parts of her personality without a formal induction of trance. The hypnotherapist would simply address a specific part of the patient's personality and anticipate the patient's responses from that perspective. This practice resulted in a profound trance effect.

We administered a hypnotic intervention to the patient, directing our attention to the part of her personality located behind her right scapula. Following this intervention, the patient switched off, experiencing tremors throughout her body. Her chin dropped onto her chest, and her hair fell forward from her forehead. Then something unexpected happened. The patient fiercely hissed at us without opening her eyes, resembling a character from a horror movie. We attempted to engage in dialogue with the emerged part of her personality, but all we heard in response were hissing sounds. We then addressed the patient by her name, and she snapped back to herself. She had no awareness of what had transpired in the past couple of minutes.

Questions regarding her conscious awareness yielded no results. We then turned our attention once again to the part of her personality located behind her right scapula and obtained a similar outcome as before. Thus, we transitioned her through different states multiple times, discovering that her consciousness resembled a television with two channels. On one channel, her own personality resided, while on the other, a hissing entity was present.

This particular case presented unique challenges for traditional hypnotic approaches. However, by employing a technique that involved communication with distinct parts of the patient's personality, we observed a profound transformation in her mental state. These findings contribute to the growing body of knowledge in the field of psychotherapy and highlight the potential benefits of alternative approaches in cases resistant to conventional methods.

It is important to note that further exploration and research are necessary to fully understand the mechanisms and efficacy of this type of hypnotherapeutic practice. Nonetheless, these preliminary results encourage further investigation into the utilization of personality-part-based communication techniques in the context of hypnosis, potentially opening new avenues for therapeutic interventions.

Thus, we can observe that classical clinical hypnosis may have no effect at all, but certain hypnotic practices can help to interact with the patient's consciousness to some extent.

Another one of our patients, also diagnosed with paranoid schizophrenia, was more talkative and even responsive to traditional forms of hypnotic induction. She came for therapy at the age of 35, with the onset of the schizophrenic process occurring at 30. Various hallucinations, perceptual illusions, deep and prolonged depression, and a loss of meaning in life began to manifest. Medication treatment with neuroleptics and antidepressants managed to alleviate most of the symptoms. However, the symptoms continued to interfere with her life and distort its quality. The patient was capable of engaging in analytical processes; during some consultations, she could reason reasonably, recall the past, and accept analytical interpretations. Occasionally, she would enter states where the quality of her communication significantly deteriorated. We noticed that to keep her in an adequate state, we simply needed to avoid certain topics in her life. Whenever we saw her slip into a negative state, we abruptly changed the conversation topic and observed how she subsequently stabilized. Her personality resembled a semi-ruined house. As long as her consciousness resided in one part, she remained completely adequate and stable. However, once her consciousness shifted to another part, she lost the adequacy of her perception of the world. During the analytical process, we discovered significant information about her personal history that had a pre-determining influence on the development of schizophrenia in her future. When she was seven years old, she was seduced by her twelve-year-old cousin, with whom she had an intimate relationship. According to her, during the course of therapy, her cousin was diagnosed with brain cancer. The development of the schizophrenic process in women who have been violated by a family member can be interpreted as a pattern that often appears in the personal histories of schizophrenic patients.

Naturally, we attempted several hypnosis sessions with her to assess the influence of trance on her consciousness and to explore the therapeutic resources within this technique. During the hypnotic induction process, contrary to our expectations, we discovered that the patient was quite hypnotizable, easily entering a hypnotic trance and experiencing a significant amount of sensory representations.

However, the most notable characteristic of her trance immersion was the constant presence of subtle demonic grimaces on her face. These grimaces would sometimes manifest as expressions of anger, pain, or suffering, alternating from one to another. We speculated that the appearance of these grimaces might lead to an escalation of negative emotional states, but it did not occur.

Upon emerging from the trance state, the patient reported feeling slightly more anxious and described the internal sensory representations as saturated with various negative emotional experiences. The imagery was predominantly black and white, with occasional bursts of red.

Over a period of three months, we predominantly employed analytical techniques while occasionally incorporating trance interventions during our work with the patient. Observable changes occurred, yet despite our efforts, we were unable to truly heal the wounded aspects of her personality. However, we discovered that we could teach her to voluntarily exit the symptomatic state.

In our opinion, the hypnotic technique neither caused harm nor provided significant benefits to the patient. Nevertheless, it was evident that the trance process could temporarily amplify the symptoms of the schizophrenic process.

Key characteristics of paranoid schizophrenia:

1. Hallucinations
2. Illusions
3. Autism
4. Impaired affective sphere
5. Associations based on secondary criteria
6. Ambivalence of thoughts and emotions
7. Problems in the volitional sphere
8. Apathy
9. Alogia (poverty of speech)
10. Anhedonia (inability to experience pleasure).

Evaluation of hypnotizability in a paranoid schizophrenic profile:

- The variations can be quite diverse. With the use of conventional techniques, the profile may not be hypnotizable at all. However, certain hypnosis techniques can induce peak hypnotic experiences.
- Trance enhances the propensity for fantasizing.
- In different cases, entering into a trance may be difficult, or specific forms of hypnotic induction may be necessary to achieve the desired result.
- Trance post-effects can have a negative bias and exacerbate negative symptoms.

When it comes to **catatonic schizophrenia**, the main manifestation of the illness is the prolonged, sometimes hours-long, immobility of the patient, known as catatonic stupor. The duration of this state can span hours, days, weeks, months, and even years.

At times, in catatonia, the patient's body is in a state of catalepsy, exhibiting a wax-like flexibility. The body can be positioned in any posture, and it will maintain fixation.

Sometimes catatonia can be negativistic, and attempts to change the patient's posture are met with strong resistance.

There is also a deeper form of catatonia called tetany, where attempts to alter the patient's position can result in such intense muscular tension that it may even cause internal organ injuries.

Sometimes catatonia can be intermittent, where, for example, a patient remains in stupor for several weeks and then unexpectedly transitions into a state of catatonic excitement. They may perform certain actions, often aggressive ones, and then return to the catatonic state. In one such case, a patient remained in a stupor for several weeks. While under the observation of doctors in a clinic, he suddenly emerged from the catatonic state, grabbed a metal bowl, and threw it at a passing orderly. The orderly managed to dodge, remaining unharmed. The doctor asked him to explain his actions some time later, to which he replied that while he was in the stupor, an inner voice repeated the phrase "move and you'll die, move and you'll die" to him. At one point, the voice told him, "if you kill the orderly with the bowl, you'll be saved; now throw it." After the patient missed, the voice began repeating that he was now doomed. In this case, we can observe that the internal vocal interpretation influences the behavior of the patient and their states.

There are three forms of catatonic excitement that can be distinguished:

Gradual speech and motor excitement are accompanied by speech emphasis and sometimes echolalia, heightened mood, and exaltation. Unprovoked laughter may occur. Impulsive actions are possible, but without disturbance of consciousness.

Acute and rapid speech and motor excitement. Behavior includes echolalia, echopraxia, and perseveration. Actions are aggressive and chaotic. Self-harm is possible.

Mute excitement. Agitation, chaotic and purposeless actions, self-inflicted harm, and harm to others.

Catatonia can also manifest through the following symptoms:

1. Mutism (silence)
2. Active or passive negativism
3. Echolalia (repeating the words of others)
4. Echopraxia (repeating the actions and movements of others)
5. Pillow sign
6. Ivan Pavlov's sign (understanding and reacting only to a quiet voice)
7. Jactitations (voluntary stereotypical rocking of the body and head)

We can hypothesize that the phrases that govern the behavior of schizophrenic individuals are implanted in their minds during childhood by someone close to them, most often their father or mother, during intensely stressful situations where the child may have felt fear and pain.

Unfortunately, obtaining detailed information about the childhood experiences of patients with such symptoms is not easy. It is often nearly impossible, so we are left with assumptions and hypotheses, but not unfounded ones.

Based on what we have observed in some patients, if the childhood experience involved intense fear and pain coupled with someone's implantation of commands like "do something" or "don't do something," this implantation may transform into a strong, uncontrollable symptom in adulthood.

For example, a woman with the rather unusual symptom of selective abulia (lack of will) sought the help of a psychotherapist. She couldn't say no to anyone, even in various contexts of her life. For instance, a stranger could approach her on the street and tell her to "follow me," and she would comply.

This selective abulia had a psychoanalytic justification. When the patient was 5 years old, she was playing in the kitchen while her mother was cooking on the stove. She somehow upset her mother, who instructed her to sit on a chair. The daughter shouted, "No, I don't want to." In response, her mother slammed her hand on the table, where there was a cup of boiling water, causing it to spill onto the child, and she yelled, "Never say no to me!"

This had a profound suggestive impact on the daughter. In fact, after that incident, she couldn't say no to anyone. Such was the power of suggestion. Indeed, intense pain and fear can open the subconscious to suggestion, and it becomes extremely difficult to free oneself from the influence of that suggestion.

However, more often, similar phrases from childhood form various phobias, obsessions, and compulsions. But we will hypothesize that similar events from personal childhood experiences can also account for the imperative phrases described above in the mind of a catatonic schizophrenic. However, this is a psychoanalytic interpretation.

When considering other factors, the causes of catatonia can be other mental disorders or physical illnesses. For example, in ICD-11, there are categories such as "catatonia associated with other mental disorders," "catatonia induced by psychoactive substances, including medications," and "secondary catatonic syndrome." Today, the belief is growing that catatonia is more often a consequence of affective disorders than schizophrenia. In any case, this question remains open.

The development of catatonic stupor or excitement can be influenced by:

Mental disorders:

- Affective disorders
- Post-traumatic stress disorder (PTSD)
- Postpartum mental disorders
- Developmental disorders in children

Neurological symptoms:

- History of cranial-brain trauma
- Brain tumor
- Stroke

Use of certain medications and drugs:

- Antipsychotics (malignant neuroleptic syndrome)
- Anticonvulsants
- Corticosteroids
- Cocaine, phencyclidine, opioids

As we can see, there are many different causes, and catatonic syndrome can occur in various conditions, not limited to schizophrenia spectrum disorders. However, for now, we will continue to associate catatonia specifically with the spectrum of schizophrenic mental disorders.

Bringing a person out of a catatonic stupor is often very challenging. However, some psychiatrists and psychotherapists may occasionally employ unconventional behavioral patterns to achieve the desired effect.

For example, Frank Farrelly used extremely extreme forms of behavior with his patients. He would start plucking hair from the legs of a patient who was stuck in a catatonic stupor, gradually moving upward from the knee toward the groin. He would say to the patient, "I will continue doing this higher and higher!" Eventually, the patient would emerge from the stupor and slap Frank. This is not a treatment method, but this example illustrates that certain behavioral maneuvers can lead a patient out of a catatonic stupor.

Unfortunately, we have not found any indications in the literature regarding any experiments with hypnotic suggestion in patients suffering from catatonia. However, we can make the assumption that, in some cases, hypnotic influence may have therapeutic potential.

Evaluation of hypnability in schizophrenic catatonic profiles:

- Undifferentiated

In the **hebephrenic subtype of schizophrenia**, the symptom progression follows the following characteristics. The behavior exhibits pronounced features such as:

- Childishness.
- Foolishness.
- Elevated mood.
- Affected mannerisms.
- Delusional ideas.
- Aggressive actions.
- Unfounded behaviors.
- Bizarre and indecent behavior.
- Giggling.
- Grimaces.
- Pranks.
- Hallucinations may be present.

This subtype of schizophrenia was first identified by Evald Hecker in his medical practice in 1878. He described this disorder as follows: "The onset during the period of sexual maturity... rapid transition into a state of mental weakness and a specific form of terminal stupidity, the signs of which could be recognized in the early stages of the illness."

The diagnosis of hebephrenic schizophrenia is most commonly made during adolescence and early adulthood (14–18 years). Without partial drug remission, almost all forms of verbal therapy are impractical.

Similar to catatonic schizophrenia, we have not found any experimental data on the use of hypnotic suggestion in patients with this symptom.

Evaluation of hypnability in an undifferentiated schizophrenic profile:

- Undifferentiated

In **undifferentiated schizophrenia**, we observe a combination of symptoms from various types of schizophrenia, making it impossible to establish a clear diagnosis.

Generalized schizophrenia manifests in a specific form of altered social behavior, sometimes with superficial relative normalcy in the patient. Let's describe the key features of the psychological processes and behavioral reactions associated with this type of mental disorder.

The individual almost completely loses their circle of familiar contacts and ceases to take care of themselves. They may go unwashed for weeks or months and not wash their clothes, resulting in a noticeable, unpleasant odor. They lose employment and educational pursuits, as well as motivation towards them.

Intellectual activities are often minimized to reading tabloids or shallow fiction literature. They may spend hours watching movies or playing online games. They develop their own life philosophy and can talk extensively about it. To an outsider, they may appear to possess a philosophical mindset. However, upon closer examination of their speech, it becomes evident that it is not a philosophical text but rather an absurd combination of meanings.

Apathy sets in, leading to significant difficulties in setting goals and following through with them. On one day, they can genuinely express to others their intention to change their life, return to university, or find employment, only to completely forget their grand speeches the next day and continue playing their online game. Their emotional life becomes reduced.

Abstract terms and words abound in their thinking and speech. Their sexual life is often either absent or dominated by autoeroticism. They encounter significant challenges in forming intimate sexual relationships, and if such relationships occur, they tend to end quickly. They are less likely to smoke, consume alcohol, or use drugs, indicating a potentially elevated level of dopamine and GABA neurotransmitter secretion. They may sometimes exhibit a tendency toward overeating.

They dislike sports and any form of intense physical activity, leading to significant muscle atrophy. This factor indicates an extremely low level of norepinephrine neurotransmitter in the brain. They often do not experience hallucinations, unlike patients with other types of schizophrenia. It is precisely because of this that cases are common where the patient's behavior is attributed by their loved ones to their personality, laziness, or other social factors.

Let's describe one case of observing such a patient and comment on their ability to interact with trance states.

A 25-year-old young man enrolled in a university where we taught the subject of psychotherapy. Initially, he showed an interest in studying and joined the psychotherapeutic group we led. He mentioned that this was already his third university enrollment. He had been expelled from previous ones due to non-attendance.

After enrolling in previous universities, he would gradually lose interest in education and stop attending classes. He followed the following unconscious behavioral pattern. Initially, he would make friends at the university and attend classes, but after six months or longer, something would switch within him. He would stay at home, watching anime for up to ten hours a day, playing online games, and hardly ever leaving the house. His spatial movement was primarily limited to the kitchen, bathroom, and toilet. He remained unemployed during this time.

After six months of this routine, he would snap out of it. He would return to the university, only to find out that he had been expelled. A similar pattern was repeated at another university with almost identical timeframes. While studying at the third university, he assured us that he would now focus on his education and complete it. In our opinion, thanks to his participation in the therapy group, his next crisis occurred only after a year and a half of studying.

He started dating a girl from another group, but she broke up with him. Then, a few months later, around New Year's, after arguing with his father, she came to his house, and they entered into a romantic relationship. They broke up after a month, and after that, he experienced a significant decline in mood and motivation in his studies. He continued attending therapy groups for some time but stopped taking care of himself, not bathing, emitting a strong odor that concerned other group members, and engaging in absurd philosophical conversations.

He soon stopped attending the group and resumed his familiar pathological routine, where he stayed at home, ate, and watched anime. He remained in this state until the end of the academic year at the university. When invited to return to the university, he usually responded that he would return soon but never showed up. After completing the academic year, he was expelled.

After that, his brother came to us and informed us that he was staying at home. The brother also mentioned that he said a strange phrase after being expelled: "Now I'll finally live!" When asked what he meant, he replied, "Now no one will interrupt me from watching anime." What happened to him afterward is unknown to us.

In all of his six-month-long home "hibernations," he exhibited almost the entire spectrum of symptoms characteristic of general schizophrenia. An interesting feature of these symptoms was that they would occur, on average, twice a year, lasting for about six months each time. We were unable to determine the cause of such a cyclic reproduction of symptoms.

During his participation in therapy and educational groups, we conducted numerous hypnotherapy sessions with him. In all sessions, he demonstrated himself as an excellent hypnotic suggestible subject. He most frequently reached medium and deep levels of trance, experiencing a significant number of sensations and meanings. However, he encountered difficulties manifesting trance phenomena. We were unable to induce catalepsy or levitation. Similar problems arose when attempting to reproduce other phenomena. Although the overall trance state could be quite deep, we have yet to find a comprehensive explanation for this phenomenon. Nonetheless, we speculate that the cyclic social demotivation experienced by the patient is naturally associated with a decrease in norepinephrine levels and an increase in dopamine levels in the brain. Additionally, we hypothesize that excessive dopamine secretion in certain areas of the brain in patients with general schizophrenia may block the ability to reproduce hypnotic phenomena. In our opinion, social activity and hypnotic activity may share a similar nature in our brain. In a typical individual, the reproduction of social actions and trance phenomena is reinforced by increased dopamine levels. In patients with general schizophrenia, this chemical motivational mechanism is disrupted both in the social sphere and during the hypnotherapy process.

Key characteristics of the general schizophrenic type:

1. Alogia: poverty of speech or lack of verbal fluency.
2. Abulia: decreased motivation and inability to initiate or persist in goal-directed activities.
3. Apathy: lack of interest, enthusiasm, or emotional responsiveness.
4. Anhedonia: inability to experience pleasure or derive enjoyment from previously enjoyable activities.
5. Autism: social withdrawal and limited engagement in social interactions.
6. Problems with emotional expression: difficulties in expressing emotions or displaying appropriate emotional responses.
7. Associations based on secondary cues: making connections or associations between unrelated things based on superficial similarities.
8. Ambivalence of thoughts and emotions: conflicting thoughts, feelings, or motivations.
9. Disheveled appearance: neglect of personal hygiene or grooming.
10. Absence or near absence of sexual life.
11. Difficulties in forming and maintaining friendships.
12. Absence of visual, auditory, and kinesthetic hallucinations and illusions.
13. Superficial impression of personal peculiarity or eccentricity.
14. Pseudophilosophizing: engaging in abstract or philosophical discussions with little coherence or depth.

Assessment of hypnotizability in the general schizophrenic profile:

1. Moderate to strong hypnotizability with possible unusual emotional affective responses.
2. Hypnosis may enhance the inclination for fantasizing.
3. Hypnosis may exhibit a tendency towards oneiric (dream-like) experiences or anxiety-phobic tendencies.

Manic-Depressive Personality Profile

Patients with manic-depressive psychosis (or bipolar affective disorder, BAR) experience cyclical episodes of intense mood elevation (mania) and mood depression, accompanied by various associated psycho-emotional and behavioral reactions. Different combinations of these states are possible, and the patient exhibits distinctly different symptoms during the two main phases of the illness.

In the manic phase, the following symptoms accompany the individual:

- Elevated mood
- Motor agitation
- Ideational and mental excitement
- Spiritual uplift
- Rapid and verbose speech
- Increased sexual drive
- Increased appetite
- Aggressive behavior
- Reduced need for sleep
- Possible emergence of grandiose delusions
- Almost complete absence of guilt or shame for actions

In the depressive phase, the following symptoms accompany the individual:

- Low mood

- Motor retardation
- Spiritual decline
- Slowed speech
- Decreased sexual drive
- Decreased appetite
- Increased need for sleep
- Feelings of worthlessness
- Suicidal impulses may occur
- Prolonged immobility
- Persistent self-condemnation and moral self-torment
- Apathy (problems with volition)
- Loss of social interest

As we can see here, the symptoms of the two stages have diametrically opposite qualities. The intensity of their manifestation can vary greatly. The course of Bipolar Affective Disorder (BAD) can occur in the following forms:

1. Periodic mania (alternating only between mania and a neutral state)
2. Periodic depression (alternating only between depression and a neutral state)
3. Regularly alternating type (mania followed by depression and depression followed by mania)
4. Irregularly alternating type (a single phase may repeat multiple times, with mania followed by mania or depression followed by depression)
5. Circular type (there is no intermission when the phases alternate regularly)

If we consider Bipolar Affective Disorder (BAD) at the level of personality accent, we will notice that the alternation of mild manias and depressions will be sublimated by the social context. In other words, both phases can be socially productive for the individual.

However, when we examine borderline and psychotic BAD, we observe significant distortions in behavior within the social context, making the individual socially maladaptive.

It is worth noting that the manic phase itself is not always malignant. Sometimes, patients genuinely enjoy life during this period. The price is paid when transitioning into the depressive phase. Let's provide an example based on our observation of a patient with a mild form of BAD.

A 28-year-old woman experiences one manic and one depressive phase once a year. Each phase lasts for 3–4 months. The manic phase occurs at the end of spring, while the depressive phase occurs at the end of autumn. During the manic phase, she becomes highly energetic, actively engages in her activities, and organizes or develops her business relationships. She starts earning significantly more money. Her libido increases, resulting in a mild fear of infidelity towards her spouse, as she knows from experience that she is capable of it in such a state. She sleeps little and experiences joy in almost any activity. When we interacted with her during this phase, she left an impression of a warm, communicative, and optimistic person. She talks a lot and constantly makes jokes. People enjoy being around her. However, when the depressive phase sets in, she spends days sitting at home, unable to go to work, lying in bed. Thoughts fill her mind that she is a failure, that nothing good will happen in her life anymore, and that she won't be able to escape this state. She sleeps a lot and has little desire for sex. Closer to spring, this phase starts to fade, and she enters a neutral interphase. This yearly cyclic pattern has been repeating for many years, and the patient has become accustomed to it. Her main complaint is the loss of almost all social communication during the depressive phase, which leads to a decline in her business and relationships. During the depressive phase, she stops attending psychotherapy sessions.

For hypnotherapy, the most favorable time is the interphase, where patients, according to our observations, demonstrate a weak or moderate level of hypnotizability. They exhibit only certain hypnotic phenomena such as hand catalepsy, hand levitation, and motor analog signaling. In the manic and depressive phases, patients either do not enter a trance state at all or have a low level of hypnotizability.

During our work with patients suffering from Bipolar Affective Disorder

(BAD), we discovered a common element in their birth history. Almost all patients with BAD were born with significant difficulties and various physical traumas. One had a clavicle fracture, another had a thigh injury, a third had forceps extraction, and so on. From this, we can hypothesize that a predisposition to manic-depressive-type disorders may arise precisely due to physical trauma during the birthing process. And cycloid affective processes that appear later in life can be seen as a certain form of abreaction and catharsis (psycho-emotional reaction) to the experienced shock and pain.

Assessment of the hypnotizability profile:

In this case, it makes sense to differentiate the effects of trance induction during the manic and depressive phases.

Manic phase:

- Moderate level of hypnotizability
- Exclusively positive orientation of trance content
- Always complete satisfaction with the trance experience
- Always satisfied with short-term psychotherapeutic dynamics

Depressive phase:

- Low or moderate level of hypnotizability
- More often, a negative orientation of trance process content
- Dissatisfaction with the trance experience

Psychopathological Personality Accents

Schizoid Accent	Psychopathic Accent	Schizophrenic Accent
Hysteroid Accent		Paranoid Accent
Manic-Depressive Accent	Obsessive-Compulsive Accent	Epileptoid Accent

The table displays the polarization of personality accents, namely:

Hysteroid Accent - Paranoid Accent

This pair is undoubtedly the true opposite on almost all psychological and physiological criteria. Hysteroids are highly hypnotizable, while paranoids are almost non-hypnotizable.

Psychopathic Accent - Obsessive-Compulsive Accent

Psychopaths are incapable of experiencing feelings of guilt and shame, whereas individuals with obsessive-compulsive accent are predominantly driven by these emotions.

Schizoid Accent - Epileptoid Accent

Schizoids are emotionally cold, withdrawn, unemotional, head-driven, rationalistic, and do not enjoy physical movement. They are not prone to alcoholism or drug addiction. Epileptoids are emotionally passionate, live through bodily sensations, are irrational, and enjoy movement. They are prone to alcoholism and drug addiction.

Schizophrenic Accent - Manic-Depressive Accent

During the manifestation of schizophrenia symptoms, we encounter a constant internal unresolved conflict and ambivalence of three types:

1. **Emotional**: simultaneous positive and negative feelings toward a person, object, or event.
2. **Volitional**: endless oscillations between opposing decisions. Inability to make a choice.
3. **Intellectual**: operating with mutually exclusive ideas and thoughts. In the manic–depressive accent, internal ambivalence seems to be divided into different temporal segments and experienced sequentially, rather than simultaneously.

In the MD accent, internal ambivalence is emphasized, as if it is divided into different time periods and is not translated simultaneously but sequentially.

By using this model for patient profiling based on the eight basic psychopathological types, we have found that with a high level of probability, we can effectively determine their ability to enter a trance state, the effectiveness of trance work, and the expected capacity to reproduce various trance phenomena.

3

Hypnotic Phenomena

There are a considerable number of perception and consciousness phenomena that can be created through hypnotic suggestion and trance work. Some of them naturally arise during the process of trance immersion, while others need to be specifically induced through trance induction. Certain phenomena can be adapted for psychotherapeutic purposes, while others are solely intended to demonstrate the capabilities of the hypnotic process. Let us explore their variety.

Eyelid catalepsy
During trance induction, a person's eyelids close and cannot be raised voluntarily. This phenomenon was observed by the mesmerist Lafontaine and the creator of the term "hypnosis," John Braid.

Eyelid lowering
Upon a hypnotic command, a person's eyelids lower. In the vast majority of cases, eyelid lowering occurs naturally and is perceived as the beginning of a hypnotic state. However, open eyes are not an indication of the absence of a hypnotic trance. Typically, the hypnotic state is perceived almost exclusively as an externally oriented process. But this is one of the misconceptions about the hypnotic process. In many cases, trance can be maintained with open eyes and even with full body mobility. However, for the purpose of

the psychotherapeutic process, transitioning the trance to an externally oriented state is often simply unnecessary.

Eyelid raising

Upon a hypnotic command, the eyelids are raised while maintaining the hypnotic state. In this case, a similar suggestion can be used, for example: "Now I will snap my fingers, and after that, your eyes will open while the depth of the trance state remains." Subsequently, additional suggestions can be given to regain control over speech function and initiate a dialogue with the suggestee.

Eyelid tremor

This is a spontaneously occurring phenomenon in which the eyelids begin to vibrate or tremble. It often occurs when the eyes roll upwards towards the brow and the head is tilted backward.

Catalepsy of the limbs and head

This is a spontaneously occurring or intentionally created phenomenon of wax-like flexibility. When a certain body part is placed in a new position, it remains independently held for an extended period of time.

Levitation of the hands

This is a spontaneously occurring or intentionally created phenomenon of unconscious lifting and movement of the hands in space. Rarely, during the induction of trance in hysterical patients, spontaneous raising of the hands into the air, sometimes accompanied by various movements, can be observed. In other cases, specific suggestions are required to activate this phenomenon.

Floppy hand syndrome

This phenomenon spontaneously occurs during hypnotic induction. The person loses voluntary control over hand movements. Regardless of the new position given by the hypnotist, the hands consistently fall downward.

Suggestion that the hands maintain a fixed position often does not work. This phenomenon can be artificially recreated in individuals who can reproduce hand catalepsy. With the command "your hand becomes floppy, relaxed, and heavy," it drops down onto the knees. According to our observations, individuals who spontaneously reproduce this phenomenon can maintain it after numerous attempts. We have seen a patient who, despite having a relative ability to enter a hypnotic trance, continued to reproduce this phenomenon throughout a year of hypnotherapy. However, at one point, her hand became stuck in a cataleptic state.

Floppy body syndrome
This spontaneously occurs in some hysterically accentuated individuals. After entering a state of hypnotic trance, the entire body deeply relaxes, causing the person to completely lose conscious and unconscious muscle tone. If not supported, the person simply falls in any direction. In this case, no commands indicating the preservation of muscle tone are effective. This phenomenon can be artificially reproduced in individuals who are not prone to floppy body syndrome through specific hypnotic commands. For example: "Your body becomes soft and pliable, you lose all control over it."

Catalepsy of the entire body
A favorite old technique of European psychiatrists, regularly demonstrated in clinics with hysteric women. During hypnotization, either spontaneously or through appropriate suggestion, the body acquires wax-like flexibility. Regardless of the position it is placed in, it remains fixed. By securing the body in an upright position, the hypnotist, with the assistance of an accomplice, can place the subject between the backs of chairs (the upper part of the back on one chair and the lower part of the calves on another), creating a small cataleptic bridge. Another version of the cataleptic bridge is possible when the subject is held by the arms and lifted above their heads (one person holds the shoulders, while another holds the legs). In this case, we observe a larger cataleptic bridge.

Another variation is the acrobatic bridge

In this case, after inducing catalepsy of the entire body, the hypnotist, from a standing position, slowly begins to arch the subject's body backward, gradually placing their hands on the floor. This phenomenon can only be achieved if there is sufficient flexibility in the thoracic spine.

Hypnotic anesthesia

The phenomenon of depriving a specific area of the body of general sensitivity. Often reproduced together with the phenomenon of analgesia, which refers to the absence of pain sensitivity in a specific area of the body. Formally, anesthesia can be considered a negative kinesthetic hallucination.

Both anesthesia and analgesia usually do not occur spontaneously in a trance state but are induced through appropriate suggestions. In a training format, the technique of analgesia can be tested through an exercise involving the application of pressure to a painful point located at the base of the thumb and index finger. Initially, pressure is applied to the point, and the level of pain sensitivity is noted.

Then, a hypnotic exercise called the "Iron Glove" is performed in an externally oriented trance format. During one of the seminars, French psychiatrist Claude Viro demonstrated the following execution of this exercise. After the pain sensitivity test on the hand is conducted without formally inducing a trance, the hypnotist begins to speak, asking the subject to imagine wrapping their hand with chain mail, like a bandage, and to imagine, hear, and feel this sensation. Then, the suggestion is given to imagine placing a large steel glove over the chain mail on the hand, which will provide protection. This visualization is maintained for 2–3 minutes.

After the visualization is completed, the hypnotist attempts to apply pressure to the painful point on the hand again. Feedback is obtained from the subject regarding the difference in pain sensitivity between the first and second application of pressure. Based on our observations, in the majority of cases, the intensity of the pain sensations decreases by 4-5 times.

Another interesting exercise we witnessed was performed by a female physician in a French clinic. She aimed to alleviate the pain in the arm of a young girl in order to take some tests without discomfort. She took a regular marker in her hand, showed it to the girl, and told her that it was a magic marker that could relieve pain when it touches the body. She then slowly approached the girl's arm with the marker, lightly touched it, and began making spiral massaging movements along the forearm using the marker's cap. After just a minute of such a procedure, the girl lost both general and specific pain sensitivity in her arm.

Once the tests were taken, the physician ran the marker cap backward along the forearm, explaining that the sensitivity was returning to the arm. At first, it may seem like magic, but in reality, this exercise is quite simple to replicate and does not even require prior hypnotic induction. The phenomenon is solely created by focusing attention on the object and establishing suggestive ideas about its function and purpose.

A completely different form of analgesia is applied during surgical proce-dures. According to available information, full hypnotic analgesia was first performed by an English physician in India during the Indian Company in the late 19th century. The records indicate that amputation surgery was performed under hypnosis for the purpose of pain control. Since then, military physicians have started using hypnosis in dentistry. More and more evidence was emerging, indicating that hypnosis could be an effective analgesic agent.

Currently, hypnotic anesthesia is used during surgical operations in numerous European and American clinics. For example, in French clinics, hypnotic anesthesia is employed during surgeries performed under local anesthesia. In such cases, hypnotic anesthesia serves as a substitute for general anesthesia.

Before the start of the surgery, the hypnotherapist begins by directing the patient's attention to various external objects. The patient undergoes 4-5 attention fixations. Then the patient is asked to close their eyes and imagine themselves in a specific trance motif, such as being on a seaside. After that, for ten minutes, the hypnotherapist, in a soft and slow voice, guides the patient on a journey through the trance motif, focusing their attention on visual, auditory, and kinesthetic sensations that the patient can experience during the hypnosis session. For example: "And you can see the yellow sand and the blue sea... And you can hear the sound of the wind and the cry of seagulls... And feel the wind blowing through your hair...". Such phrases are repeated cyclically many times.

When the patient has been in the trance for more than ten minutes, the surgeons begin the surgical intervention. During the procedure, the hypnotherapist remains beside the patient and continues to accompany them with their voice through the trance motif. This continues until the end of the surgery. The gradual transition out of trance begins when the operation is completed and the sutures are applied.

Naturally, the patient has a choice before the surgery: either to undergo it with full medication anesthesia or to choose local and hypnotherapeutic anesthesia. In the case of choosing the latter option, there is always the possibility, if the hypnotic form of anesthesia does not work sufficiently well, of switching the patient to full medication anesthesia. However, in the vast majority of cases, this is not necessary. Hypnotic anesthesia is used with people of various age groups: children, adults, and elderly individuals. According to observations by French medical professionals, postoperative recovery is faster for individuals who choose hypnotic pain management. There has also been an increase in self-confidence among individuals who undergo hypnotic anesthesia.

During the training format for the implementation of the technique of hypnotherapeutic anesthesia and analgesia, it is possible to use small needles to puncture the skin on the hands or forearms. The depth of the puncture is superficial, just enough for the needle to pass through the epidermis. In addition to the above-mentioned methods of creating hypnotic pain management, direct suggestion can also be employed. For example: "Your hand ceases to feel pain, the sensitivity in it decreases to a minimum, and it is protected from any external interference." Working with various metaphors is also possible, for instance: "You are standing on the shore of a frozen lake, piercing a hole in the ice and inserting your hand into it, feeling a strong coldness in your hand spreading up to your shoulder.

Your hand freezes and is covered with a layer of ice; you cannot feel anything except the coldness in it." This is an example of a metaphor that can be vividly developed during trance, adding more descriptive elements to depict sensations of different qualities.

Usually, when suggestion or metaphor (or both) are successfully activated in trance, a person does not feel any pain during the needle puncture. Sometimes the sensation is simply very weak and superficial.

Bleeding cessation

Hypnotic techniques can be used to attempt to stop minor bleeding. An interesting example of an experiment with blood cessation during gum surgery was shared by Claude Viro in a seminar. In one instance, during gum surgery where hypnoanalgesia was applied, the patient experienced severe bleeding that the doctor could not stop. Seizing the opportunity, the hypnotherapist decided to try to stop the bleeding using hypnosis. He suggested to the patient that they were in front of a lever that controlled the intensity of the bleeding, and they could touch it to adjust its settings. Then he suggested that, in the patient's imagination, they visually changed the lever, reducing its intensity to a minimum. Within a minute, the bleeding actually ceased to flow intensively. As an experimental continuation, he then suggested to the patient that they reverse the direction of the lever. The blood started flowing intensely again. Finally, he suggested the patient return the setting to the minimum, and once again, the suggestion worked. In this case, we can see an example of using functional visual metaphors to interact with and potentially alter not only a person's state but also the course of certain physiological processes.

A similar example of working with functional visual metaphors can be found in the works of American hypnotherapist Leslie LeCron, who was active in the 1950s and 1970s. Here's the story of a case he encountered. Once, a patient came to LeCron for a session and complained about a toothache, mentioning that after the psychotherapy session, they would have to visit a dentist to have it extracted. LeCron suggested using hypnosis to anesthetize the toothache, and the patient agreed. LeCron induced a hypnotic state and suggested that the patient was in a "consciousness control room," instructing them to find the button to turn off the toothache on the control panel. He then asked the patient to mentally press the button. Afterwards, he brought the patient out of a trance. Remarkably, the pain was indeed turned off. Subsequently, the patient went to the dentist. When they returned for the next session with LeCron, they reported that the entire dental procedure had been surprisingly painless, which amazed both the patient and the dentist.

Regarding functional visual panels, it's worth noting that Richard Bandler extensively applied them in his psychotherapeutic method called DHE (Design Human Engineering), which he developed in the mid-1980s. Bandler significantly expanded the functional application of these panels and created a range of techniques that allow for the alteration of numerous states, whether in collaboration with a psychotherapist or independently. Similar DHE techniques will be presented in the practical section of the book.

Hypnotic hyperesthesia

By hypnotic hyperesthesia, we understand the emergence of various sensations in the body that are not typical in the ordinary waking state of consciousness. For example, this may involve the experience of warmth or coldness, heaviness or lightness, vibrations, or sensations of movement within the body, and so on. This phenomenon can occur naturally during trance induction or can be artificially induced through suggestion.

Hypnotic Amnesia

This phenomenon refers to the partial or complete loss of the ability to remember a specific period of time in a patient. During hypnotic suggestion, amnesia can occur spontaneously or be induced. In almost all cases, spontaneous amnesia is formed only during the period of hypnotic induction. For example, a patient may remember the beginning of the hypnosis session and the moment of coming out of it, but forget what exactly happened during the trance induction. This phenomenon is quite commonly observed and often appears during the induction of deep levels of hypnotic trance.

Hypnotic amnesia can also be suggested for the patient. We provided a similar example in the section of the book dedicated to the hysteric profile of personality. In our opinion, this profile is almost ideal for reproducing this phenomenon. With representatives of other profiles, even highly hypnotizable ones, reproducing this phenomenon is not often successful, or it creates an *illusion of amnesia*—a phenomenon similar to amnesia that gives the feeling that the memory is still there but there is no desire to recall it at the moment.

Richard Bandler once shared a story about successfully suggesting to a patient during a hypnosis session that he had forgotten he ever smoked. The patient spent several days wondering why his smoking acquaintances kept offering him cigarettes. Eventually, the amnesia naturally disappeared. Inspired by this, we decided to conduct a similar experiment but with a slight variation. In one hypnosis laboratory, we took one of our students with a hysteric profile of personality who despised nicotine and cringed at the smell of cigarette smoke. We induced her into a state of deep hypnotic trance and suggested to her that she had been smoking cigarettes for a long time and enjoyed it. Then we brought her out of trance, left the room with her, and offered her a cigarette. She calmly took it and happily lit it. We then re-induced her into trance, removed the previous suggestion, and brought her back to the waking state, where she again reacted very negatively to nicotine. Formally, this could be called *mnesic illusion*, a phenomenon where a person becomes convinced that something occurred in the experience that did not actually happen.

We performed another experiment with the same student to create selective amnesia. We suggested to her that she forget how to use the Ukrainian language and that her native language be English. It is worth noting that she knew English at a basic level. After coming out of trance, she did not understand Russian words addressed to her and responded in English phrases. At our request, she took out her passport from her bag. After she failed to read anything from it, she exclaimed, "Oh my God, I can't read this text!" Then we re-induced her into a trance and canceled the previous suggestions. Such experiments vividly demonstrate the ability of our consciousness to recreate various hypnotic phenomena associated with memory functioning.

Hypnotic Recall

This trance phenomenon allows the resurfacing of forgotten fragments in memory through hypnotic suggestion. It can occur spontaneously or through appropriate suggestion. Spontaneous hypnotic recall may manifest during hypnosis as the recollection of forgotten parts of one's personal history. These parts of personal history are often emotionally charged and require psychotherapeutic processing. These memories can emerge as full-fledged internal films and images, where the person immediately recognizes which memory they are dealing with and to which time period it belongs.

Cathartic Remembrance

Sometimes, cathartic remembrance may occur, which involves a strong emotional abreaction such as laughter, tears, vomiting, and so on. For example, during a hypnotic regression into early childhood, our patient began to cry while remaining in a hypnotic trance. When we brought her out of the trance state and asked what she specifically remembered from her childhood, she replied that in her recollection, she became a six-year-old girl again, and her mother wanted to take her to school, but she didn't want to go and started crying. In this case, during the hypnotic induction, we did not provide any suggestions for the patient to recall a specific memory. What manifested was a spontaneous expression of cathartic hypermnesia. Sometimes, the intense expression of emotions during trance induction can occur without consciously recognizing the exact memory fragment from which it arises. However, we most often observed such phenomena when working with the holotropic breathwork technique, where individuals can laugh, cry, and scream without fully realizing the source of the emotional abreaction.

An interesting example of unconscious strong emotional abreaction was witnessed during one of Bert Hellinger's seminars. Instead of using his systemic constellation method with a patient, he created a hypnotic regression using physical perinatal anchoring. He embraced the patient in a circle with his arms and then asked her to start freeing herself from his therapeutic embrace, which triggered her experience of reliving her birth. The patient spent about 15 minutes going through the "birth paths" out of Bert's embrace and then fell to the ground. Afterwards, the participants helped her lie down on chairs next to Bert, resting her head on his lap. She remained there for another 20 minutes. Throughout this process, Hellinger described the metaphor of a journey up the staircase of life, where each step symbolized a year of the patient's life. Ascending the stairs recreated the phenomenon of hypnotic progression in her consciousness. Hellinger carefully observed the patient's nonverbal reactions to each year of her life, and if he noticed that a particular emotion began to surface, he would pause for a while. In some childhood years, the patient exhibited body tremors and tears. Around the third or fourth year, she started vomiting. Hellinger commented that she had experienced intense emotional struggles that year. From the age of 5–6 and into adulthood, no significant negative experiences were observed.

Another example from our practice involved a patient who had attempted suicide by hanging four years prior to seeking psychotherapy, resulting in partial retrograde amnesia for the last two years of her life. We attempted to help her retrieve the forgotten fragments using hypnotic work. In the hypnotic session, we used an externally oriented trance. We placed pieces of paper on the floor in a line, symbolizing the timeline, and the paper scraps represented fragments of memories, both recoverable and forgotten. Initially, we asked her to step on the pieces of paper that symbolized the recoverable memories. Stepping on them, she accurately described their content. Then we asked her to step on a sheet that symbolized one of the blocked memory fragments. Initially, nothing happened, but after 10–20 seconds, the blocked memory fragment began to unfold. In this case, when working with externally oriented trance, we can see the application of the technique of working with the timeline, a spatial metaphor that significantly facilitates the search for memories in the mind.

Hypermnesia

If we are discussing the phenomenon of hypermnesia, it allows us to retrieve not just any memory fragment but its detailed content. For example, during training on the use of hypermnesia in hypnotic suggestion, we invite students to try visualizing a beloved children's book after recreating a hypnotic regression into childhood. They are instructed to open the book to a specific page and attempt to read the text written there. After the training session, they return home and check if they have successfully recalled the specific text indicated on the given page.

Transderivation Search

The process of memory retrieval is one in which a particular sensation or emotion is taken as a starting point to find the desired memory fragment.

Let's provide an interesting example from our practice. During a group psychotherapy session, one of our students mentioned experiencing a strange feeling of nausea when attempting to relax her tense trapezius muscles. We asked her to sit next to us, applied pressure to her trapezius muscles to reproduce the negative sensation, instructed her to close her eyes, and gently induced a light trance state. We then suggested that the sensation she experiences when pressure is applied to her trapezius muscles would guide her into the depths of her memory and reveal the memory fragment from which this sensation originated. When we brought her out of trance, she shared that she recalled when she was ten years old, her parents took her to a masseur who had a strange look in his eyes when working on her. She remembered that the feeling of nausea occurred when he was massaging her. "Most likely, he had a strong sexual attraction toward me," the young woman said.

Positive Hypnotic Hallucinations

The phenomenon of positive hallucinations occurs when a person sees, hears, or feels something that does not exist in reality. For example, they may see an implanted image of an apple on the table, a hovering ball in front of their eyes, or an imaginary person sitting on a chair. The hallucination can be either suggested or spontaneous, depending on the type of suggestion given by the hypnotic suggestor. If the hallucination is auditory, it could be someone's speech, a simple sound, or even a melody. A kinesthetic hallucination may manifest as a sensation of touch, the feeling of the body floating in weightlessness, and so on. Hallucinations can be tentatively categorized as true or false. True hallucination cannot be distinguished from real objects, while false hallucination markedly differs in quality from actual perceptions.

Positive hypnotic illusions differ from hallucinations in that a person perceives, sees, hears, or feels a real object in a distorted manner. For example, a real apple may appear purple, a male voice is perceived as female, or a dry hand feels wet.

Let's provide an example of creating true hallucinations with one of our students during a seminar. We induced a deep hypnotic trance in a student with a hysteroid personality profile. When she reached a sufficient depth of trance and began demonstrating catalepsy and levitation of both hands, we suggested to her that she was traveling ten years into the future. This created an additional trance phenomenon of age progression, where we could project our ideas of the future as sensory experiences. Then we instructed her that with a snap of our fingers, her eyes would open, and while remaining in a trance state, she would see a sphere in front of her that would show her glimpses of her future. We snapped our fingers, and her eyes opened slightly, squinting. It was clear that she was focusing on something in front of her. We then re-induced the trance with closed eyes for a few more minutes, followed by post-hypnotic suggestions, and eventually brought her out of the trance.

After coming out of the trance, she told us about her experience. When she opened her eyes in the trance, she saw a round sphere with fuzzy edges, about 40–50 centimeters in diameter. She looked inside the sphere and saw herself with children and a husband (at the time of hypnosis, she was not married and had no children) on an island. She felt a surge of energy and happiness.

If we continue discussing age progression, we can describe its various variations. For example, Milton Erickson used age progression with patients who didn't know how to achieve a certain life goal. He created a hypnosis session with the patient and progressed them into a hypothetical future where they could achieve that goal. While the patient remained in their subjective representation of the future, the therapist asked them how they had already achieved their goal. The patient, associated with the situation of accomplishment, described in detail how they had achieved it. Upon coming out of trance, Erickson simply relayed to the patient what he had heard during the trance. In this case, we see how information derived from the projection of personal future representations can be utilized.

Another intriguing example is the technique of working with hypnosis on people who are dying from cancer. This is not a method of treating cancer but rather an emotional preparation for the process of dying. Patients were put into a hypnotic trance and then progressed to the moment of death. The goal was for the patient to find their own representation of where their consciousness would reside after death. Then, when the patient progressed to that state, the hypnotherapist would interview them about their experiences, ask them to say goodbye to their loved ones, and let go of the world. Patients who underwent this form of regressive hypnosis underwent significant changes in their attitudes toward the world, themselves, and the process of death and dying, significantly reducing emotional distress.

The technique we used at the time for treating death anxiety in patients was effective. Let's provide a similar example. A 40-year-old woman had been experiencing intense fear during air travel for many years. She often resorted to heavy drinking during flights to numb her anxiety and unease, but even that didn't always help. In our interaction with her, we attempted the following approach. We induced a trance state and recreated a fantasy of an airplane crash that she had experienced. Then, we asked her to imagine a series of dead bodies of people involved in the crash. The next step in working with the trance motif was to have her envision herself lying among the deceased. When this was visualized, we uttered the phrase, "It's all over now." Tears started streaming down the patient's face as she intensely relived the sensation of being beyond the boundary of life. Subsequently, we brought her out of the trance and asked for feedback on her well-being. She felt as if something had been purged from within. A week later, she flew on a plane to visit her daughter in Prague. When she returned and came to see us, she reported flying without fear for the first time in her life.

Similar techniques involving age progression beyond life are not new and have been part of Hindu and Buddhist practices for centuries. The essence of these practices involved meditating on the image of oneself as a deceased individual. Some monks would deliberately visit cemeteries to engage in prolonged contemplation and meditation on the actual bodies of the dead. Indeed, the associated experience of being beyond the threshold removes fear and unease.

In neuro-linguistic programming, a technique called "Old Bones" was developed, utilizing the phenomenon of age progression for individuals seeking advice regarding their current life situations. This technique can be applied both in a hypnotic format and as a pattern without direct hypnotic induction. In either case, the structure of "Old Bones" is a modified version of Milton Erickson's technique involving age progression. With this technique, the patient is induced to believe that they have aged significantly and can, from the perspective of extensive life experience, offer themselves in the past adequate and constructive advice and recommendations.

Age regression

The hypnotic phenomenon of age regression is similar in its creation to age progression, with the exception that the hypnotic suggestion is directed backward in time instead of forward. This phenomenon was a favorite among hypnotherapists in the late 19th and early 20th centuries. Some hypnotherapists even used it as a standardized template, considering it their primary therapeutic tool. Some believed that it was necessary to return the patient to a traumatic experience and evoke a cathartic reaction (J. Breuer), through which a healing effect could be achieved. Others implanted false memories to alleviate a person's suffering (P. Janet), while some helped patients in a state of age regression to complete unfinished business (R. Bender).

We have previously described the cases of J. Breuer and P. Janet in our book. R. Bender, through the technique of completing memories, assisted Vietnam veterans suffering from PTSD. For example, one of his patients experienced painful reminiscences (visual flashbacks) in which he relived the scene of his friend's suicide multiple times. He suffered from severe depression, and during one of his military helicopter flights, he simply jumped out of the door. R. Bender regressed his patient to the traumatic situation and, in a trance, concluded it differently. He suggested to the patient that he had successfully boarded the helicopter and retrieved his friend's body. Then he transported them back to America. The trance visualization of this scene significantly alleviated the patient's emotional suffering.

As Russian psychologist B. Zeigarnik discovered in her research, we are much more likely to hold memories of unfinished or improperly completed events in our memory. R. Bender's work demonstrates how we can help a patient release their attention from a sense of incompleteness through hypnotic techniques. Although this release may not be complete and may differ from literal real-life closure, in the practice of hypnotherapy, we can observe a genuine therapeutic effect solely through trance visualization.

Negative hypnotic hallucination.
Negative visual hallucinations occur in consciousness when a person does not see, hear, or perceive an actual existing object. Nevertheless, even when the phenomenon of negative hallucination is created, the process of perceiving surrounding objects continues to occur; the individual simply loses awareness of what has been perceived. Let's provide an example to clarify this thought further.

Stephen Gilligan shared a story about experiments with creating negative visual hallucinations. Individuals were induced into a hypnotic trance state, and it was suggested that they would negatively hallucinate any furniture in the room. Then they were asked to open their eyes and walk in a straight line toward the opposite wall. On their path, a table was placed. The patient would approach the table but then walk around it. When later questioned about why they deviated from a straight path toward the opposite wall, the patient would respond that they did not know; they simply felt like it. Similar results were obtained with other participants in the experiment. This indicates that the process of perception continues to occur, but on a conscious level, the person is not aware of what they perceive. However, their unconscious reactions still indicate that sensory information continues to reach the brain, be processed, and generate appropriate responses to external stimuli.

A somewhat similar experiment was conducted by doctors with patients suffering from anterograde amnesia. This form of amnesia occurs when a person loses the ability to remember or retain anything after a traumatic experience. All memory before the traumatic event continues to be preserved, as well as the memory of the last 15-20 minutes of the most recent experience. Therefore, after this short period of time, any event falls out of memory and can no longer be consciously recalled. Doctors attempted the following approach. They approached an anterograde amnesic patient, holding a handheld electric shocker in their hand, shook their hand, and simultaneously shocked them. Then they left and returned after half an hour, when the patient had already forgotten about the previous handshake. When they reached out their hand for a handshake again, the patient refused. When asked why they refused, the patient could not formulate a reason for their behavior.

As in the case of hypnotic negative hallucinations and anterograde amnesia, we can see that conscious control over certain mental processes is lost, but these processes themselves do not disappear, and the unconscious part of the mind continues to adequately react to the world.

Hypnotic phenomena of time illusions

There are various phenomena of time distortion that can occur during trance induction. Some of them occur spontaneously and accompany the trance process, while others can be created through specific suggestions. One of the most commonly encountered trance phenomena is compressed time. It often arises simply as a result of deep immersion in a hypnotic state.

And sometimes, the deeper the trance, the stronger the compression of time. Compression usually occurs at a rate of 2−3 times per second. For example, if a patient was in a trance state for 30 minutes, upon exiting, they may comment that it felt like only 10 minutes had passed. Observing patients experiencing such time compression, we have found that almost all of these trance sessions were emotionally rich, possessed significant therapeutic potential, and led to constructive changes. The presence of the time compression phenomenon, in our opinion, indicates a deep rapport between the hypnotherapist and the patient. It reflects the patient's internal readiness for positive transformation. Often, during the manifestation of time compression, hypnotic amnesia can spontaneously occur for the duration of the trance induction.

The phenomenon of extended time is encountered much less frequently and, in our opinion, is a consequence of the patient's inability to integrate an internal conflict that may be unexpressed in the conscious realm during trance induction. Typically, this phenomenon is accompanied by negative emotions, ominous premonitions, and dark or black-and-white images. After a trance session with such time distortion, patients often feel uncomfortable. However, despite this discomfort, this phenomenon provides indications of a significant internal conflict that requires additional psychotherapeutic exploration.

There is an interesting story about Milton Erickson's work with a patient who had a very peculiar symptom. She would go to sleep and dream that she was going on a vacation by the sea and spending many days there. The dream was wonderful, except for one drawback: she wouldn't wake up in reality and continued sleeping for several days at a time while her consciousness was enjoying the vacation. Once, she was out of contact with her loved ones for over a week. When they went to her home, they found her peacefully asleep. She had been sleeping continuously for over a week, and her body was in terrible condition. She was taken to the hospital and later referred to Milton Erickson for consultation, seeking his assistance. The legend goes that Erickson worked with her only once, using a hypnotic trance, in which he suggested that she would be able to continue having similar dream journeys in the future, where she could spend a week or more, but in reality, it would only take a couple of hours.

In essence, one could say that he taught her to expand time in her dreams during trance. We have never encountered a similar phenomenon of hyperextended time in the process of hypnotic induction. However, we have observed this phenomenon in the dreams of some patients. They would describe dreams in which they lived for several weeks, months, or even years, and upon waking up, it felt as if they remembered many days spent in some other place. It is worth noting that descriptions of such dream phenomena are very rare. Additionally, it is interesting to note that after dreams with hyperextended time, people experience intense and unusual sensations and emotions, which are more often positive than negative.

In our observations, the phenomenon of absent time did not spontaneously manifest during the trance process, although we acknowledge that it could potentially occur. To understand what this phenomenon represents, it is important to note that for each person, the representation of time is always at the level of bodily sensations. In other words, we deal with the perception of time. We feel that time is passing. Each of us may have our own subjective representation of it. And, naturally, any sensation in the body can be turned on or off using hypnotic inductions. The phenomenon of absent time, in its form, resembles hypnotic analgesia, where we disable sensitivity to pain in a specific area or throughout the entire body.

Hypnotic phenomena of alternative personalities

Our personality consists of fragments, different parts that have been formed during different periods of personality development. These parts interact with each other in a specific way, like employees of the same company. Some parts are more friendly towards each other, while others are not. Each of these parts can have different values and beliefs.

For example, one part may prioritize work and career advancement, another may prioritize friends and socializing, and yet another may prioritize spirituality and self-development. Our integrated personality is a compromise among these parts. In mentally healthy individuals, there is always a core personality that governs the other subpersonalities. Volitional control emanates from this core personality. Some subpersonalities may be stable, while others may be traumatized. A stable subpersonality is always in effective interaction with the core personality.

For example, if the core personality primarily manages work and career and one of the subpersonalities is focused on friendships and leisure activities, and both of these parts are stable, then the person can effectively integrate these aspects into their life without experiencing internal conflict. However, if one of the parts is traumatized, its manifestation can lead to internal conflict because what one part desires may be completely contradictory to the desires of another part. For instance, the work-oriented part may insist that "you're not earning enough; you need to work more; you can't afford to rest." In response, the part associated with leisure activities may say, "forget about work, let's meet up with friends and have a good time." If one part is significantly stronger than the other, the weaker part is repressed in the unconscious. However, when two parts are roughly equal in strength and the person cannot choose one over the other, they experience internal conflict, which can only be resolved by finding a compromise between these two parts. This is an example of a possible neurotic disorder.

It is important to understand that conflicts can arise among multiple parts of the personality. Sometimes, it is not just a conflict but a full-fledged struggle. In such cases, neurotic disorders can develop into borderline personality disorders or psychoses. In mild personality disorders, the conflict can be consciously recognized. In more severe cases, one part of the personality may have no awareness of the other parts.

In some instances, multiple core personalities can coexist within an individual's consciousness. In certain psychiatric cases, clinicians have identified up to 70 core personalities, which can vary in age, race, and gender. However, these are critical forms of multiple personality disorder. In milder forms, there may be only 2–3 personalities of the same gender, age, and race, sometimes without a change in name.

As an example, let's consider a case from an American clinic involving a woman with symptoms of multiple personality disorder. She had two core personalities with different names. During the psychiatric evaluation, the doctors conducted a blood test and discovered that she had diabetes. After some time, when she transitioned into her alternative personality, another blood test was conducted, and an astonishing finding emerged—the second personality did not have diabetes at all. The test was repeated several times while the patient was in different personalities, consistently confirming that the symptoms of diabetes manifested exclusively in one personality.

We are not aware of similar observations or examples, and it would be incorrect to make generalizations based on a single case. However, we can hypothesize that any physical or mental illness is a reflection of a personality disorder. As part of the mosaic of assertions, we can provide an example of a belief existing in psychospiritual and psychotherapeutic circles that any illness is a reflection of a moral violation. Through analyzing numerous cases in our work with patients, we find multiple confirmations of this belief.

Hypnotic suggestion often provides unique opportunities for working with such a disorder. In hypnosis, one can communicate with any personality, understand them, activate or deactivate them, and even attempt to reconcile different parts with each other.

When it comes to individuals who do not suffer from multiple personality disorder, it is possible to temporarily create the phenomenon of multiple personalities under hypnosis. This can be done for experimental purposes or with psychotherapeutic intentions.

For example, the technique of interacting with different parts of the personality in hypnosis involves directly addressing one of them, saying, "Now I would like to speak with your joyful personality," or sad, or anxious, whichever you prefer. After the statement, the person usually transitions into an alternative personality, and communication can be established with that part.

For instance, starting with the phrase "I welcome you," the part responds in some way, and the dialogue continues. Sometimes, upon emerging from trance, the person may continue to remember their conversation with the alternative personality, while other times, the dialogue is amnesic.

During the transition to the alternative personality, the suggestible individual's nonverbal communication almost always changes. Their posture, gestures, bearing, tone, tempo, depth, volume of voice, and so on may differ from the main personality. What an artificially induced alternative personality can express may be unfamiliar to the primary personality. Hence, this technique can be used for hypnoanalysis.

We provided a simple example of implementing this technique in the section of the book dedicated to the schizophrenic accentuation of personality, where we described our interaction with a patient suffering from paranoid schizophrenic personality disorder.

For instance, hysteric personalities, when using this technique, can provide vivid representations of their parts. Representatives of other psychopathological profiles usually display less intense manifestations of different parts of their personality. However, everything is connected to the intensities of emotions hidden within them.

It is also worth noting that different parts of the personality may have different psychopathological profiles. One part may be psychopathic, while another may be epileptoid. This information should be taken into account during the psychopathological profiling of the personality.

Stage hypnotists can create interesting variations of this phenomenon.

The phenomenon of induced animal role
For example, inducing a person to transition into an animal role, such as a cat, dog, or any other animal. After appropriate suggestion, the person begins to exhibit behavior characteristic of the suggested animal image while in an externally oriented trance state for a certain period of time. Sometimes, consciousness forms amnesia during this period.

Hypnotic phenomena of awakening creative abilities
Numerous experiments have been conducted using hypnosis to activate latent creative abilities in individuals. A Ukrainian psychiatrist has demonstrated examples of implementing this technique on volunteers whom he hypnotized, suggesting that they become famous artist or musician, and then allowing them to draw or play musical instruments. People who

underwent such techniques were often amazed when they viewed or listened to the results of their activity. According to their accounts, the induced and expressed skills in hypnosis were previously inaccessible to them. These experiments were conducted not only by medical professionals but also by stage hypnotists for the purpose of entertaining the audience. The essence remained unchanged.

The recreation of creative ability can be divided into two main practices. The first involves inducing an alternative personality, often a known one, who possessed or possesses certain creative abilities. The second involves inducing the creation or enhancement of creative skill without altering the personality. In our opinion, the first practice is much more effective. However, this hypothesis still needs to be tested.

When examining the activities of artists, musicians, writers, and representatives of other forms of creativity, one can discover their specific methods of self-inducing trance states to enhance their creative abilities. An interesting method was employed by the artist Salvador Dali. He would sit in front of a blank canvas, take a spoon in his hand, hold it over a plate, and wait until he started to fall asleep. When this happened, he would drop the spoon, awakening due to the sound of its fall. Afterward, he would take a brush and attempt to depict on the canvas the unusual images that appeared in his consciousness on the border between wakefulness and sleep. The "Salvador Dali creativity pattern" can be easily reproduced without a spoon and plate, but with the help of hypnotic induction. However, the images obtained through this method will likely differ from those in dreams. The states of trance and sleep are significantly different, even at the level of brain rhythms—measurable electrical oscillations. Let's briefly delve into this topic and indicate the frequencies at which the brain operates when a person is asleep, in a hypnotic trance, or awake. We will discuss the following brain rhythms: delta rhythm, theta rhythm, alpha rhythm, beta rhythm, and gamma rhythm.

· **Delta rhythm**. The frequency of oscillations ranges from 1 to 4 Hz with an amplitude of 20–200 µV. This rhythm is associated with restorative processes that naturally occur during sleep. An excess of delta rhythm during wakefulness predisposes to the impairment of various cognitive functions.

· **Theta rhythm**. The frequency of oscillations in this rhythm ranges from 4 to 8 Hz with an amplitude of 20-100 µV. It is registered in the frontal area and hippocampus. Activation of the theta rhythm occurs during the transition from relaxed wakefulness to light drowsiness. This rhythm is specifically observed in individuals in a state of hypnotic trance and other forms of altered states of consciousness. Theta rhythm often transitions into delta rhythm naturally. It can also naturally arise during chronic fatigue and stress. This rhythm is sometimes referred to as the "twilight" rhythm, which serves as the most appropriate metaphor for its function.

· **Alpha rhythm**. The frequency of oscillations varies within 8–13 Hz with an amplitude of 5-100 µV. It is predominantly registered in the occipital and temporal regions of the brain. This rhythm is associated with a relaxed state of wakefulness that occurs when we close our eyes and begin to relax. A decrease in alpha waves occurs when a person actively engages in tasks requiring visualization. Additionally, a decrease can be caused by emotions such as anger, anxiety, fear, or worry.

· **Beta rhythm**. The frequency of oscillations ranges from 14 to 40 Hz, with oscillation amplitudes reaching up to 20 µV but typically ranging from 3 to 7 µV in a normal state. It is registered in the frontal and central gyri, as well as extending to the posterior central and frontal gyri. This brain rhythm is associated with a state of active wakefulness, cognitive processes, and focused problem-solving. It diminishes during motor activity and tactile stimulation and is more active with open eyes. An increase in beta rhythm is a response to stressful factors.

- **Gamma rhythm**. The frequency of oscillations varies within 30–100 Hz, with typical oscillation amplitudes up to 15 μV. It is registered in the precentral, frontal, parietal, and temporal regions of the cerebral cortex. The gamma rhythm is observed during tasks that require maximum concentration and focus.

From delta rhythm to gamma rhythm, we observe a gradual increase in the frequency of the rhythm from 1 to 100 Hz, accompanied by subsequent changes in the functional characteristics of the brain.

Inducing theta rhythm in human brain activity opens the doors to its unconscious structures while maintaining the ability to interact with them. This can lead to healing trance states, the activation of extraordinary creative abilities, and the control of physiological body functions and states of consciousness. The specific method of generating this theta rhythm becomes a matter of personal choice. The entire spectrum of techniques, from shamanic chanting and dancing to Ericksonian hypnosis and generative trance, can be suitable.

Brain rhythms	Frequency of oscillations	States
Delta rhythm	1-4 Hz	Sleep, narcotic sleep, deep sedation
Theta rhythm	4-8 Hz	Altered states of consciousness, trance, hypnosis, exhaustion
Alpha rhythm	8-13 Hz	Relaxed wakefulness
Beta rhythm	14-40 Hz	Active wakefulness
Gamma rhythm	30-100 Hz	Hyperactive wakefulness

Brain Rhythms

The human brain exhibits various rhythmic patterns known as brain rhythms. These rhythms are characterized by their specific frequency of oscillations and are associated with distinct states of consciousness. Understanding these brain rhythms is crucial to comprehending the complex workings of the mind.

The delta rhythm, with a frequency ranging from 1 to 4 Hz, is primarily observed during sleep, narcotic sleep, and deep sedation. It represents a state of profound mental rest and restoration.

The theta rhythm, oscillating between 4 and 8 Hz, is linked to altered states of consciousness such as trance, hypnosis, and even exhaustion. During these states, the mind enters a realm where perception and awareness undergo significant shifts.

Moving on to the alpha rhythm, which ranges from 8 to 13 Hz, we enter the domain of relaxed wakefulness. This rhythm becomes prominent when we close our eyes, seeking relaxation and tranquility. It reflects a state of calm and serenity, often associated with a meditative or reflective mindset.

Transitioning to higher frequencies, we encounter the beta rhythm, with oscillations spanning from 14 to 40 Hz. This rhythm dominates during active wakefulness, when the mind is alert, focused, and engaged in cognitive tasks. Beta rhythm signifies heightened mental activity and concentration.

Lastly, we arrive at the gamma rhythm, which encompasses frequencies between 30 and 100 Hz. This rhythm corresponds to a state of hyperactive wakefulness, characterized by intense mental engagement, heightened sensory processing, and maximal concentration. It is prevalent during tasks that demand exceptional cognitive capabilities.

By deciphering and comprehending the intricacies of these brain rhythms, we can gain profound insights into the functioning of the human mind. Exploring their interplay and significance contributes to our understanding of consciousness, cognition, and the vast potential of our mental capacities.

Hypnotic Phenomenon of Motor Analog Signaling
During the process of hypnotic work, the human body can exhibit various motor signals. These can manifest as slight tremors or twitches in the hands, legs, and head, as well as spontaneous changes in their position. Each of these unconscious movements holds significance and reflects changes in trance states. In order to transform these subtle motor movements into a fully-fledged language of communication, the establishment of specific hypnotic frames becomes necessary. These frames enable the unconscious suggestee to express themselves in an orderly and clear manner.

It is likely that Leslie LeCron was one of the first to apply motor analog signaling in the 1950s and 1960s in America. In his work with patients, he created a simple framework for the unconscious patient to respond to the psychotherapist. The framework was as follows: "If your unconscious wants to answer 'yes,' let it raise the index finger of the right hand. If it wants to answer 'no,' let it raise the left finger." Once this framework was established, the psychotherapist would begin asking questions to the unconscious patient, carefully observing the resulting movements. The movement of a specific finger would indicate a particular response from the unconscious. Often, the patient may not be aware of their own finger movements, as they occur unconsciously.

LeCron initially proposed using such a form of communication with the unconscious for hypnoanalysis, which involves uncovering the root cause of existing symptoms. He also suggested a set of basic questions that could be asked of the patient during hypnoanalysis, utilizing motor analog signaling.

These questions are now known as "**LeCron's Keys**"

1. **Conflict**. Is the symptom a result of any past conflict? This question can be posed in two forms, using the terms "external conflict" and "internal conflict." External conflict refers to any altercation, fight, or similar events. Internal conflict encompasses dilemmas in decision-making, the inability to make a choice, conflicts of conscience, and actions.

2. **Motivation**. Is there any hidden internal motivation that leads to the emergence of the symptom? The term "positive intention" is commonly used in psychotherapy today. Behind any symptom, there may be a concealed benefit. Although the person may not consciously understand the cause of the problem, analyzing their life situation can reveal that they are not receiving something important without the symptom. A simple example would be an elderly person who frequently falls ill and receives a lot of attention from their relatives. If the illness were absent, they might lose the necessary attention.

3. **Suggestion effect**. Is the symptom a result of any past suggestion? Indeed, several symptoms arise as a consequence of negative suggestions made to us during childhood or other periods of time. Many inappropriate beliefs about one's sexual life are passed down by mothers and grandmothers to their daughters and granddaughters.

Let's recall a case where a patient described how her grandmother would "brainwash" her during childhood. The grandmother would take her to the window, point to an arch in the building, and tell her, "Do you see, my dear, one evening when you're walking there, five boys will catch you, pin you down, and one of them will violate you." Such suggestions do not necessarily determine a person's life, but they certainly have an impact, reflecting changes in certain aspects of behavior.

4. **Elements of "organic speech."** Is the symptom a result of using "organic speech"? This point requires further clarification. In our speech, we often employ verbal metaphors that can directly influence bodily sensations, bypassing their figurative or abstract meaning. Examples of such metaphors include phrases like "Why are you so sour?", "You'll break your neck," "Lose your head," "Your hands are growing from the wrong place," "Everything is twisted," and so on. Theoretically, each metaphor used in the right context and at the right time can have an impact on physical and mental well-being. This was believed by Lekron, who once shared a case involving a lawyer who complained of a bad taste in his mouth. Despite undergoing medical examinations that revealed no underlying illnesses, the symptom persisted. Lekron employed motor analog signaling with the client to uncover the cause of the symptom, and a positive response was linked to the element of "organic speech." Subsequently, Lekron began questioning the patient about whether he or someone in his surroundings had used words related to a bad taste shortly before the onset of the symptom. Indeed, the patient quickly found an answer to this question. He revealed that during that time, he was handling a case in court, defending a person whom he knew to be guilty. However, he managed to prove the person's complete innocence in court, which caused him to experience feelings of guilt. He would then mention to acquaintances that the case had "bad taste." Such self-suggestion, intertwined with feelings of guilt or shame, could

manifest as a symptom. In this case, the use of such words provides the unconscious mind with an alternative means of communicating with the conscious sphere about what it represses or suppresses. On the other hand, it should be noted that, in our opinion, if there is no repression or suppression of negative emotions in a specific life situation, the likelihood of these types of phrases manifesting as symptoms is quite low.

5. **Identification**. Is the onset of the symptom a result of identification with another person? Sometimes, a symptom arises from our identification with a close individual. On an unconscious level, our conscience can "compel" us to share their fate in order to satisfy our social instinct. The topic of symptom inheritance through identification is extensively explored and interpreted by systemic family and transgenerational therapy. We will not delve into this topic in detail here, as it deserves a separate book.

6. **Masochism**. Is the symptom a result of masochistic tendencies? It would be more accurate to refer to this point as the "need for self-punishment." "Guilt is a sense of balance," said Bert Hellinger, a German psychotherapist, during one of his seminars. When we commit an act that goes against our conscience, we seek ways to balance the "amoral" action with a symptom that may restrain us from engaging in similar actions in the future. Thus, a symptom is always a form of unconscious resistance to our own actions or the actions of individuals with whom we have a psycho-emotional connection.

7. **Painful experiences from the past**. Is the symptom a consequence of painful experiences from the past? This point highlights the connection between experiencing negative sensations and emotions from the past and the current symptom. Let's provide a simple example: During a consultation with a psychoanalyst, a patient confessed that she had a strong internal, unconscious prohibition against using swear words.

After some time, they discovered the cause of her symptom in the patient's childhood. When she was around 5 years old, she overheard profanity on the street and then decided to share her discovery with her mother during dinner. In response, her mother took her to the bathroom and washed her mouth with household soap. This form of upbringing may not be ecologically sound, but it seems to have been quite effective.

Naturally, there can be many more keys to uncovering the cause of a symptom than those listed by Lekron. However, they would involve questions that provide further details on a specific point from his list.

If we return to the general topic of motor analog signaling, it is worth mentioning that it is not necessary to limit the variety of unconscious responses to only "yes" or "no." Different finger movements can be assigned to responses such as "don't know," "don't want to talk about it," "you don't need to know that right now," and so on. Similarly, you can work with a list of different answers. For example, you can ask the unconscious mind, "What would be the best activity for me right now?" with options like a) "Work," b) "Take a walk," c) "Eat," d) "Sleep." In this case, each answer option can be assigned to different fingers of one hand, or other answer options can be used.

An interesting application of motor analog signaling is found in Neuro-Linguistic Programming (NLP) and the technique of six-step reframing, where the therapist uses unconscious responses not only to gather specific information from the past but also to initiate or stop certain mental and neurophysiological processes in the present. For example, asking the unconscious mind, "Creative part of the personality, can you find new ways to manifest the positive intention of the part of the personality responsible for the symptom?" vividly illustrates this example. As a result, the number of questions that can be asked expands significantly. Let's refer to these types of **questions as process keys**. Here are some examples of these keys:

· Unconscious mind, can you immerse consciousness in a deep hypnotic trance?

- Unconscious mind, can you show the cause of the symptom?
- Unconscious mind, can you initiate the process of psychotherapeutic transformation?
- Creative part of the personality, can you demonstrate a variety of constructive solutions to the situation?
- Part of the personality responsible for the symptom, can you show what you truly want to achieve?
- Wise part of the personality, can you reveal any new meaning for the existing situation to help me better understand it?

And so on. The questions can be very diverse, and their combination can create individual psychotherapeutic algorithms.

By the way, it is worth mentioning that motor analog signaling does not necessarily have to be performed after inducing a hypnotic trance. The process of verbal communication with the unconscious mind and its parts itself creates a trance-like process. Therefore, essentially, it is only necessary to establish the framework of therapeutic communication, assign response options to the fingers, and begin the communication itself. However, for some individuals, performing this phenomenon after a trance induction may be more effective.

Hypnotic phenomenon of jactation

This is a relatively rare trance phenomenon that sometimes occurs during public performances by stage hypnotists who use prolonged monotonic types of hypnotic induction. In this case, a person's body may start rhythmically swaying from side to side or making circular movements clockwise and counterclockwise. Sometimes there can be an uncontrolled rhythmic raising and lowering of the arms. Similar phenomena have been observed during group hypnosis sessions with Ukrainian hypnotist V. Kashpirovsky. Based on our observations, the usual type of trance induction does not spontaneously produce this phenomenon. However, when we attempted to recreate Kashpirovsky's working style in a hypnosis laboratory, we found that some participants started exhibiting similar hypnotic rocking phenomena.

Hypnotic taste and smell illusions

This hypnotic phenomenon creates taste distortions when consuming food in a trance state. It is difficult to trace the original context in which this phenomenon was first practiced, whether in a clinical or stage setting. However, it is more commonly practiced by stage hypnotists for entertainment purposes. Most often, during a hypnotic trance, the suggestion is given that the person will now taste a delicious sweet fruit or something similar, and then they are given a bitter onion or a sour lemon to try. If the suggestion is successful, the true taste is not perceived at all. The person can eat a bitter onion, crying from the onion's smell irritating their eyes, but at the same time, they can comment on its amazing taste qualities without showing any facial muscle reaction to the bitterness. Naturally, along with this, a hypnotic illusion of smell is also created. This phenomenon can also be turned into taste and olfactory hallucinations by suggesting to the person that they are holding a fruit that does not actually exist.

Hypnotic paralysis

The phenomenon of hypnotic paralysis, in the overwhelming majority of cases, requires intentional induction. Although we have seen a few cases where it occurred spontaneously in hysterical patients during the creation of catalepsy of the arm. In such cases, while remaining in a hypnotic trance, the person retains the ability to communicate and can even stand up and move around, but their arm remains frozen and paralyzed. Willpower does not lead to the removal of paralysis. In other cases, paralysis of the hands and the entire body is created through specific hypnotic inductions.

Hypnotic phenomenon of rebirth

In describing the phenomenon of hypnotic regression, we have already touched upon this topic when discussing the work of Bert Hellinger. In a hypnotic state, the experience of rebirth can be induced by regressing the patient to the moment of their birth. To stimulate association with this memory, it is necessary to perform bodily imitative actions. For example, placing the patient in a hypnotic state on a mat in the fetal position. Then, with the assistance of a helper standing beside the patient, they embrace the patient, simulating contact with the mother in the intrauterine state. Subsequently, spasms of the uterus are imitated by the helper applying pressure to the patient's body from all sides. Following this, pulling movements are made to evoke neurophysiological associations with the process of traversing the birth canal.

Formally, this description corresponds to the technique of V. Reich-O. Rank, "Birth of a New Child," which was demonstrated to us by Alexander Danilov. The psychotherapeutic aspect of this practice is based on the theories of Otto Rank, who introduced the concept of "birth trauma" into psychoanalysis and hypnoanalysis. According to O. Rank, during the process of birth, a person undergoes a significant amount of emotionally and physically painful states, which are then suppressed and can potentially contribute to neurotic and even psychotic processes in the individual's personality. Re-experiencing this event can lead to catharsis—a psychoemotional cleansing of consciousness from these emotions and feelings.

In a section of the book dedicated to the manic-depressive profile of personality, we commented on our observations regarding the fact that difficult and problematic childbirth can potentially lead to the formation of a manic-depressive accent in the personality or even its full-fledged psychotic manifestation in the future. Therefore, in our opinion, in such cases, the hypnotic re-experiencing of birth can possess exceptional psychotherapeutic potential.

Let us present our observations in a slightly different trance context. During holotropic breathing sessions, patients sometimes regress on their own to the moment of birth and begin intensely re-experiencing it without any external involvement.

Once, we observed a patient during holotropic breathing who became associated with the birthing process, and she believed that she was the one giving birth and that the baby was emerging through her birth canal.

However, she had never experienced childbirth before. We interpreted this case as an associated re-experiencing of her own birth through the mother's image. We have not encountered any other similar cases, so we refrain from making any generalizing statements on this matter.

Hypnotic Phenomenon of Regression into Past Lives

Russian psychiatrist and hypnotherapist V. Raikov practiced a fascinating form of hypnotherapy with alcoholics in the 1960s and 1970s. By inducing them into a state of hypnotic trance, he regressed them along the timeline, first into early childhood, and then suggested that they transition from their current life to their past incarnation in their consciousness. Patients began to recall and share their experiences in this state, describing who they were and what they did. V. Raikov then suggested that they look from there into their future incarnation, where they would die, be reborn, and descend into alcoholism in the next life. The realization of this was often shocking for the patients. According to V. Raikov, many of those who experienced this process eventually quit drinking or significantly reduced their alcohol consumption.

Many years ago, together with my students, we experimented with inducing the experience of past incarnations through hypnotic suggestion and discovered a remarkable phenomenon. The majority of students who reenacted this phenomenon easily regressed into the experience of their past incarnation and provided detailed feedback about who they were and what they did.

It is difficult to determine the nature of this phenomenon. Rationalistic reductionists would argue that we are dealing with fantasies of the patient's unconscious mind. Transpersonal psychologists, on the other hand, would claim that we are dealing with genuine experiences of past incarnations. At present, we cannot fully confirm or refute either viewpoint. Therefore, let us focus on the fact that such experiences can be reproduced, analyzed, and integrated into other forms of therapeutic work, yielding significant therapeutic results. Let me provide an example from the psychotherapeutic work of Stanislav Grof, who utilized the method of holotropic breathwork. One of his patients had been plagued by a psychosomatic symptom for the past 20 years. She suffered from persistent frontal sinusitis and maxillary sinusitis, which did not improve regardless of the treatments she received. During a holotropic breathwork session, she regressed into a memory of one of her past incarnations and recalled being a young woman in an English medieval village, regarded as a witch by the villagers. They caught her, tied her to a board, and submerged her head into the water of a lake, resulting in her death. In the holotropic trance, she fully relived the process of her death. After some time following the psychotherapeutic session, she began to notice that the symptoms of frontal sinusitis and maxillary sinusitis started to recede. The symptoms disappeared and never returned. Stanislav Grof's books contain several similar cases of working with patients and their regressions into past lives.

Based on our observations and the observations of other psychotherapists who have employed this phenomenon in therapeutic practice, we can affirm its ability to produce a powerful therapeutic effect, sometimes unattainable through other hypnotic methods.

It is worth mentioning our findings in working with this phenomenon. Following the concept of regression, we attempted to recreate the phenomenon of hypnotic reincarnational progression in a hypnotic laboratory with students.

Hypnotic reincarnational progression
We simply induced students into a hypnotic state and then suggested to them that they were becoming associated with their future incarnation. Similar to the previous phenomenon of hypnotic reincarnational regression, most of our students began to re-experience experiences not related to their own personality. Some did so superficially, while others provided highly detailed accounts. Interestingly, we observed a physiological phenomenon in individuals who were in this state and provided feedback on what was happening to them. The more detailed information they commented on, the faster their pulse and breathing became, and they experienced trembling in their hands and sometimes throughout their entire body. We cannot fully interpret such vegetative reactions. However, it can be assumed that

during the reproduction of this phenomenon, several areas of the brain are activated. To fully confirm this assumption, it would be necessary to repeat this experiment using MRI equipment.

By activating this hypnotic phenomenon, we initiate unconscious processes of intensive analysis of existing experiences and the projection of assumptions about what they might lead to in future incarnations, assuming that such incarnations exist. However, it is important to note that these projections may be influenced by our desires and fears. In any case, we have found that the material obtained after such hypnoanalysis possesses significant psychotherapeutic value and can be used in the process of psychotherapy.

Phenomenon of false hypnotic paralysis

During hypnosis, you may encounter not only the phenomenon of complete hypnotic paralysis but also its false variant. What does it entail? The patient is aware that they are in a trance and theoretically capable of moving, but a volitional impulse is formed in their consciousness, making them unwilling to move. When prompted by the hypnotist to try to overcome the paralysis on their own, the patient usually manages to do so after several attempts, typically taking 5–20 seconds. This indicates that a certain form of paralysis did exist but was in a more controllable state. When patients who successfully emerged from this state voluntarily provided feedback, they described the process of emerging as similar to attempting to break free from sticky shackles or making progress in a viscous swamp.

Vectors of hypnotic phenomena

Positive hallucinations (illusions)	Negative hallucinations (illusions)
Catalepsy (paralysis)	Levitation (motor analog signaling)
Hyperesthesia	Anesthesia
Hypermnesia	Amnesia
Age progression	Age regression

4

The Use of Hypnotic Phenomena in Psychotherapeutic Practice

In psychotherapeutic practice, there have always been a range of phenomena that have been and will continue to be beloved tools of therapists. These include hypnotic progression and regression, catalepsy, levitation of the hands, and motor analog signaling.

Indeed, these phenomena can be more than sufficient for the treatment of various conditions. However, this does not mean that other phenomena cannot be used as psychotherapeutic tools.

Hypnotic phenomena serve various purposes within the hypnotic trance.

Hypnotic phenomena can serve as clear indicators that the trance has been induced and the patient is receptive to suggestions.

Different phenomena can act as diagnostic criteria for assessing the depth of the induced hypnotic trance and the patient's ability to reach such depths. This, in turn, can provide valuable insights into the patient's specific psychopathological profile. Only individuals belonging to certain psychopathological profiles are capable of fully reproducing certain hypnotic phenomena. For instance, we have observed genuine negative hallucinations exclusively in individuals with a hysteroid profile.

Hypnotic phenomena can trigger changes in the patient's consciousness. For example, during a trance state, the client's arm may be lifted, inducing catalepsy. The hypnotherapist then establishes a framework for change, suggesting that the arm will gradually descend, controlled by impulses from the unconscious. As the arm lowers, a pleasant, warm sensation of joy and happiness increasingly arises in the patient's consciousness. Additionally, one can introduce the criterion of touching the leg with the hand, explaining that when the hand reaches the leg, a new and unusual healing process will initiate in the patient's consciousness. The specific unfolding of events during the lowering of the arm and the touch of the knee can be tailored according to your preference. Furthermore, an alternative approach can involve not lowering the arm from catalepsy but initiating the phenomenon of hand levitation. In this case, we can suggest allowing the unconscious mind to spontaneously move the hand in space, and while the hand levitates, the wise part of your personality will explore new ways to solve the existing challenge.

Ernest Rossi, one of Milton Erickson's closest students, demonstrated another interesting variation in the use of catalepsy and levitation of the hand in a psychotherapeutic context. This technique was later named "Ernest Rossi's Hands."

The execution of the technique is as follows: First, the hypnotherapist identifies the symptom they will work with. Then, a trance is induced, during which catalepsy is created in the patient's hands. Next, the hypnotherapist verbally associates the patient's right hand with the existing symptom and the left hand with the potential solution existing in the unconscious. A hypnotic induction is then given to prompt the patient's unconscious to begin moving the hands slowly and spontaneously in a trance state. As the hands move, existing unconscious resources that can be used to address and treat the symptom are awakened. The hands start moving; they may travel through space and interact with each other. Often, at the end of the movement, they come together, symbolizing the point of finding an acceptable solution at the conscious or unconscious level. However, there are cases where the hands do not come together and even move apart, indicating the patient's internal resistance to finding a solution. In such cases, it is necessary to either continue the hypnotic session by adding specific interventions that can help activate the correct path to finding a solution or to bring the patient out of the trance, discuss possible causes of unconscious resistance, and attempt to understand them at the conscious level. Then, the technique can be attempted again.

"**Ernest Rossi's Hands**" can be a universal technique applicable to almost any type of symptom during hypnotic work. Based on our observations, this practice has shown good results in working with addictive behaviors. The only important aspect of this form of hypnotic work is the activation of full catalepsy in the hands and their subsequent unconscious movement. In some cases, the movement may be intuitive and semi-conscious, but its effectiveness is diminished. This practice represents an expanded form of working with motor analog signaling, where the unconscious creates an external representation of internal change processes through the movement of the patient's hands.

One very interesting way of using the hypnotic phenomenon in trance is as a metaphor for change and transformation. An example of such work was shared with us during one of the seminars by Alexander Danilov, who discovered a fascinating form of utilizing hypnotic hand catalepsy in the treatment of male erectile dysfunction.

Danilov would induce the patient into a hypnotic trance and then create catalepsy in the hand, keeping it in a vertical position with a clenched fist. He would then suggest to the patient a comparison between the cataleptic hand and the ability of the penis to achieve a similar state. Thus, the hand in catalepsy became a neurophysiological metaphor for the erectile function of male genitalia.

This example demonstrates how different phenomena can be used as metaphors in trance work. Let's provide analogies with other phenomena.

For instance, the hypnotic phenomenon of anesthesia can be employed to address emotionally traumatic situations. To do so, the patient is regressed to the problematic emotional context, followed by the induction of the anesthesia phenomenon and its testing by applying pressure to a pain point or pricking the skin with a needle. Afterward, an analogy is drawn between the emotional sphere and pain sensitivity, making the anesthesia metaphor a representation of insensitivity to psychotraumatic experiences.

The cataleptic bridge phenomenon can serve as a powerful metaphor for resilience in the face of life's difficulties. The working strategy can be similar to the previous example. The patient is either progressed into or regressed into the desired context, the cataleptic bridge phenomenon is created, and it is associated with the necessary process or phenomenon.

Visual hallucinations can be an excellent metaphor for the ability to see a way out of a situation when others cannot. Taste illusions can serve as a metaphor for changing the perception of a situation.

By analogy with the examples mentioned above, any hypnotic phenomenon can be transformed into a metaphor for transformation. For ease of use, let's describe an algorithm using hypnotic phenomena as metaphors for transformation.

The structure of utilizing hypnotic phenomena in therapy practice is as follows:

1. Identify the problematic context.
2. Select a hypnotic phenomenon whose metaphor can provide a solution in this context.
3. Induce trance.
4. Associate with the problematic context.
5. Recreate the chosen hypnotic phenomenon.
6. Associate the hypnotic phenomenon with the problematic context, making it a metaphor for transformation.
7. Provide post-hypnotic suggestions.
8. Bring the patient out of a trance.

Certainly, it is worth mentioning that not all phenomena can be reproduced with every patient. It is best to start training in the application of this practice with simpler phenomena and explore in which cases their metaphors for symptom work can be most applicable.

The more difficult it is to reproduce a phenomenon in trance work, the stronger its metaphor for transformation is. Although this is only a hypothesis that is challenging to confirm or refute.

Even if you can only elicit one elementary phenomenon in a patient, such as catalepsy of the hand, using cause-and-effect language, you can integrate it into a certain part of the transformative trance process.

5

Hypnotic Trance Depth Levels

Different hypnotherapists have proposed their own understanding of the existing levels of hypnotic trance depth. For example, August Forel identified three primary levels:

1. **Somnolence**
2. **Hypotaxis**
3. **Somnambulism**

Somnolence refers to a light, drowsy state that often occurs during the initial stages of hypnotic induction. In this state, the hypnotic subject remains fully aware and in control of themselves, hearing and understanding the suggestions given to them. Their eyes may begin to close, and new images may emerge in their consciousness, accompanied by bodily sensations. This state is reminiscent of the transitional phase between sleep and wakefulness, when one is aware of not being asleep but anticipates being engulfed by sleep. Based on our experience, this state is often more than sufficient for suggestions and the execution of psychotherapeutic algorithms. Some simple hypnotic phenomena can already manifest at this level, such as hand catalepsy. To induce catalepsy in this state, or even without trance induction at all, Betty Alice Erickson recommended touching the patient's hand with one's own hand and very slowly, inch by inch over several seconds, beginning to lift it upwards. With successful execution, the hand will eventually remain suspended in the air. Furthermore, this state is well-suited for re-creating hypnotic age progression and regression. The depth of emotional experience at this level may not necessarily be intense, but it is adequate for psychotherapeutic changes.

At the level of **hypotaxis**, the trance state deepens significantly. The individual begins to immerse themselves deeply in the trance state, experiencing a variety of sensations. In this state, the sense of voluntary control over the trance process may be lost. The subject continues to hear the hypnotherapist's speech, but comprehension of its meaning is greatly diminished. It is relatively easy to create phenomena such as catalepsy, levitation of the hands, cataleptic bridge, amnesia, hypermnesia, anesthesia, hypnotic illusions, and hallucinations in this state.

At the level of **somnambulism**, an individual delves into the deepest levels of hypnotic trance, where they are barely aware of what is happening to them. The time spent in trance is often subject to amnesia. All, or almost all, hypnotic phenomena can be reproduced. Any hypnotic command becomes a command for the neurophysiology of the individual, corresponding to Ivan Pavlov's phase of ultra-paradoxical inhibition of the cerebral cortex.

The division of hypnotic depth into three sections is practical and allows for relatively easy verification of a patient's state. However, during inter-actions with a large number of patients in a hypnotic state, one eventually begins to notice that each level of depth of the three mentioned above has gradations, sometimes quite distinct and evident.

For example, in the 1930s, Ukrainian hypnologist and physiologist E. Katkov attempted to differentiate the model of three levels of hypnotic trance depth proposed by August Forel into a more detailed model by subjectively dividing each level into three further sublevels. As a result, a model of nine levels emerged. According to Katkov, each sublevel provided a clearer classification of the states occurring when transitioning to a new depth level.

The spectrum of the nine levels started with the description of a light superficial trance at the first level and reached the deep unconscious somnambulistic state at the last level. As we understand it, Katkov's model was created based on the generalization of observations of patients in hypnotic states. In his description of the levels of hypnotic trance, Katkov actively employed the terms introduced into brain physiology in the early 20th century by Ivan Pavlov. These terms refer to the first and second signal systems. Let us provide a brief explanation of these concepts.

By the signal system, Ivan Pavlov referred to the system of conditional and unconditional reflexive connections in the higher nervous system of animals and humans. He distinguished between the first and second signal systems.

It was believed that the first signal system is well developed in animals, while the second signal system is likely to be developed only in humans. Ivan Pavlov believed that only humans are capable of forming concepts in their consciousness that are detached from circumstances. The first signal system is imagery, which is activated upon the perception of a specific external stimulus or word without additional associations. The second signal system involves an associative series and can be referred to as discrete.

Some of Pavlov's assumptions turned out to be incorrect, as modern ethology has found numerous examples of thinking displayed by animals. In the 1970s, scientists even succeeded in teaching some monkeys to communicate using sign language. For instance, the laboratory gorilla Koko knew over 2,000 words, was capable of constructing sentences, lying to experimenters, and even making jokes. These processes in an animal's mind are simply not possible without the activity of the second signal system.

Eugene Katkov's Model of Hypnotic Trance Levels

First Segment of Hypnotic Levels:

1. Gradual decrease in the activity of the cerebral hemispheres' cortex. Thought control.
   Suggestions are easily achieved.

2. Cortical tone is reduced.
   Eyelids close.
   Under suggestion, the eyes easily open.

3. Cortical tone significantly decreased.
   Inhibition of the second signal system.
   Relaxation.
   Raised arm falls.
   The patient hears surrounding sounds.

Second Segment of Hypnotic Levels:

1. Cortical tone is reduced.
   Rapport zone emerges.
   Gradual general inhibition.
   Catalepsy. Analgesia.
   Transitional state.
   Significant drowsiness is noted.
   Raised arm remains briefly.
   No interest in sounds.

2. Waxy catalepsy.
   Greater inhibition of the second signal system.
   Initiated automatic movement weakens.

3. Suggested illusions are realized with closed eyes.
   The arm bounces.
   Slow jerky movements.
   Anesthesia of the nasal mucosa.

Third Segment of Hypnotic Levels:

1. Rapport zone is fully established.
   Amnesia.
   Activity of the first signal system.
   (Dropping the raised arm—Platonov symptom)
   Skin irritation triggers hallucinations.

2. Almost complete inhibition of the first signal system.
   Visual hallucinations.

3. Hears only the hypnotist.
   Words have a stronger impact than actual stimuli.
   All types of positive and negative hallucinations.
   Amnesia.
   Instantaneous hypnosis.
   Ultra-paradoxical phase of brain activity, where any suggested command is instantly realized at the neurophysiological level, contrary to actual sensory stimuli.

New Model of Hypnotic Trance Levels

Working with a group of students in one of the hypnotic laboratories, our goal was to experimentally, rather than simply based on observational generalizations, create a map of the possible existing levels of hypnotic trance.

To achieve this, we set up the following experimental framework. Each person in the group took turns being hypnotized, either by us or our assistants. After a light hypnotic induction, it was suggested that the subject was at the first level of hypnotic trance. They remained in that state for a while, then were brought out of the trance and asked to describe their experiences. We repeated this procedure with other participants.

As a result, we found that the majority of people's perceptions of the first level of hypnotic trance were almost synonymous. We then created a generalized description of this level.

Throughout the course of the experiment, we used the same technique to induce the second, third, and fourth levels of hypnotic trance, and so on. Each time, we obtained new, similar descriptions of the subsequent levels.

We discovered that approximately the first four levels corresponded to Auguste Forel's description of the state of somnolence. At each of these levels, the subject continued to be aware that they were being hypnotized and could distinguish words, but with each level, their state deepened, becoming less controllable. By the 3rd or 4th level, individuals began experiencing catalepsy of the hand and body, spontaneous age regression, and false hypnotic paralysis.

The next 5-8 levels, as described, corresponded to the state of hypotaxis. The phenomena of hand levitation, anesthesia, and analgesia—hypnotic paralysis of the hands and body began to appear. The subject still maintained awareness that they were being given trance induction suggestions, but the meaning of the words gradually faded from their conscious sphere. The first signs of visual hypnotic hallucinations emerged, although true hallucinations had not yet occurred.

From levels 9 to 12, we discovered states that corresponded to the description of somnambulistic trance. At levels 9–10, individuals almost lost awareness of what was happening and manifested nearly all hypnotic phenomena, including both true positive and negative visual hallucinations. We did not test the depth of anesthesia, but the students did not react to simple painful stimuli used during hypnotic trance training.

By levels 11–12 (more often the twelfth), the subject had simply switched off completely and had no conscious awareness of what was happening to them. Not all students reached high levels. Some remained at a maximum of 5–6, others at 9–10. Any attempts to deepen their trance were unsuccessful, leading us to conclude that there were specific neurophysiological barriers that prevented further progress to deeper levels of hypnotic trance.

Approximately 20% reached the 12th level of hypnotic trance under step-by-step induction. By stepped induction, we mean sequentially introducing the subject to the necessary level, going through each previous level one by one. The subject is first induced into the first level of trance, then the second, third, and so on, spending some time at each level.

Any attempts to induce trance levels deeper than the twelfth led the subjects to provide feedback on states that corresponded entirely to the twelfth level. We cannot understand why the group we worked with had a limit of 12 levels.

Initially, we thought that the number of these levels might vary among individuals, but when we tested our twelve-level gradation of hypnotic trance in training programs for hypnotic suggestion on people who did not participate in the research, we repeatedly confirmed the corresponding states with the levels of hypnotic trance depth.

In our opinion, this model still requires confirmation and further development with a larger number of hypnotic suggestibles. However, for now, we simply offer this model for consideration and testing. The test of this model can be performed using a simple hypnotic exercise.

Exercise: "Induction of Twelve Levels of Hypnotic Trance"

1. Induce a light trance state in the subject for one minute.
2. Provide a brief induction: "You are now entering the first level of hypnotic trance."
3. Then, pause for 10–20 seconds and ask the person to describe their sensations in their body and mind without opening their eyes.
4. Monitor their nonverbal body and speech signals.
5. Repeat steps 2-3-4, incrementing the trance depth by one, until you reach the 12th level of trance.
6. Provide a suggestion to exit the trance state.

If possible, perform this exercise with several individuals and compare the data obtained. Additionally, when considering the data, we recommend taking into account the psychopathological profile of the hypnotic suggestible, as the ability to reach deep levels of hypnotic trance, the formation of different hypnotic phenomena, and the intensity of their representations may vary depending on it.

Description	Hypnotic Phenomena	Psychopathological Profiles
Level 1: Mild relaxation, shifting focus inward	Light hypnotic progression or regression	True psychopath Paranoid Manic-depressive Schizophrenic Obsessive-compulsive Schizoid Epileptoid Hysteroid, sexual psychopath
Level 2: Possibly a slight increase in breathing and heart rate; reduction in cognitive processes	Motor analog signaling	
Level 3: Deeper relaxation, emergence of richer internal sensory representations, possibly the beginning of reproducing integrated images or inner movies	Possibility of mild hand catalepsy	Paranoid Manic-depressive Schizophrenic Obsessive-compulsive Schizoid Epileptoid Hysteroid, sexual psychopath
Level 4: Intense immersion in sensations while maintaining connection to reality	Light hand levitation	Manic-depressive Schizophrenic Obsessive-compulsive Schizoid Epileptoid Hysteroid, sexual psychopath
Level 5: Gradual loss of the need to fixate attention on the external world, the meaning of the hypnotherapist's words gradually fading from attention	Cataleptic bridge	Obsessive-compulsive Schizoid Epileptoid Hysteroid, sexual psychopath
Level 6: Feeling as if under a dome Expansion of internal sensory representations	Mild anesthesia and analgesia	Schizoid Obsessive-compulsive Schizoid Epileptoid Hysteroid, sexual psychopath
Level 7: Mild memory gaps, slight loss of body contour sensation	Temporal distortions Strong catalepsy and levitation	
Level 8: Near-complete loss of connection to reality, abundant sensory representations	Possible induced mild illusions and hallucinations with eyes open	
Level 9: Very active interaction between the conscious and unconscious mind Sense of wholeness and clarity Willingness to follow hypnotic commands Sense of depersonalization	Mild negative hallucinations with eyes open	Obsessive-compulsive Schizoid Epileptoid Hysteroid, sexual psychopath
Level 10: Disorientation in time, loss of understanding of what is happening	Deep anesthesia and analgesia Full visual hallucinations with eyes open	Epileptoid Hysteroid, sexual psychopath
Level 11: Almost complete disengagement of conscious reactions	Full negative hallucinations with eyes open Full alternate personality in external trance	Hysteroid, sexual psychopath
Level 12: Complete absence of conscious reactions to the world	All or nearly all phenomena, depending on individual characteristics	

Model of Hypnotic Trance Levels

The data in this table is approximate and can vary significantly among representatives of different psychopathological profiles, as well as the order of reproducing phenomena. Therefore, the table represents one possible way to organize states. A personal description can be created by performing the aforementioned exercise of inducing the twelve levels of hypnotic trance. The table also indicates the approximate levels of hypnotic trance that individuals with different psychopathological profiles can reach.

The model of the twelve levels of trance can be used in the format of meditative self-induction into trance. In this exercise, various psychotherapeutic processes can be initiated independently. Let's provide an algorithm:

Exercise "Therapeutic Self-Induction of the Twelve Levels of Trance":

1. Sit comfortably in a chair or on a comfortable stool in a position that is comfortable for you, and close your eyes.
2. Determine the task that you would like to address in the trance state.
3. Give yourself a suggestion in the form of the following phrase: "Now I will immerse myself in the depth of the hypnotic trance, and as I descend to each subsequent level, my unconscious will activate the resources of my personality and my body to solve the task I have set. When I reach the twelfth level of the hypnotic trance, I will stay there for a maximum of X minutes and then naturally return to the waking state."
4. Say out loud or silently to yourself, "I am descending to the first level of hypnotic trance."
5. Stay in this state for one to several minutes.
6. Repeat steps 4 and 5, each time increasing the depth of the trance by one level, until you reach the twelfth level.
7. When a natural exit from the hypnotic trance occurs, take note of at least three key changes that you have observed within yourself during the process of trance self-induction.

Modify the content of the exercise as needed.

By following this algorithm, you can explore and utilize the therapeutic potential of the twelve levels of trance. Remember to adjust the exercise according to your specific needs and objectives.

In addition to the model of the twelve levels of hypnotic trance, we can propose another way of organizing the depth of trance states: the model of meta-trance levels. Transition to a meta-trance level can be achieved through a repeated procedure of initial trance induction when a person is already immersed in a hypnotic trance state. The procedure for creating a meta-trance is as follows:

1. Induce the subject into a light trance level.
2. Expand the sensory representation in the hypnotic trance.
3. Obtain verbal feedback from the subject.
4. Create a motive in the trance where the subject realizes themselves sitting on a chair next to you.
5. Suggest to the subject that they are now entering a trance within the trance.
6. Obtain feedback from them in this state.
7. Bring the person out of the trance within the trance first, and then out of the trance completely.

This exercise can be deepened by transferring the subject to more meta-trance levels. For example, a trance within a trance that is within another trance. We have noticed in our work with this model that the deeper the meta-trance level, the more confusion the consciousness experiences during the transition, and the more strange and unusual the sensory representations become.

The induction of a meta-trance level can be used either as a form of deepening the trance or as an internal trigger that sharply shifts the focus of attention from current trance experiences. By utilizing this technique, it is possible to explore the potential of meta-trance states and their impact on the therapeutic process.

6

Motives of Trance and Their Application in Psychotherapy

By the term "motive of trance," we refer to a fixed sensory representation created by the hypnotherapist that has spatial characteristics in the subject's consciousness. A motive for trance can be static or dynamic. In a static motive, the spatial characteristics remain unchanged throughout the suggestion induction. A dynamic motive reflects spatial changes in the internal imagery associated with the hypnotherapist's induction.

The motive of trance is not simply an imposed visualization but specifically a spatial visualization. Elementary examples can include a beach, a forest, mountains, and so on. In the non-directive form of hypnotic induction, it is possible to suggest an arbitrary motive for trance chosen by the conscious or unconscious subject.

During the process of hypnotic induction, various methods of utilizing the motives of trance can be employed. Different styles of hypnotic induction can vary greatly in their approach to using trance motives, ranging from almost always incorporating them to completely omitting their application. Therefore, motives of trance are not a mandatory tool for trance induction but rather provide an additional framework for working with the patient's conscious and unconscious mind.

With the help of trance motives, it is relatively easy and effective to program therapeutic algorithms for trance work. Here are a few examples:

A therapeutic algorithm aimed at increasing self-confidence and assertiveness can be programmed using the motivation of standing on top of a mountain, feeling strong and powerful, while visualizing positive self-affirmations.

To address emotional healing and forgiveness, the motive of walking along a peaceful beach can be utilized, symbolizing the release of emotional burdens into the calming waves.

For enhancing creativity and problem-solving abilities, a dynamic motive of exploring a mystical forest can be employed, where the subject can encounter symbolic representations of their challenges and find creative solutions.

These examples illustrate how the motives of trance can be incorporated into the therapeutic process, providing a powerful tool for guiding and influencing the patient's experience within the hypnotic state.

Exercise "House of Emotions. Overcoming Anxiety"

1. Imagine yourself in front of a private house in a garden.
2. Enter the house and visualize that after the entrance door, you see three new doors. On the left, there is a gray door; in the center, a green door; and on the right, a colorful rainbow door.
3. Go through the gray door, where you will find a gray room and a gray version of yourself. This represents your anxiety. Approach it closely and imagine that golden light flowing from your heart into your anxiety, gradually filling it. Continue doing this for about one minute.
4. Enter the green door, where you will find a greenish version of yourself. This represents your calmness. Make eye contact with this part of yourself and observe how bright green light flows from its eyes into yours. Continue doing this for about one minute.
5. Go through the colorful door and see a colorful version of yourself in the space. This represents your joy and fulfillment in life. Observe how colorful rainbow dust is carried by the wind from this version towards

you, enveloping you from all sides. Continue doing this for about one minute.

6. Visualize yourself stepping out of the house into a beautiful meadow. Sit in a lotus position, listen to the birds sing, feel the breeze, and sense the grass beneath your feet. Merge with nature. Continue doing this for about one minute.

7. Thank your unconscious mind for its assistance in getting rid of negative emotions, and ask for the positive changes to be extended for as long as possible.

Exercise "Communicating with Parts of the Self. Treatment of Paranoia"

1. Imagine a seaside shore as you walk along it. Look around, listen to the sound of the wind and the waves, and feel the sand beneath your feet.

2. Find a version of yourself on the shore that slightly differs from you, represented by darker and gloomier colors. This represents your paranoia. Approach it and engage in communication with it.

3. Look at it and say the following phrases: "You are a part of me (pause). I see you (pause). I wanted to get rid of you (pause). But you reflect my actions, speech, and thoughts (pause). I cannot remove you, but I can transform you into something better (pause). I accept you as you are (pause)." Touch it with both hands and let the golden color flow into it through your hands. Continue doing this for about one minute.

4. When it is filled with the golden color, merge with it. Observe your sensations.

5. Look behind you and see a wise version of yourself, bright and radiant. Approach it and look at it. Address it with the words: "You are my wise part (pause). I see you (pause). I need your help in my task (pause)." Visualize it extending its hands towards you. Touch its hands with yours. Observe how bright light flows from its hands into yours. After some time, you become a colorful version of it.

6. Express gratitude for it and continue walking along the shore.

7. After a while, sit on the shore in a lotus position, gaze at the sea, listen to the sounds of the wind, and feel the sand beneath you. Merge with nature.
8. Thank your unconscious mind for its assistance in completing the pattern.

These patterns can be used in the form of regular targeted visualization or in the format of hypnotic suggestion.

Let's provide a list of possible motifs that, in our opinion, are most applicable for trance work:

1. City.
2. Private house.
3. Forest.
4. Meadow.
5. Field.
6. River, lake, sea, ocean shore.
7. Mountains.
8. Road.
9. Flying in the air above the ground.

The preference for a specific trance motif can be a matter of choice for both the hypnotherapist and the patient. For example, before a hypnotic session, the patient can be asked in which particular trance motif they would feel most comfortable during the session. Sometimes, the trance motif should remain unchanged due to its strong connection to the therapeutic algorithm's meaning. For instance, visiting different rooms in a house. However, based on our observations, there are no strict rules that must be followed in the process of using trance motifs. The motif is merely a favorable background that can be dispensed with if necessary.

Now let's provide an example of a preliminary algorithm to determine a favorable motif that can be used in psychotherapeutic work.

Exercise "Determining the Motive of Trance"

1. Induce a light hypnotic trance.
2. Provide the following request to the unconscious suggestor: "I welcome your unconscious mind. We will now work on a specific task, and I would like to ask you which particular motive of trance could produce the most favorable effect for our work. If you can demonstrate this phenomenon, please do so now."
3. Once the motive of trance is presented to the conscious mind of the suggestor, it is possible to express gratitude to the unconscious mind for its assistance and smoothly transition to the implementation of the therapeutic algorithm, if applicable.

We can suggest an exercise for independent meditative trance work with the motive of trance.

Exercise "Dynamic Motive of Trance"

1. Sit in a chair or on a comfortable stool.
2. Determine the task you want to work on in a trance state.
3. Determine the motive of trance that can be beneficial for this particular work, using the algorithm from the previous exercise.
4. While in the trance, perform self-induction:

   "My unconscious mind, my friend. Transform this motive of trance into an inner film that I will watch for the next X minutes. I ask you to depict the process of finding a solution in this film. When my inner film reaches its end, continue to keep my consciousness in a hypnotic trance for a few more minutes, and then naturally bring me out of it. If you can begin creating the solution film, immerse me in a sufficient level of hypnotic trance and start the process right now."
5. After exiting the hypnotic trance, identify three key changes that you have experienced during the trance work.

7

Styles and Vectors of Hypnotic Work

In the modern world of hypnotherapy, there is a conditional division of hypnotic work into two main styles: directive and nondirective. Sometimes attempts are made to distinguish the philosophy of a third, separate style, but in our opinion, it often boils down to various intermediate variations along the continuum of directiveness and nondirectiveness with slight changes in values and beliefs and the addition of new technical tools.

Stephen Gilligan provides an example of his attempt to identify the existence of a new style that is different from the two previous ones. Gilligan defines the directive style, the nondirective style, and his generative style as follows:

Directive style of hypnotic work prioritizes the knowledge and representation of the hypnotist themselves regarding what should and should not be suggested to the patient. The hypnotist becomes the standard bearer of what is right and wrong. Their suggestions are direct and imperative, leaving no room for the patient's own choice.

Nondirective style of hypnotic work, or **Ericksonian** style, prioritizes the unconscious wisdom of the patient, who, for various reasons, cannot bring it into their life. The hypnotist themselves do not act as the standard bearers of knowledge on how the patient should or should not change. Instead, they merely assist the patient in awakening the wisdom of their unconscious. The key belief here is that the conscious realm of the patient is not competent, while their unconscious is competent. To achieve good results, the hypnotist should primarily communicate with the patient's unconscious.

Generative Style of Gilligan's Hypnotic Work introduces the philosophy that both the conscious and unconscious mind of a person are wise. However, symptoms arise due to the inability to build a bridge between them. The task of the psychotherapist, according to Gilligan, lies in constructing this bridge and establishing a proper connection between the conscious and unconscious minds.

This idea can be quite innovative in the field of hypnotic work. However, we can find a nearly synonymous model in one of Carlos Castaneda's books, which is part of the Mexican shamanic tradition rather than the psychotherapeutic tradition. Carlos Castaneda writes about two key positions of perception inherent in humans: the position of the mind and the position of silent knowledge. He also points out that the connection between these positions is a two-way bridge. When a person establishes this connection, they gain personal power. Castaneda referred to the process of establishing this connection as "clearing the connecting link with intent."

While the terminology used by S. Gilligan is Ericksonian, the meaning is almost identical to Castaneda's model. It is difficult to ascertain whether Gilligan's idea was derived from Castaneda or independently created. Nevertheless, the incorporation of this model into the psychotherapeutic context has created an exceptionally positive vector that, in our opinion, continues to evolve. However, it still resembles the old-fashioned Ericksonian style with intriguing innovations.

In our view, the main characteristic of this style of work is the preference for an externally-oriented trance process. The therapist uses voice modulation and specific speech patterns to induce a light trance state in the patient. According to Gilligan, this state allows the "filters of consciousness" to relax. In this state, the hypnotherapist engages in a slow conversation with the patient, which resembles an interesting blend of regular verbal therapy and

Ericksonian hypnotic suggestion. Indeed, this format of work serves as a highly original and productive framework for psychotherapeutic interaction, and it also becomes a matter of stylistic preference for the therapist. All styles—directive, nondirective, and generative—can be effective. The key to this effectiveness lies in the competent application of each method and the ability to understand the patient's profile in order to vary one's instrumental technique.

We believe that Gilligan makes a methodological mistake in his attempt to categorically separate himself from the philosophy of Milton Erickson, reducing his ideas to the belief that Erickson was solely focused on communicating with the unconscious. To be frank, that was only a part of his practice. One of Erickson's key beliefs regarding the theory of psychotherapy was that it could not afford the luxury of fixed beliefs. This belief formally established the metarule of being open to new experiences in practice, constantly seeking something new, and the necessity of applying a practical methodology that bypasses the patient's resistance. And if a patient easily enters a trance state simply by giving an imperative command, any nondirective intricacies are a manifestation of the psychotherapist's lack of understanding regarding why they do what they do.

Therefore, we would argue that in addition to the basic nondirective style, Milton Erickson created (although not everyone realized it) an **integrative form of trance work**. The goal of this style was not stylistic preference but rather the ability to adapt one's approach to a more effective style according to the current need. Formally, due to its logical and categorical nature, the integrative style can be called the **metastyle of hypnotherapy,** as it serves as a category in relation to specific styles of hypnotic work. However, the metastyle cannot be simply a collection of hypnotic tools; it is merely a philosophy that enables one to be more effective in the process of creating hypnotic induction.

As soon as the integrative style is viewed as a wild cocktail of hypnotic techniques from various directions, we observe an **eclectic style of hypnotic work**. This style effectively combines parts of the techniques and beliefs of other styles. The eclectic approach in hypnosis can only be subjective, resulting in a wide variety of variations. Therefore, formally, we have described five styles of hypnotic philosophy and work. In our opinion, any attempts to add anything more would only offer different variations within the five proposed styles.

In addition to styles, we would also like to consider eight main vectors of hypnotic work that can be used in psychotherapeutic practice:

1. Hypnoanalytic.
2. Suggestive.
3. Provocative.
4. Humanistic.
5. Behavioral.
6. Transpersonal.
7. Cognitive.
8. Somatic.

Each of these vectors represents a distinct approach and orientation within the field of hypnotherapy. By understanding and utilizing these vectors, therapists can tailor their interventions to meet the specific needs of their clients, leading to more effective and comprehensive treatment outcomes.

Hypnoanalytic Vector

This vector focuses on key beliefs:

1. The cause of the symptom lies in the patient's past.
2. By recognizing the cause, it is possible to influence the symptom in some way.
3. Hypnotic techniques should be applied to regress into the past in order to become aware of it, understand the underlying behavior, or influence it in some way.
4. Hypnotic regression can also be used to search for psychoemotional

resources needed in the present and future.

This vector can serve as an auxiliary set of methods in other forms of psychotherapy, reducing the time spent searching for the cause of the symptom, such as in psychoanalytic processes.

The primary technical arsenal of this vector provides various methods of hypnotic regression, symptom awareness, and influence on it.

Techniques and metaphors of hypnotic regression include:

1. **Staircase metaphor.**

   The person visualizes themselves descending or ascending a staircase, associating this process with the movement along the timeline in any direction.

2. **Elevator metaphor.**

   The person imagines entering an elevator, where the floor buttons represent the years of their life. They press one of the buttons and await their arrival.

3. **Television metaphor.**

   The person creates an image of being in a room and sitting in front of a television. The remote control can switch channels backward and forward. Each channel represents a year of the patient's life.

4. **Regression through hand catalepsy.**

   The suggestor induces a trance and creates catalepsy in the hand. Then they suggest that as long as the hand remains at a certain height, the person remains at their current age. They give a suggestion to the unconscious suggestor to slowly lower the hand. As the hand descends, the person gradually regresses into the past. When the hand reaches the leg, the unconscious associates the suggestor with a memory containing the cause of the symptom.

5. **Regression through spatial movement.**

The patient is positioned in a specific spot in the room, representing the present. Another point on the floor is chosen, symbolizing a past memory associated with the symptom or its creation. The space in between represents the timeline. The suggestor instructs the patient to gradually move through space toward the designated memory, sequentially reviving intermediate memories. They suggest that when the patient reaches the designated position, the necessary memory moment will reemerge in their consciousness. It is better to perform this technique with closed eyes after inducing at least a shallow level of hypnotic trance. However, this practice can also work without specific hypnotic induction. The fact that the person gradually traverses the timeline creates and deepens the hypnotic state.

6. **Hypnotic regression using motor analog signaling.**

The patient is induced into a light hypnotic state, and motor analog signaling is established on the fingers, enabling unconscious responses of "yes" and "no." A series of questions is asked, regressing the patient into the past:

- Does the unconscious mind of the patient know a situation from their life that became the cause of the symptom?
- Can the patient, at a conscious level, recall the content of the memory associated with this situation?
- Can you regress the patient to that memory now?

7. **Hypnotic regression through touch.**

The patient is induced into a hypnotic state, and it is established that they will transition to the necessary state in the past through a clap on the shoulder. Then one or several claps are given on the shoulder. Sometimes, such a sharp trigger technique for hypnotic regression can be sufficient.

Suggestive Vector

When working with this vector, the main focus is on direct suggestions aimed at the transformative process. Direct or indirect suggestions that provide clear instructions to the conscious and unconscious patient form the fundamental framework of hypnotic suggestion.

Direct suggestions have an imperative nature and a clear referential index: "You are entering a state of hypnotic trance." In other words, there is no choice to comply with the message or not, and there is a clear indication of the recipient of the message. Depending on the conforming or negativistic profile of the ego, reactions to direct suggestion can be diametrically opposed. A conforming ego profile will induce a psycho-physiological response to the suggestion without any resistance. For individuals with such a profile, repeating a specific command a few times will result in its reproduction in their consciousness or behavior. However, when dealing with a negativistic profile, direct suggestions may encounter various forms of resistance. These can include ignoring the suggestion, displaying aggressive reactions, misunderstanding, incorrect interpretation, and so on. Such defense mechanisms can operate in consciousness at different levels of intensity and manifest in various life contexts. In essence, the presence of at least a minimal level of a negativistic profile is a sign of personal maturity. Its complete absence or exaggerated potential may indicate strong neuroticism or problems in ego structure formation.

Since the overwhelming majority of individuals have at least a minimal negativistic profile, the usual flow of hypnotic phrases like "you sleep, you fall asleep, you enter hypnosis" will not always be effective. To bypass existing ego defense mechanisms, a considerable number of tricks have been developed in hypnotic suggestion. For example, Milton Erickson emphasized working with a hypnotic voice and non-directive verbal interventions. When referring to Erickson's voice, it is primarily slow, soft, and elongated. For the vast majority of people, this vocal pattern almost automatically induces a light trance state, even if the semantics of the voice do not include any formal hypnotic interventions. In our opinion, this sound pattern triggers a regression to infancy, when a mother would pick up a crying child and sing lullabies in a slow, gentle voice. This conditioned reflex exists in almost all individuals. It is also important to note that throughout our lives, we develop an emotional resistance to louder and faster speech patterns. Although some stage hypnotists occasionally manage to use this speech pattern by inducing a hypnotic state through conscious overload with rapid suggestive speech, it is worth emphasizing that hypnotic speech is any speech to which a person is not accustomed. Any change in speech characteristics in any direction can trigger hypnotic effects when used correctly:

- Fast speech - slow speech;
- Loud speech - quiet speech;
- Soft speech - firm speech;
- Melodious speech - monotone speech.

Proper utilization of changes in speech characteristics in any direction can evoke hypnotic effects.

Stephen Gilligan, who integrated the sound algorithm of Milton Erickson's hypnotic work into his practice, referred to sound as the heart of trance. And indeed, playing with speech sounds in hypnotic work can work wonders. However, it should be noted that a hypnotic state can be achieved even without using speech at all. We will revisit this topic when discussing the somatic vector of hypnotic work. Ericksonian practitioners have a wide variety of hypnotic patterns. For example, Betty Alice Erickson has a deep and melodic vocal pattern. Her trance speech seems to be sung. Jeffrey Zeig uses a more monotone and high-pitched voice, reminiscent of a radio announcer. Ernest Rossi sometimes makes his voice even softer than his teacher, Milton Erickson. Stephen Gilligan's voice has depth and resonance. Directive hypnotherapist Alexander Danilov employs a loud and exalting voice with a fast speech rate. Many other variations exist. However, describing the sound characteristics of the vocal patterns of well-known hypnotherapists and hypnotists is a challenging task; they must be heard. In our observation, every practitioner of hypnosis eventually develops their own individual sound pattern. In Ericksonian hypnosis, significant attention is given to the state from which a person generates hypnotic speech because the sound you transmit directly depends on it. If you are calm, confident, and serene, you will convey this state to the person through your speech, just like any other state you are in during the process of hypnotic work. Therefore, for novice practitioners of hypnosis, the ability to create a balanced state in oneself before and during hypnotic work should be their number one task. One of the most powerful beliefs that can support the "right" state is that "whatever happens to the patient in hypnosis is always beneficial," regardless of whether the patient enters hypnosis or not, does it quickly or slowly, and so on. Holding such a frame of mind significantly increases the likelihood of success compared to worrying about whether something will work or not. Any reaction from the patient to hypnotic suggestion is feedback. If one style of hypnotic work doesn't work, it is possible that you are simply trying to open the door with the wrong key. And sometimes finding the right keys can take a considerable number of hypnosis sessions with patients who have a high level of resistance. Legends about Milton Erickson's work tell stories of him attempting to hypnotize such "difficult" patients for many hours. For others, he had to develop completely new and original methods of hypnotic induction to guide them into a hypnotic state. If you apply a monotonous technique, you will eventually find that it works well only on certain individuals. Therefore, we view the skill of a hypnotherapist as a creative ability to transform their approach in order to find the optimal triggers to influence the patient's consciousness.

One of the most unconventional forms of hypnotic work introduced by M. Erickson in hypnotherapy was the use of metaphors. M. Erickson discovered that metaphors, analogies, and stories that enter the associative sequence of consciousness begin to live their own lives, gradually changing and reprogramming a person's behavior and emotional reactions. Metaphors operate on an abstract level, expanding an individual's map of the world, primarily through the unconscious. There is no need for a person to deliberate, analyze, or search for a specific meaning within a metaphor. Simply hearing it is enough, and the unconscious mind begins to seek parallels in the person's own experience, creating a new mosaic.

Metaphors are applied to the most emotionally charged experiences, current problems, tasks, or life challenges. Importantly, they often encounter little conscious resistance from the patient, as they lack direct instructions for action and fixation on the patient's own personality. It is worth noting that metaphors, fairy tales, and stories are among the universal methods of learning known to us since early childhood. It is during this time, through metaphors, play, and direct imitation, that we begin to learn various behavioral patterns. We hear a fairy tale in childhood and unconsciously start associating ourselves with its characters, attributing their qualities and emotional reactions to ourselves. Favorite childhood stories can become a metaphor for an entire person's life, influencing it for better or worse, depending on multiple personality and environmental factors.

For example, a person may adopt both the positive qualities of the fairy tale protagonist, such as wit and physical strength, as well as indirect qualities like laziness or a tendency to seek trouble and absurd ways of relating to reality. Not all parts of a metaphorical tale necessarily influence consciousness. Sometimes only certain aspects are activated. For instance, psychologists in Moscow conducted a study on the favorite childhood fairy tales of women with alcoholism. It was found that 3 out of 4 of them adored the tale "Beauty and the Beast" during their childhood. The relationship strategies of these women with men were built on the model of searching for a "beast" and the hope of transforming them, often resulting in disappointment due to the inability to accomplish this transformation. Although in the fairy tale, the beast eventually becomes a handsome prince, in reality, the embodiment of this aspect of the tale does not necessarily occur. The metaphors that govern the life of an alcoholic are entirely different.

Similar effects can be observed with full-fledged artistic books, movies, stories about specific individuals that deeply resonate with us, and so on.

Metaphors that govern our consciousness determine the focus of our attention, personal preferences, and motivation towards something or its absence. A symptom existing within a person's personality can be either a result of limited metaphorical maps of the self or the experience of a crisis element within one of the existing metaphors. This should also be kept in mind when attempting to change a symptom through metaphorical reprogramming of the self. The fewer metaphors that govern a person's life, the more their life path resembles a movie that cannot be controlled. Various diverse metaphors integrated within the self allow for the establishment of a meta-position in relation to existing experiences and the opportunity to actively exert willpower in order to change elements of one's life path. Older metaphors, especially those concerning the life path of a person's parents, may possess a particular power over unconscious processes, but nonetheless, openness to experience can eventually reshape and transform the existing self. In such cases, the therapist's task becomes to select or create the appropriate metaphor for change and present it to the patient.

One very interesting variation of working with metaphors was employed by M. Erickson, using the technique of "My Friend Joe," in which he instructed the patient through the description of cases involving other patients. For example, he would say that just yesterday, there was a patient sitting here with a very similar problem and a very similar life situation to the patient he was currently working with. He would then simply recount the story of the patient, describing what they said and how they interacted. This story could be a real account of his work with a patient or a fictional story in which he incorporated all the necessary analogies and metaphors that he believed could be healing for the patient. In my personal conviction is that this method is one of the best for creating non-directive suggestions. Even if the patient's conscious mind ignores the content of the story, their unconscious mind will still take something from it.

The suggestion and the necessary method of problem resolution should be encoded within the structure of the analogy or metaphor, and whether it is real or not, in our opinion, does not hold significant value for the therapeutic effect. Although in our practice, we prefer to use realistic therapy metaphors. However, this is a matter of choice and preference for the therapist themselves. For instance, in my belief, hypnotherapy with young children should primarily be based on working with imaginary fairy tale plots that contain embedded suggestive elements. Let's provide a simple example of a symptom existing in a child and the method of working with it through metaphorical storytelling.

Let's take the symptom of bedwetting. The therapeutic fairy metaphor could be as follows:

"Once upon a time, there lived Little Red Riding Hood in a house with her grandmother. She lived a good life and had no worries, except for one problem that constantly bothered her. Whenever it rained, the roof of the house leaked, and water dripped directly onto Little Red Riding Hood's bed. She would wake up wet in the morning and feel sad about it all day long. Little Red Riding Hood was still young and unable to fix the roof herself. Her grandmother was too old to do it as well. One day, Little Red Riding Hood learned from her grandmother that there were three woodcutters living in the forest. They were strong, grown men who could repair the roof if they were called. However, her grandmother warned her that there was also a gray wolf living in the forest who could eat her, so seeking help could be dangerous. Little Red Riding Hood was scared for a while and hesitated to go to the woodcutters. But waking up in a wet bed was so unpleasant that she finally decided to embark on the journey. She left her home in the morning and walked all day long towards the woodcutters' house, following the path her grandmother had indicated. Halfway there, she met the Gray Wolf. He approached her and asked where she was going. She replied that she was going to the woodcutters to ask them to fix the roof. The Wolf advised her to be careful because there was a Cunning Fox living in the forest who could interfere with her plans. However, the Wolf offered to accompany her to the woodcutters' house to keep her safe. Little Red Riding Hood was surprised at first, but then she felt relieved and agreed. And so they went together. As they walked through the dense forest, they encountered the Cunning Fox. He emerged and asked them where they were going. They replied in unison, 'We are going to the woodcutters to ask for their help in fixing the roof.' The Fox said that they should be cautious on their way because there was a Tricky Hare in the forest who could not be trusted. They were surprised once again, but then felt glad and continued their journey together. The three of them walked through the forest, and eventually they reached the woodcutters' house. 'Where would you be without me?' said the

Tricky Hare. 'The woodcutters went deep into the forest to collect firewood today.'
He informed them that he could lead them to the woodcutters. The Cunning Fox
warned Little Red Riding Hood not to listen to the Tricky Hare, and the Gray Wolf
said that both the Fox and the Hare were untrustworthy. Little Red Riding Hood
looked at them and said, 'I know the way myself. I will reach the woodcutters'
house and wait for them there. Thank you for your help.' She continued on her
own, leaving her helpers behind. She arrived at the woodcutters' house and was
not disappointed. They had already returned home with the firewood. 'You did
the right thing by following your grandmother's instructions rather than listening
to the forest animals,' the woodcutters said. Little Red Riding Hood returned with
the woodcutters to her grandmother's house. They easily and quickly repaired
the roof. 'You are all amazing,' said the delighted grandmother, and she treated
them all to pastries. After this adventure, Little Red Riding Hood always woke up
in a dry bed."

Let's comment on the structure of the fairy metaphor. Little Red Riding
Hood represents the child with the symptom. The rain dripping on the bed
symbolizes the symptom itself. The animals in the forest represent the
child's fears. Her decision to follow her own path represents a rejection
of actions based on fear. The woodcutters represent the resources of the
unconscious. The return and roof repair symbolize the final positive changes.

The structure of the fairy tale can vary and be adjusted to suit the child's
personality, making the story more appealing to them.

We have provided just one example of a therapeutic metaphor to highlight
the particularity of its structure. There can be numerous versions and
variations of such a practice. The fairy tale itself can be very brief or lengthy,
with a vast amount of details. The way the tale is narrated can be in a simple
storytelling style or incorporate hypnotic patterns.

A detailed description of this practice is beyond the scope of this work, as
it deserves a separate book. For now, we will simply note its key features to
understand the basic principles of its application.

The non-directive form of hypnotic work can involve the use of various
tricks to create or enhance the hypnotic effect.

Furthermore, within the context of discussing the suggestive aspect of hypnotherapy, it is worth addressing the topic of positive and negative suggestions. This refers to suggestions that utilize resourceful words and suggestions that negate non-resourceful words.

Here are some examples of such suggestions:

Resourceful words:

- You are in a trance.
- You are relaxing.
- You feel warm.
- You feel good.
- You are recovering.
- You are improving.
- You think about the positive.
- You are winning.
- Your strength is growing.
- You are moving forward.
- You are finding.
- You are on your way.

Negation of non-resourceful words:

- You are not awake.
- You are not tensing up.
- You don't feel cold.
- You don't feel bad.
- You are not getting sick.
- You are not deteriorating.
- You are not thinking about the negative.
- You are not losing.
- Your strength is not diminishing.
- You are not standing still.

The reader, having read the left and right columns one after another, surely noticed that the emotional reactions to the words in them differ significantly. Words from the first column often evoke stronger and warmer reactions. Words from the second column, despite their positive meaning, more frequently evoke emotionally uncomfortable reactions.

In order to understand a spoken or written word, our brain creates a sensory representation for it, and the amygdala, a region of the brain, begins to generate an emotional response to that representation. Our amygdala does not perceive the negation prefix "not" before a word, so an induction of the type "not" + non-resourceful word will prompt it to produce negative emotional reactions.

In modern forms of hypnotic suggestion, particularly in Ericksonian hypnosis and NLP, the exclusive use of resourceful statements during trance induction with a known goal is often advocated. Indeed, according to the majority of suggesters who have experienced both types of trance, a trance with resourceful statements is warmer, brighter, and more pleasant.

This raises the question of whether the induction of the type "not" + non-resourceful word will have only negative consequences. This question becomes even more acute when we turn to the works of hypnotists from the late 19th to the early 20th century, such as A. Forel, P. Janet, Platonov, and others. In their works, dozens of examples of hypnotic inductions are cited, which they used in treating their patients, with subsequent observation of how their symptoms disappeared.

The most important thing that needs our attention is that a significant portion of their inductions consisted of negating non-resourceful states and adding resourceful ones. At one point, we posed a similar question to ourselves and began experimenting with the use of hypnotic phrases of both types on our patients. We discovered that patients could respond excellently to both resourceful suggestions and the negation of non-resourceful ones. Both types of suggestions had a significant impact.

The most important conclusion we drew for ourselves was not that phrases of the first and second types should be used, but that their correct application yields the best effect.

Our conclusions were as follows:

The negation of non-resourceful phrases should be used more moderately and not dominate the induction.

If the negation of a non-resourceful state is used, it is desirable to follow it with a resourceful suggestion. In fact, this style of suggestion, where two types of phrases are used alternately, can add an additional dimension to trance induction.

There are different types of negations of non-resourceful states. For example, the phrase "you no longer think about it" is quite neutral and applicable. However, the phrase "you will not be sick and unhappy" is better replaced with "you will be healthy and happy."

The construction of primary target suggestions is better done in a positive format.

Towards the end of the session, it is preferable to give more positive suggestions to ensure that the patient exits the trance with a warmer and more positive emotional background.

On some educational programs, we have heard absurd statements from experts claiming that the unconscious mind does not perceive the prefix "not." However, that is not the case. The experience of many seasoned hypnotherapists, including ourselves, suggests the opposite. If the amygdala generates an emotional reaction to a word or other impression, the left prefrontal cortex of the brain is fully capable of inhibiting the amygdala's response. Furthermore, it is the left prefrontal cortex that constantly protects us from strong sensory representations of various negative images and words. If this didn't happen, we would constantly exhibit inappropriate behavior. In the hypnotic trance state, the left prefrontal cortex does not completely shut down and is capable of filtering bundles of negative sensations that penetrate the realm of consciousness. However, this occurs in different individuals with varying degrees of intensity. It is because of this variation that the belief emerged that only resourceful phrases should be used.

Significant elements of the suggestive vector are specific verbal technical techniques that can deepen the hypnotic state or help effectively implant various elements of hypnotic content. Many of these technical techniques were developed by Milton Erickson, while others were created by his students. Let's provide examples of verbal hypnotic patterns and discuss ways to apply them:

Analogical marking

Milton Erickson conducted an interesting experiment with schizophrenic patients in a clinic. He recorded their speech on an audio tape, carefully listened to it, and transcribed only the words on which the patients placed intonational accents. When he read these words in succession, he discovered that their content directly revealed the patients' main emotional issues. Erickson concluded that we unconsciously mark the words we consider more emotionally significant with an intonation emphasis. It is worth noting that psychologists studying the psychology of deception, independently of Erickson, came to a similar conclusion. For example, Aldert Vrij reports that a person who believes in their words is more likely to raise the volume of their speech. On the other hand, a person who does not believe in what they say will intuitively make that part of the speech quieter. As we can see, simply increasing the volume of spoken words is not necessarily a criterion of message truthfulness, but it can be an indicator of intense emotions underlying those words. Erickson drew another conclusion from his findings: What if we intentionally mark certain words with an increase in volume? Will the listener unconsciously perceive them as more emotionally significant? Erickson started practicing this method of suggestion and found that it worked very well. He would select several words he wanted to implant in the patient's mind, and while in a trance, he would speak various phrases, marking the chosen words with an increase in volume.

An exercise to practice this pattern could be as follows:

· Choose three words that you will mark during the hypnotic process.
· Induce a trance in the patient.
· Begin giving various trance commands that include the pre-selected

words.
- Mark these words by raising the volume of your voice and making slight changes in intonation.

Brief general questions

These questions help create an atmosphere of uncertainty and non-directiveness. It is recommended to pause after them, allowing the patient to generate any conscious or unconscious responses to the question:

- Is it really so?
- Could it be?
- Isn't that the case?
- Isn't it true?
- Really?
- Perhaps so?

Alignment with current experience

These truisms help establish conscious and unconscious rapport with the patient. They should be used more frequently when dealing with strong resistance in the patient's reactions:

- You hear my voice.
- You are sitting on a chair.
- Your eyes are open.
- The trance is somewhere nearby.
- Something inside is changing.
- Something within you is ready for change.
- You have plenty of resources.
- Your unconscious knows.

Double binds

These phrases help create a "choice-without-choice" situation in the patient's consciousness. Regardless of which answer the patient chooses, they agree with the suggested suggestion:

- Do you want to enter a trance state now or a bit later?
- Will your right hand or your left hand enter the trance state first?
- Will you enter a trance state while standing, or do you need to sit down?
- Before entering a trance state, will you say something or remain silent?
- Are you aware that you are already entering a trance state?
- Before going into a trance state, do you need to see, hear, or feel something?
- Do you prefer to enter a trance state quickly or slowly?
- Do you realize that you are already deeply in a state of hypnotic trance?

Conversational presupposition questions

When we create a presupposition, we partially allow the patient to re-experience the suggested suggestion:

- Can you imagine yourself already in a trance state?
- Do you know how to relax?
- Are you ready for change?
- Oh, what will you think when you reach a deep, hypnotic trance?

Semantic boundary violation

Such phrases create confusion in the mind and connect the patient to sensations they have likely never experienced before:

- The trance feels you.
- Your wisdom knows about your task.

- Changes tend to come unexpectedly.
- The unconscious speaks to you.

Inappropriate pauses

Creating these pauses allows for the activation of personality's projective mechanisms and engages the patient in conscious or unconscious "completion" of the hypnotic state:

- You are starting to descend... into a state of hypnotic trance.
- Anticipation of change is emerging... in your consciousness.
- Your wise part of your personality... speaks to you.
- You are ready... for positive transformations.
- Active transformation... is happening within you here and now.

Utilization

This is a universal technique frequently employed by Milton Erickson to address various forms of resistance from patients during hypnotic suggestion and other psychotherapeutic interventions. Through such phrases, the patient's statement is framed, creating the illusion that their statement becomes merely the beginning of the hypnotherapist's command.

Patient: I don't think I can.

Therapist: Yes, you cannot until you sit in the chair.

Patient: I can't change.

Therapist: Yes, you cannot change until you envision how you act.

Patient: I am not hypnotizable.

Therapist: Yes, you are not hypnotizable until you relax.

Linking language

Words "and" and "but". The word "and" creates a sense of flow in the hypnotic induction. The word "but" helps frame the patient's resistance:

- ...and you are diving into a trance, and your body relaxes, and you start to become more aware.
- You may feel tense, but despite that, a trance begins to emerge.

Provocative Vector

This vector of hypnotherapy involves a preference for inducing a patient into hypnosis through specific pattern interruptions and various dramatic techniques of interaction with patients in trance and bringing them out of it. It is frequently used in stage hypnosis, where the creation of a dramatic effect is essential. In hypnotherapy, it is just one of the ways in which the therapist interacts with the patient.

One of the key methods for deactivating defensive mechanisms in a patient's consciousness is pattern interruption. Our consciousness functions cyclically and stereotypically, and it develops a kind of "immunity" to everything familiar. New and unusual experiences are perceived more intensely and have high suggestibility potential. When we perceive a new sensory information block, our perceptual apparatus maps it and tries to adapt the new experience to existing world interpretation schemes. However, this process takes a certain amount of time, which is ideal for creating hypnotic suggestions.

Pattern interruption, or breaking the perception template, is a favorite technique of the old directive school and an integral part of Ericksonian hypnosis. There can be various versions and variations, ranging from simple and unremarkable to amusing and sophisticated. Let's provide a few examples to grasp the general principle behind their creation.

187

For instance, Richard Bandler suggests extending the hand for a hand-shake, then suddenly grabbing the other person's hand, swiftly bringing it to the client's face, and saying, "Notice how your focus of attention changes as you look at the spot on your hand and gradually continue to immerse yourself in the state of hypnotic trance." Then the hand is smoothly brought towards the client's forehead. If the pattern is successful, the client is already in a basic hypnotic state. Further interventions follow to deepen the client's hypnotic work.

In another presentation, R. Bandler slowly approached his patient, smirked mischievously, symbolically spat on his hands, demonstratively rubbed them together in front of the patient's face, and then touched the base of his eyebrows with the palms of his hands, tilting his head slightly backward. The patient plunged into a deep trance.

Once, Milton Erickson applied a different version of pattern interruption using a handshake during one of his public appearances. He came on stage and called a person whom he intended to hypnotize. As soon as the person approached him, Erickson extended his hand for a handshake. The person responded with a handshake, but at the last moment before their hands met, Erickson unexpectedly squatted down and spent about ten seconds tying his shoelaces. The client was slightly bewildered by the confusion. Erickson then stood up, stared intently into the client's eyes, and said, "Now you can simply relax and allow the hypnotic trance to come in some unusual and special way for you."

Alexander Danilov performed the pattern interruption technique in the following manner. After inquiring about the client's well-being with a calm, slow voice, as soon as the client started talking about their state, Danilov quickly leaped towards the client, placed one hand on the back of their head and the other on their forehead, tilted their head backward, and began giving hypnotic interventions: "You're sleeping, falling asleep, entering the state of hypnosis."

Let's list various forms of hypnotic pattern interruptions that can be used during the process of trance induction.

Classic Hypnotic Techniques

In this brief section, we would like to provide a concise list of hypnotic induction techniques that were used by the old masters of hypnosis. Many of these techniques are no longer commonly employed in clinical hypnosis, but they demonstrate their applicability and effectiveness in practice. Based on some of these techniques, one can construct not only the process of inducing a hypnotic state but also the entire hypnosis session, including the emergence from it. So, here they are:

Celsius Technique – gentle, monotonous skin stimulation.
The hypnotherapist performs light stroking movements on the surface of the patient's skin, such as the hands, head, and back. The touch is light, sometimes barely touching the skin's surface.

Shabardyo-Labardyo Technique – light neck scratching.
The hand is placed on the patient's neck and begins upward movements towards the nape and downward to the atlas vertebra. The movement gradually slows down, and the hand remains on the neck, providing gentle support.

Abrutz Technique – stroking without touch.
The hypnotherapist starts to perform stroking passes without physical contact all over the patient's body, focusing on the head, neck, arms, and torso. The Abrutz Technique pairs well with the Celsius Technique and can smoothly transition between the two.

Lasègue Technique – finger pressure on closed eyelids.
The hypnotherapist holds the subject's head so that the thumbs rest on the closed eyes, while the other fingers are placed on the occiput. Gentle pressure is applied to the closed eyes, accompanied by a gradual, slight backward tilt of the head. A gentle vibration of the head can also be created.

Sharco Technique – rubbing the scalp.

The hypnotherapist places the hand on the subject's crown and begins circular stroking movements either clockwise or counterclockwise. The touch is gentle, not applying excessive pressure, and gradually slows down, creating a calming effect.

Gaupp Technique – hands placed on the occiput.

One hand is placed on the occiput, and with the other hand, the head gradually tilts backward. The hand can perform stroking and vibrating movements.

LaFontaine-Braid Technique – fixation on objects.

Initially, a glass bottle was used, with its shiny neck held above the subject's head. For several minutes, the subject had to gaze unwaveringly at the neck, and then close their eyes and transition into a hypnotic state. Over time, numerous variations of this technique emerged, which were employed by mesmerists and later hypnotists. One of the most popular variations, at one time widely depicted in cinema, involved the use of a swinging pocket watch on a chain before the subject's gaze. This technique becomes more refined when the watch or any other object swings slightly above the eyes rather than directly in front of them. The eyes remain constantly focused on the object. In this form, the speed of induction into a hypnotic state can be significantly increased.

Bremo Technique – eye fixation.

There are two versions of this technique. In the first, the hypnotherapist simply fixes their gaze on the subject's right or left eye and stares intently without blinking. In the other version, the hypnotist gazes not directly into the subject's eye socket but at an imaginary or real object behind their head. This variant is much more hypnotic, and sometimes it is possible to put someone to sleep without approaching them or saying anything. In our opinion, when using the simple intense gaze technique, a specific verbal induction is still necessary. The preferred eye for fixation is the leading eye, which is usually the right eye for most individuals. If there is a need to determine the subject's leading eye, you can perform a simple test. Extend your right arm in front of you and focus on your outstretched thumb. Then start looking at some object beyond the thumb. Next, alternately close your right and left eye. When the leading eye is closed, the thumb will appear to shift position. With a non-leading eye, the opposite will occur.

Jean-Martin Charcot Technique – sudden sound impact.

After focusing attention on a point or any other object for some time, a sharp sound, noise, or clap can induce a sudden transition into a hypnotic state. For example, one could fixate their attention on a point in front of them and then produce an unexpected clap of the hands. Alexander Danilov frequently used a sudden foot stomp on the floor during his seminars, followed by commanding the patient to "Sleep!" or by seizing and tilting their head backward while keeping a hand on their forehead.

Abbé Faria Technique – the command "SLEEP!!!"

This is a sudden and unexpected command given by the hypnotherapist to the subject. If the command is delivered unexpectedly and disrupts the subject's expectations, the likelihood of entering an altered state increases. In this case, the hypnotic effect can be attributed to the fear itself, which is generated during the execution of this command.

Alexander Danilov suggests an interpretation that the hypnotic fear induced by this technique can be equated to the phenomenon of the "playing dead" reflex – an instinctive action observed in certain animals and crustaceans in life-threatening situations. This reflex simulates death, causing predatory animals to lose interest in pursuing them. For example, the Virginia opossum simply "plays dead" when threatened, and its anal glands start releasing an unpleasant odor. Similarly, hamsters curl up when danger looms. The armadillo rolls itself into a perfect ball when sensing danger, while the pangolin curls up and releases a foul-smelling fluid from its anal glands. The list goes on.

This evolutionary interpretation is quite original, and we speculate that some hypnotic states induced by sudden, unexpected actions are indeed based on the "playing dead" reflex. Perhaps this reflex has been preserved in human neurophysiological reactions as an atavism, which was inherent to some of our ancestors in earlier stages of evolution.

Constam Technique – placing the hand against the wall and then releasing it. This technique is more of a neurological activation practice for hand levitation than a hypnotic induction technique. However, if necessary, the Constam Technique can be used as a starting point for hypnotic induction.

Nazraliev Technique – approach and withdrawal.
Gradually approaching and then withdrawing from the subject, the hypnotist initiates a hypnotic state of consciousness. If accompanied by verbal trance induction, it only enhances the effect of this technique.

Techniques for Rapid Hypnotic Induction

Sudden blow to the face.
Alexander Danilov repeatedly demonstrated this technique of rapid trance induction at his seminars. He would abruptly approach the subject, blow strongly into their face, and then, while the subject was in a state of confusion, place his hand on their forehead and tilt their head backward. Afterward, he could swiftly raise the subject's hand, inducing catalepsy.

Swinging pendulum before the eyes.
The simplest way to perform this technique is by using the finger of the hand. However, pendulum clocks or any other object can also be suitable. The hypnotist places their hand with an extended index finger in front of the subject's eyes and instructs them to focus on the tip of the finger. Then, the hypnotist starts swinging their hand from right to left. Within 30–60 seconds, the subject's eyes may reflexively close, and they enter a trance

state. Three levels of pendulum swinging can be employed.

Clapping on the palms.
The subject's palm is placed opposite the hypnotist's palm in front of their face. The hypnotist stares intensely into the subject's eyes, lifts their other hand, and claps it onto the subject's hand from above while commanding, "Sleep!"

Crossed movement of the palms.
The subject is asked to hold out both palms in front of them. The hypnotist places their hands on top of the subject's hands and gives the instruction that when the hypnotist's hands move, the subject's hands should follow them as if stuck to them. Several times, the hypnotist raises both hands up and down simultaneously. Then, abruptly, one hand is raised upward and the other downward, creating confusion for the subject. At this moment, the command "Sleep!" is given.

Gradual raising of the gaze toward the ceiling.
The subject is asked to fixate their attention on a point in front of them and slowly and smoothly raise their gaze upward toward the top of their head. When the gaze is nearly at the destination point, the hypnotist claps their hands sharply and gives the command, "Sleep!"

Placing palms on the eyes.
The hypnotist slowly approaches the subject, positions their palms in front of the subject's eyes, and then gradually places the base of their hands on the subject's eye sockets, slightly tilting their head backward while commanding "Sleep!" This technique was demonstrated by Richard Bandler in one of his presentations.

Jerking of both hands.
The hypnotist approaches the subject, holds their wrists with both hands, and instructs them to gaze at the ceiling. Then, the hypnotist jerks the

subject's hands slightly downward and forward, commanding, "Sleep!"

Jerking of one hand to the side.
The hypnotist asks the subject to turn their head and gaze as far to the left as possible. Then, the hypnotist grabs the subject's right wrist and jerks it to the right and downward, commanding, "Sleep!"

Attention fixation on a vibrating object.
Initially, the hypnotist asks the subject to extend their right hand in front of their head and focus on their index finger. Then, the hypnotist places their own finger in front of the subject's finger and starts rapidly vibrating it, gradually bringing it closer to the subject's brow. When the finger touches the brow, the command "Sleep!" is given.

Confusion through refocusing attention.
Standing next to the subject, the hypnotist sharply points their finger upward and to the right or upward and to the left. As soon as the subject's head starts turning toward the pointer, the hypnotist places their hand on the subject's forehead, tilts their head backward, and gives the command, "Sleep!"

Dual hand movement.
Standing behind the subject at a distance of a couple of centimeters, the hypnotist extends their hands horizontally in front of the subject's face. The hands are held still for a moment with the palms facing upward and then quickly placed on the subject's face, slightly tilting their head backward. At this moment, the command "Sleep!" is given.

Attention trap.
The subject is asked to close their eyes and count aloud up to ten. Then, it is stated that when they reach ten, the hypnotist will touch their hand, and after that, they will enter a hypnotic trance. When the subject counts to three, the hypnotist places their hand on the subject's forehead, tilts their head slightly backward, and gives the command "Sleep!" Then, when the word

"ten" is said, the hypnotist grabs the subject's hand and abruptly raises it upward, aiming to create instant catalepsy. This technique works well for patients with a high level of hypnotic induction resistance.

Humanistic Approach

The humanistic approach in hypnotherapy places special emphasis on a non-directive form of work. Formally, it was Milton Erickson who pioneered the humanistic approach in hypnotic work. This approach revolves around a specific attitude towards the patient, seeing them as someone who already possesses all the necessary resources to solve existing problems. In this approach, the hypnotherapist's task is not to guide the patient towards clear criteria for recovery but to allow the hypnotic trance to create the best possible state out of the available resources. The work focuses on activating the resources of the unconscious and involving them in the context of the tasks. During the process of hypnotic trance, the patient learns to communicate and interact with their wise, creative, and healing unconscious, in order to retain this skill and use it independently in their life.

One of Milton Erickson's students, Stephen Gilligan, fully developed the ideas of humanism in his hypnotic work. He shifted the focus of hypnotic work from the patient's unconscious to the connection between the conscious and unconscious mind. We have already discussed him briefly before. Gilligan's work differs from Ericksonian work more in the philosophy of approach, although he, together with his colleague Robert Dilts, created a decent new arsenal of models and instrumental techniques.

For example, S. Gilligan introduces the acronym **COACH**:

C - Centered: This state reflects an individual's ability to rely on their center, both literally and metaphorically.

O - Open: Openness refers to the ability to embrace new experiences, receive feedback, and interact with both external and internal resources.

A - Aware: Awareness allows for understanding, drawing conclusions, and implementing their results in life.

C - Connected: Connectivity signifies the ability to maintain contact with external and internal resources.

H - Holding: Holding implies the ability to preserve and utilize newly acquired experiences.

According to Gilligan, this acronym represents the five essential states required for effective transformation in individuals. Prior to most of his hypnosis sessions, he intentionally and sequentially induces these states in his patients, upon which he builds the hypnosis session.

During his hypnosis work, S. Gilligan often utilizes four transformational mantras that, in our opinion, beautifully embody the spirit of the humanistic approach in hypnosis work.

Four Transforming Mantras by S. Gilligan

During the process of psychotherapeutic and hypnotic work, various repetitive emotional patterns may emerge, manifesting fragments of the unconscious and conveying specific informational messages. It can be said that the symptom and all its manifestations are forms of unconscious communication. And the symptom will continue to be active until it is heard and understood. The main task of the psychotherapist is to establish communication with the symptom and help the patient listen to its speech.

In this case, the following phrases are appropriate:

1. "This is interesting!"
2. "I'm sure there is meaning in this."
3. "Something is trying to awaken (or heal)."
4. "I welcome you!"

These phrases can be effectively used both in regular verbal therapy and during the process of trance induction by incorporating them into the hypnotic script. The ways to use them are as follows:

1. "You have a 'symptom,' and it's interesting."
2. "I'm confident it holds a special meaning for your unconscious."
3. "Through its manifestation, something undoubtedly wants to heal within you."
4. "I welcome this part of you."

By using these transforming mantras, the therapist creates a supportive and curious attitude towards the symptom, encouraging the patient to explore and engage with it. It helps establish a therapeutic alliance with the unconscious and facilitates the healing process. These mantras serve as linguistic tools that promote understanding and integration of unconscious material, leading to transformative change.

Stephen Gilligan's model of hypnotic mantras can be significantly expanded with the following hypnotic therapeutic phrases:

1. "This is wonderful!"
2. "Something important is happening right now."
3. "I hear what wants to speak within you."
4. "I'm listening to you very attentively right now."
5. "I'm ready to hear what you want to tell me."
6. "What is manifesting has a place in the world."
7. "Tell us what you want to convey."
8. "All my attention is now focused on you."
9. "What you're sharing now will be heard."
10. "You're speaking about what has been excluded."
11. "I'm glad you're ready to communicate with me now."
12. "Thank you for your communication."

Such phrases can serve as excellent ecological language for the communication between the psychotherapist and the symptom manifested in the patient.

We can also draw very interesting verbal tools from the phrases used by Bert Hellinger in his therapeutic meditations, which are a variation of Ericksonian hypnosis. He deserves credit for adding numerous new patterns of meaning to this form of work, beautifully combining hypnotic and psychotherapeutic aspects. Let's provide examples of such phrases.

Bert Hellinger's Powerful Hypnotic Phrases

If these phrases are used outside the context of hypnosis, the patient repeats them after the psychotherapist. In a hypnotic context, it is sufficient to simply hear them from the hypnotherapist. The active imagination of the unconscious associates the person with these interventions and brings about the necessary changes.

To this, I say "Yes"

This intervention involves accepting any significant element in the patient's unconscious. Psychotherapy is largely based on concepts of acceptance and wholeness. Symptoms arise when a person tries to turn a blind eye to what exists, to exclude it from their life, forget about it, and not think about it. When the therapist manages to find the missing, excluded link, such an intervention can help people accept it and create a sense of connection with it. This message can be directed to a part of the individual's personality, for example, an image of oneself from the past that is rejected or not accepted for some reason. Any symptom is a deep inner need of a person to say "Yes" to some part of themselves or their life. The intervention can be modified to the phrase "To you, I say 'Yes!'. In this case, the acceptance phrase can be directed at a forgotten, deceased, or excluded family member, a former sexual partner, or a friend from the past.

I don't know the depth of this secret.

This intervention pays tribute to a part of the unconscious or a member of the personal environment. This phrase embodies the acceptance of the situation, the desire for knowledge and understanding, and the beginning of active interaction with the present.

I accept this now.

This intervention involves active acceptance, a declaration of current intention, and a way to bring it into the present. This phrase can serve as a final point in the formation of the transformation impulse.

I will hold life firmly.

In the final stages of working with the symptom, this hypnotic phrase has a potent potential, activating beneficial processes in the mental and physical spheres.

There is a place for this in my heart.

This phrase is a somatic metaphor for accepting what has been excluded, repressed, or suppressed. It is most optimal to use it in relation to a person who is significant to the patient and has a direct or indirect connection to the symptom. Proper application of this phrase can significantly improve the patient's state.

In my body, there is a place for this.

This somatic metaphor is almost analogous to the previous one but operates on a slightly more abstract level in relation to the symptom.

In my family, there is a place for this.

Another metaphor of acceptance is more oriented towards an individual who has a connection to the symptom. The origins of this metaphor lead us to the theories of family psychotherapy, which consider the individual's symptom as related to the psycho-emotional processes of the family as a whole.

In the future, I will do something good with this.

This is an excellent hypnotic phrase that creates an assumption of unconscious constructive positive future planning. When what can be corrected is done, it is essential to establish a vector for introducing positive changes into the contexts of future experiences. This intervention briefly and elegantly provides such an opportunity.

I have the right to feel this emotion.

The last word of the phrase can be replaced with any necessary emotion in the context of working with the symptom. These words can represent any emotion, but it is often more appropriate to use emotions or states that need to be expressed but are prohibited by the individual. For example, these could be joy, sadness, anger, fear, and so on.

Behavioral Vector

The primary focus of attention in behavioral hypnotherapy is the teaching of new reactions to problematic contexts to the patient, using methods closely aligned with the theories of Ivan Pavlov's reflexology and B.F. Skinner's operant conditioning.

Rarely, in the context of hypnotic suggestion, are the theories of behaviorists discussed. However, during the process of hypnosis, the application of principles from these schools can have significant therapeutic potential. For example, modern NLP hypnosis widely integrates them into its practice. Let us first outline the key principles of this vector:

1. A symptom is a neurophysiological imprint in the client's brain that has arisen in response to specific stimuli. For instance, if a person is attacked by a dog and becomes scared, the fear emotion becomes imprinted in their consciousness. Now, whenever they see any dogs, the person experiences the emotion of fear.
2. This imprint has been reinforced by neurophysiological reactions due to contextual and internal factors.
3. In the process of hypnotherapy, we can modify the established reaction to external stimuli using various instrumental techniques.
4. Direct or indirect suggestions may or may not be utilized in behavioral hypnotherapy sessions.

5. Deep hypnotic states enhance the new imprints created by behavioral instruments.

6. Behavioral work in hypnosis occurs through the visual, auditory, or kinesthetic sensory channels of perception, or a combination of these channels.

Submodalities and Behavioral-Hypnotic Work

Our emotional reactions to internal images, sounds, and sensations are directly linked to the way they are sensorially encoded. Emotions will vary greatly depending on their quality. For example, a black-and-white, distant, and small image evokes subtle emotions, while a colorful, close, and large image elicits stronger emotions. Not only can the intensity of emotions vary, but the emotions themselves can differ as well. For instance, a more joyful image will possess brighter color content, while a depressive image will be characterized by black and gray tones, and so on. A sound coming from behind can be alarming, a child's voice may not be taken seriously, and a soft voice may symbolize trust. A warm and bright sensation arising from sunlight interweaving is likely to be interpreted as joy.

Such qualitative characteristics of internal images in NLP have been termed submodalities and have become actively employed as fundamental technical tools in this form of therapy.

Let's provide examples of some submodalities that, when altered, can vary emotional reactions:

Visual	Auditory	Kinesthetic
Color	Volume	Warmth/Coldness
Brightness	Spatial Position	Hardness/Softness
Distance	Intonation Characteristics	Mobility/Stability
Size	Rhythm	Spatial Localization on or in the body
Mobility/Stability	Melodiousness/Monotony	Relaxation/Tension
Magnitude	Musical characteristics	Pleasure/Pain
Presence/Absence	Personification of Voice	Fullness or Emptiness

Now let's present examples of psychotherapeutic work utilizing the modification of submodalities in different sensory modalities.

Visual Submodalities

When dealing with differentiated object-phobic reactions, their internal sensorial visual representations are always large, vivid, and very close to the patient's face. It is worth trying to suggest reducing the size of the representation, making it dull, and moving it away from the face, as the intensity can significantly decrease or even disappear altogether.

The suggestion phrase could be as follows: "Your fear decreases in size, becoming small and microscopic, becoming dull and inconspicuous, moving away from you towards the horizon line, where it vanishes completely." This can be a form of hypnotic submodality work with unpleasant experiences.

Conversely, if we want to suggest something positive and constructive through this practice, we act in reverse: "The joyful future becomes big, even enormous, filling the entire inner screen. It fills with bright, vibrant rainbow colors and approaches you closer and closer."

Sometimes, to significantly change the emotional reaction to an internal image, it is sufficient to modify just one submodality that encodes it. If a strong change in emotional reaction occurs by modifying only one submodality, it is referred to as critical. A vivid example of working with a critical submodality was shared with us by Sid Jacobson during an NLP seminar, where he worked with the visualization effect of a white flash.

The technique initially involves recalling a moment when the patient could see the operation of a welding machine or a bright fireworks flash. Then, they are instructed to think of an unpleasant image that triggers any unpleasant emotional reactions. Afterward, three times, with each snap of the fingers, they are asked to "flash" the problematic image with bright white light, as if burning it. In the overwhelming majority of cases, if the technique is executed correctly, the intensity of emotions towards the image significantly diminishes or disappears completely.

During the hypnotic work, the critical modality can be activated as follows: "You can recall an image that is unpleasant to you and simply observe it for a while. Then, after some time, you begin to notice how a bright white, dazzling light emanates from within the image, burning it from all sides and turning it into a stream of bright white light that is a little difficult to look at. Then the light fades away, leaving only an emptiness that will be filled with a new positive experience in the future."

To determine which specific submodality is critical, it is necessary to test them in work with the patient. For example, patterns of sudden contraction of the negative image into a dot or its abrupt removal to the horizon line can possess an excellent critical submodality effect. Similarly, work with critical submodalities can be employed to create a positive effect.

For instance, a person who contemplates a potential future achievement but lacks dynamic imagery, meaning they recreate a static photograph in their mind rather than a film, may doubt the possibility of realizing their dream in action. Sometimes, transforming the internal photo into a video and observing the unfolding events for a while can instill confidence in the individual.

In the format of hypnotic induction, it may appear as follows: "To start, you can envision your future as a fixed, static image in front of you and simply observe your emotional reactions to it for a while. And then, you can imagine beneath this image something like a switch button that, when pressed, transforms the picture into a film, vividly and colorfully displaying the perspective of your amazing future."

Auditory Submodalities

To describe the work with auditory submodalities, one therapeutic case from our practice is particularly relevant. One of our patients complained that her two-year-old son would constantly throw tantrums when she called him to eat in the kitchen. He would simply refuse to eat, and at times, the mother had to exert tremendous efforts to feed her rebellious child.

We asked the patient to imagine that the therapist himself is her son, Misha, and to call him with the same tone of voice she usually uses to call Mikhail. She uttered the phrase, "Come eat!" loudly, quickly, and aggressively, which even evoked strong negative reactions in us. Then we asked the patient to call us to lunch with that voice if we were ourselves and not Mikhail. The patient said the same phrase softly, slowly, and calmly. We observed our most positive reactions to that voice.

Afterward, we asked the patient to use this second voice, which she had just voiced, to call her son in the evening. The next day, the patient returned and reported what had happened in the evening after our therapy session. Her son responded excellently to the soft voice, actively devouring his well-deserved meal. However, when the patient attempted to call her son with her old voice, he immediately retreated and reacted with a hasty escape.

The tone, intonation, and timbre of the voice, as well as its speed, can be significant submodalities that either facilitate or hinder hypnotic induction. For the vast majority of individuals, a soft and slow voice automatically evokes trust, as it is a childhood auditory imprint of a soothing maternal voice. A harsh and rough voice is more likely to induce tension and resistance, although numerous exceptions to this rule can be found.

For example, like our aforementioned patient, who strongly resisted the soft and slow voice because her mother had always tried to manipulate her with it. On the other hand, individuals accustomed to obeying a loud authoritarian voice due to family tradition or professional specificity will better perceive a more assertive and loud hypnotic induction. Therefore, in such cases, there cannot be strict recipes, although we would recommend starting to work with an unfamiliar hypnotic subject using a soft and slow voice and then, based on the patient's emotional reactions and calibration, modifying the hypnotic induction as necessary.

If it is possible to determine which specific characteristics of the voice inspire more trust, it can significantly assist in working with a patient's resistance during the hypnotic induction. We will devote considerable attention to working with visual-auditory spatial submodalities in the chapter on psychogeographic positioning.

Kinesthetic Submodalities

In working with kinesthetic submodalities during psychotherapy, the spatial-body direction of movement sensations in the body and the looping of their reproduction are often utilized. Richard Bandler developed a variety of practices within his psychotherapeutic system called NHR (Neuro-Hypnotic Repatterning).

Bandler devised an intriguing pattern of therapeutic work with fears, employing kinesthetic submodalities. He would extensively inquire about the details of the sensory sequence experienced by the patient during a phobic reaction. He would identify where and in which part of the body the first sensation appears, the direction it takes, and how it qualitatively changes. After tracing the spatial path of sensations in the body, Bandler would induce a light hypnotic state and cyclically induce the described sensations in reverse order. Following such a procedure, the phobic reaction significantly diminished or even disappeared altogether.

Similarly, Bandler could repeatedly induce positive states in a patient or transfer a positive state from one patient to another. With one person, he would elicit the specifics and details of experiencing a particular positive state, such as the quality and location of the sensations in the body and the direction of their irradiation. Then, with another person, he would induce a trance state and suggestively model the sequenced experience of the positive state.

Bandler also discovered that by repeatedly reinforcing the looping pattern of sensations, its sensory effect could be intensified multiple times.

To summarize the aforementioned points:

1. Every human state comprises a set of body sensations.
2. A state is activated through the sequential activation of these sensations.
3. Deactivation of a state occurs when the sensory cycle is run in reverse.
4. Through repeated and multiple reproductions of the pattern in a cyclic format, a state tends to intensify and grow.
5. By modeling a state as a sequence of sensations experienced by one person, it can be transmitted to another individual or a group of people.

Example: A person describes feeling warmth and light in the center of their body, followed by an increasing flow of this warmth and light expanding into the chest, then filling the arms, neck, and head, resulting in a deeper relaxation in the body. In this case, the feedback from the individual itself becomes the text of hypnotic suggestion.

Similarly, it is possible not only to model states but also to construct them. The hypnotherapist, based on their considerations, combines key sensations that may arise in a person's consciousness to compose the text of hypnotic suggestion.

For example, the text of a hypnotic suggestion could be: "You can feel a gentle, pleasant tingling and warmth on the surface of your feet, which first fills the lower part of your legs, the calf muscles, quadriceps, and thigh muscles." The sense of an increasing flow instills a particular sense of confidence, providing a feeling of support and foundation.

The flow expands in the lower part of the body, creating a sense of fullness that continues to grow and fills the entire body—the arms, neck, and head—with pleasant warm electric impulses, fostering a unique sense of confidence and comfort in both mind and body and allowing the unconscious to seek and discover new creative ways to address existing personal challenges.

Another method of dismantling pathological states in a patient's consciousness is to introduce new non-standard elements into the sensory strategy of the state.

For instance, as previously described, we learn from the patient the detailed sensory strategy for activating the negative state, including the sensations that arise in different parts of the body.

Let's assume it includes a feeling of coldness in the solar plexus (1a), followed by a spasm in the abdomen (1b), tension in the chest (1c), and a slight tremor in the hands (1d). We have four elements of the pathological sensory strategy that we want to disrupt.

Next, we select 2-3 positive sensations in the body, such as warmth and relaxation in the collarbone (2a) and a sense of strength in the muscles of the back (2b). Then, with the person closing their eyes or inducing a light hypnotic state, we bring to their consciousness the stimulus that previously triggered the pathological reaction, and after that, we embed the positive sensations into the negative strategy using the following pattern: 1a, 2a, 1b, 2b, 1c, 2a, 1d.

Thus, we create changes in the processing of sensory information. The addition of new elements is more likely to interrupt the old sensory pattern. In cases involving intense emotional experiences, it is possible to repeat this procedure 2-3 more times, using different positive sensory embeddings.

Working with **modeled states** in the process of hypnosis brings a touch of the philosophy of psychological structuralism, which considers any psychological processes as collections of sensations. Edward Titchener, the founder of **structuralism**, probably never imagined that his scientific concepts would find an interesting adaptation in the field of hypnotic work.

During the induction of a hypnotic state, we often deal with an abstraction that finds a specific realization in the patient's consciousness. If we were to survey a large group of people and ask them to describe the sensations they experience in their bodies when feeling joy, we would find common denominators shared by many individuals, but their experiences would likely not be identical. Therefore, detailed suggestions of states introduce a new dimension to the process of hypnosis, allowing for more precise therapeutic work.

In order to model a state, it is necessary to identify 3–7 sensations accompanying it in various representational systems: visual, auditory, kinesthetic, vestibular, gustatory, and olfactory. However, in the vast majority of cases, kinesthetic sensations and occasionally visual sensations are required. By visual sensations, we do not mean strict, semantically loaded images but rather changes in submodality characteristics of perception.

Important criteria include the sequence or simultaneity of the sensations, the gradations of their intensity, and their location in the body. Once this information is gathered, a "snapshot" of sensations can be created and utilized with various patients during hypnotherapy. Here are a few examples of such "snapshots":

- A warm brightness emerges in the center of the body, vibrating and expanding to fill the entire body, limbs, and head with pleasant relaxation.
- A pleasant coolness arises in the feet and spreads across the skin, concentrating warmth inside the body, which overflows with energy and vibration. The coolness penetrates the mind, making it clear and sharp.
- Strength and vibration arise in the hands and legs, making the body collected and whole. The sense of balance fills the body, and every movement becomes coordinated and easily controllable.

It is worth noting that this approach allows for the modeling of not just different states but specifically sensory strategies for recovering from various psychological disorders such as fears, anxieties, and worries. To find such a sensory strategy, it is necessary to identify an individual who has suffered from a sensory ailment and then healed from it. This can also apply to sensory strategies for effective motivation or decision-making, where a person relives sequences of specific sensations during the execution of an effective action.

The topic of state modeling is extensive and goes beyond the scope of this book. In this chapter, we define the general characteristics of the topic and how it can be used in the process of hypnotic work. It should be added that Edward Titchener was the first psychologist to begin modeling states, although he did not attempt to do anything with the products of his modeling. As we know, he often assigned his students tasks that required them to describe the physiological acts of the body in detail through sensations.

Abraham Maslow became interested in modeling states of perfection and other constructive states. He attempted to find common denominators in the personalities of individuals he considered self-actualizing. The field of personality and state modeling was greatly expanded and explored by practitioners of Neuro-Linguistic Programming (NLP) such as John Grinder, Richard Bandler, Robert Dilts, Michael Hall, and others.

Anchors and Behavioral-Hypnotic Work

In NLP and various other forms of psychotherapy, the term "anchor" is synonymous with Ivan Pavlov's concept of a conditioned reflex. To understand what it represents, we must refer to the original sources. Ivan Pavlov believed that a conditioned reflex is an acquired reflex that arises during an individual's lifetime and is not genetically fixed. He also believed that it is formed based on unconditional reflexes, which are genetically determined reflexes inherent in individuals from birth, such as salivation, sweating, sexual instinct, etc.

Ivan Pavlov's research on conditioned reflexes revealed that a new stimulus can trigger a reflexive response if it has been presented with an unconditional stimulus for some time. We can recall Pavlov's well-known experiment with a dog, in which the dog was given meat (the unconditional stimulus), and upon seeing it, the dog began to salivate. The experimenter also presented the sound of a whistle or a bell (the conditioned stimulus) to the dog. After some time, the experimenter observed that the dog started salivating when the conditioned stimulus was presented.

Interestingly, this process was also independently discovered by Edwin Twitmyer, approximately during the same period as Pavlov. Pavlov believed that throughout life and as individuals gain experience, a whole system of similar conditioned reflex connections is formed in the cerebral cortex of the brain, which determines behavior and forms its basis. Pavlov referred to this system of conditioned reflex connections as the "dynamic stereotype."

To form a conditioned reflex, at least one unconditional stimulus and a neutral stimulus are necessary. The neutral stimulus becomes conditioned when it is presented simultaneously with the unconditional stimulus. The conditioned stimulus should dominate the activity of the nervous system, while the future conditioned stimulus should be neutral. It is preferable to repeatedly pair the stimuli, where the unconditional stimulus is activated first, followed by the conditioned stimulus (e.g., presenting food first and then the sound signal). Consistency in the surrounding environment is also desirable.

It is worth mentioning that transferring one conditioned stimulus to a new stimulus is also possible. The process of conditioning will simply have a lower intensity. Although we do not know if Pavlov conducted experiments of this kind, we are confident from our psychotherapeutic practice with humans that such conditioning works. For instance, let's assume that a dog that already has a conditioned reflex of salivation to a sound signal can transfer the salivation response if it is subsequently presented with alternating sound and light signals, causing salivation in response to both. In NLP, this process of combining two conditioned or unconditioned stimuli is called collapsing or anchoring, and the process of combining can occur through visual, auditory, or kinesthetic representational systems. Specific combinations of anchors are also possible. There can be numerous examples, and we will provide a structured exercise that can be performed to understand the essence of the process.

Exercise: "Visual Anchors Collapse"

1. Pair work.
2. One person selects a stimulus—a reaction they want to change.
3. The other person, in conversation, identifies stronger positive emotional images that exist within the partner.
4. Then, in a specific location near themselves, the patient must imagine the positive image, fixate on it with their attention, and hold it for some time.
5. Afterward, they imagine the negative image and shift it onto the positive one, allowing the second person to "absorb" it.
6. Feedback is then given on the resulting changes.

If the positive image is about the patient winning first place in a major sports competition, and the second image is about their wallet being stolen, the strength of the nervous system's reaction to the first image will likely remain stronger and transform the reaction to the second image.

The crucial factor is the required intensity of the positive stimulus. If it is insufficient, the transformation of the second image may not occur in the usual manner.

Possible variations include blending two states and generating a third state that combines the elements of the previous two. If the negative stimulus is significantly stronger than the positive one, a negative transformation will occur.

Similar studies were conducted by behaviorists. John Watson performed an experiment with an 11-month-old boy named Albert, where a stimulus— a white, fluffy rat—was presented to him, causing him to laugh and smile. Then, a metal gong was struck behind him, eliciting fear and crying. The negative stimulus was repeatedly presented in conjunction with the sight of the rat. After a certain number of exposures to the negative stimulus, the boy began displaying a negative reaction to the rat even without its presence. Psychologists later discovered that the boy's negative reaction generalized even to white fur, causing him to cry upon seeing it. Subsequently, the boy was taken away from the clinic where he was located, and his fate remains unknown. It is possible that his negative reaction to white rats and white fur persisted throughout his life. Interestingly, this story became a starting point for the emergence of behavioral therapy in the United States in the 1950s. Therapists aimed to develop procedures in which negative stimuli could be associated with neutral or even positive reactions. Many of these procedures still exist and are practiced today.

Exercise: "Auditory Anchors Collapse"

1. Pair work.
2. The first participant asks the second to close their eyes and recall a strong positive experience they have had.
3. Then, the first person creates a rhythm with their fingers or an object on the table. Other arbitrary sounds can also be made.
4. Following this, the first person asks the second to imagine a less resourceful experience with lower intensity than the positive one.
5. Once the second person starts imagining the experience, the first person exactly reproduces the sound they made during the visualization of the positive experience.
6. Feedback is then given on the resulting changes.

Exercise: "Kinesthetic Anchors Collapse"

1. Pair work.
2. The first participant asks the second to imagine a positive, resourceful experience.
3. After the second person begins imagining it, the first person presses their fingers on an arbitrary point on the second person's shoulders or knees with a specific intensity for 5–10 seconds.
4. Afterward, the second person is asked to imagine a less resourceful experience with lower intensity than the initial positive one.
5. Once the less resourceful experience is imagined, the first person

presses the same spot on the body that was activated during the work with the resourceful experience. The pressure is applied with the same intensity as before.

6. Feedback is then given on the resulting changes.

Using Anchors During Hypnotic Suggestion

1. Let's provide examples of how working with different types of anchors can be applied both during trance induction and directly during the therapeutic process.
2. Trance induction using visual anchors: Imagine a representation of yourself in the current space and time.
3. Then, imagine a fragment of a dream you have experienced floating just above your head.
4. Next, return to the initial representation and slowly move it upwards towards the second one, merging them together and allowing the second image to absorb the first. Close your eyes and observe the resulting changes.

This form of exercise can be performed both individually and in pairs. If the exercise is done individually, before starting self-induction, choose the goal of entering a hypnotic state. For example, express your intention out loud: "I would like to connect with my deep wisdom," "I would like to better understand myself in the current situation," or "I would like to find inner resources to understand how to proceed." Vary your intention as needed.

If the exercise is performed in pairs, after closing the eyes, the hypnotist can begin delivering direct suggestions. In this exercise, we chose a trance-inducing image related to sleep. This image can also be varied depending on the need and replaced with other images associated by the patient with a dreamlike, trancelike, or any other altered state of consciousness they have experienced.

Similarly, visual anchors can be used directly in the process of hypnother-apy. For example, when the patient is already in a trance, an induction can be given to visualize positive and negative images together. Then, the suggestion can be given that the negative image begins to move towards the positive image, and as it gets closer, it is absorbed and assimilated by it. In this case, for effective transformation, it is necessary for the positive image to be significantly stronger than the negative one.

It is also possible to use a visual-spatial overlay of 3–4 positive images to enhance the power of the positive effect. An even stronger effect can be achieved by using the "Anchor-Cross" technique during the trance state.

Exercise "Anchor-Cross"

1. Pair work.
2. Identify a negative experience that will be addressed during the hypnotic trance.
3. Determine four positive experiences that will serve as healing tools during the trance work.
4. Induce trance.
5. During the trance, have the subject imagine a symbol representing the negative experience, approximately 5 cm in size, positioned to their left.
6. On their right, have them imagine four positive symbols arranged in a cross shape, leaving enough space between them to accommodate the negative symbol later.
7. Suggest that the negative symbol gradually moves towards the center of the "positive cross."
8. Suggest that as it moves towards the center, it gradually absorbs and assimilates the positive symbols. Each element of the cross actively incorporates the negative experience, transforming it into pure understanding.
9. Once the transformation is complete, allow the subject to remain in the trance state for some time.
10. During this period, provide the suggestion: "Allow your wise unconscious mind to complete the transformation in the most ecological

way."

11. Bring the patient out of the trance.

12. Obtain feedback from them regarding the changes that have occurred.

Induction of trance using auditory anchors:

1. Pair work.

2. The first participant asks the second participant to close their eyes and imagine a moment of falling asleep, a fragment from a dream, or any other trance experience they have previously had.

3. After that, the state is anchored by a specific sequence of sounds.

4. Steps 2 and 3 are repeated two more times, with each repetition involving a change in both the trance image and the sound associated with it.

5. Then the second participant is asked to close their eyes and shift their gaze to the middle of their forehead.

6. The first participant begins to sequentially produce all three anchored sounds for 1–2 minutes.

7. Afterward, verbal induction of trance suggestions can be initiated.

Auditory anchoring of states and their transfer to the context of other states can be performed immediately after trance induction. During hypnosis, suggestions can be given to associate positive experiences with them. Once this experience is created in the subject's consciousness, it can be anchored with a new auditory signal. Then, when needed, this auditory anchor can be activated. For example, by giving a command to recall a negative experience and then activating the auditory anchor.

Induction of trance using kinesthetic anchors:

1. Pair work.
2. The first participant asks the second participant to recall and associate it with any dream or trance experience they have had before.
3. Then the first participant anchors a new state in the second participant by touching a specific point on their shoulder or knee for 5–10 seconds.
4. Steps 2 and 3 are repeated two more times, each time creating an anchor at the same bodily location but using different dream or trance experiences. Thus, a triple stack of anchors is created, with trance states layered on top of each other.
5. After that, the first participant chooses a different point on the second participant's arms or legs, touches it, and gives an intervention: "While I maintain fixation on this point, you are in a normal waking state. The closer my finger gets to the stack of anchors, the deeper you will immerse yourself in a trance state. When my finger reaches the stack of anchors, your eyes will close by themselves, and you will enter a deep hypnotic state." In this case, the technique combines working with kinesthetic anchors with the technique of state scaling.
6. Then the first participant starts slowly moving their finger from the first point to the second point.
7. Once the second participant's eyes close, verbal suggestions can be introduced as needed within the context of the practice.

Transpersonal Vector

Hypnotic work with the transpersonal vector is primarily based on specific forms of interaction between the patient and archetypal structures of the personal and collective unconscious.

Carl Jung, the creator of the concept of archetypes or primordial images, mainly used them for analytical work, seeking correlations between personal life experiences and dream imagery in mythical and abstract forms of the psyche. As far as we know, during his medical studies, C. Jung was interested in hypnosis and spiritualism. As an experimental practice, he would induce alternative personalities in the individuals he worked with. In the spiritualist-hypnotic tradition, such individuals were called mediums. He would then engage in dialogue with these alternative personalities. Unfortunately, very little information is available about C. Jung's hypnotic practice. It is known that such practices were present in several generations of his family. Spiritualistic séances were practiced by his mother Emilia, his grandfather Samuel, his grandmother Augustina, and his cousin Helen Preiswerk. It is challenging to evaluate the spiritualistic-hypnotic legacy of one of the greatest psychologists of the 20th century. We will limit ourselves to mentioning that this form of work occurred during the early stages of his life. Spiritualism, which was popular entertainment among the aristocracy in the 19th and early 20th centuries, represented, in our opinion, a form of mystified hypnotic work. A person capable of reaching a level of somnambulistic trance due to their spiritual system of values and beliefs, as well as the contextual rules, provided feedback that corresponded to the expectations of the questioners. The most popular form of spiritualistic work involved inducing the alternative personality of a deceased individual and communicating with them through a medium in a state of somnambulism. Essentially, if we are dealing with a hysteroid accentuated suggestible individual, the technique of a spiritualistic séance can be easily reproduced in a regular hypnosis session. It can be fascinating to observe the sometimes shocking information that can come from a suggestible individual.

For experimental purposes, we have repeatedly reproduced this phenomenon in a hypnosis laboratory with our students. We usually followed the following algorithm:

1. Selected the most hypnotizable student.
2. Induced a trance state.
3. Induced the personality of a deceased individual.
4. Engaged in conversation with the suggestible individual, asking various

questions, for a duration of 10–20 minutes.

5. Then brought the suggestible individual out of the trance state and obtained feedback on the experiences that occurred during the trance induction process.

Without unnecessary mystifications, we can assert that the hysteroid accentuated personality will unconsciously play into the context of trance and amplify the semantics of trance work and the emotional intensities experienced during it. However, the dramatic nature of this hypnotic phenomenon can truly impress the audience observing the process. While working with this practice, we have discovered its significant psychotherapeutic potential. Formally, such a practice can be used in the format of **hypnodrama** when there is a need to address unresolved psychoemotional patterns related to significant deceased individuals in the patient's life.

Let's provide a possible example. If a patient has strong emotions associated with a deceased loved one, in the context of group dramatic psychotherapy, a trance state can be induced in one of the participants, temporarily suggesting the personality of the significant deceased individual. Afterward, a dialogue can be constructed between the patient and the hypnotic suggestion. Powerful hypnotic phrases described earlier, such as "I see you," "In my heart, there is a lot of space for you," "In my family, there is a lot of space for you, and "In memory of you in the future, I will do something good," can be used during the dialogue. Then, the hypnotic suggestibles can be questioned about their reactions to the uttered phrases. If necessary, the discussion can continue until the patient's consciousness experiences a sense of resolution of the problematic emotion or a vector indicating how it can be achieved. Similar practices are utilized by Bert Hellinger in his systemic constellations. However, he does not employ literal hypnotic induction; instead, he provides interventions for the substitute to feel the necessary role and act based on their own sensations. For therapeutic effect, this is often more than sufficient. Inducing a deep hypnotic state in this context can create excessive behavioral and emotional drama that is not essential for the psychotherapeutic process.

The utilization of Carl Jung's concept of archetypes, created in the past, is beginning to find resonance in the practices of various hypnotherapists. For example, we have witnessed on numerous occasions how Alexander Danilov induced various archetypal images in patients during hypnosis sessions. His favorite induced archetypal images were the warrior archetype, the shaman or shamaness archetype, and the mother archetype. The induction of archetypes was primarily used to amplify the intensity of experiencing the induced resourceful state.

In our work, we would like to present a list of archetypes that can be used in trance work, which can add an additional dimension to it, and briefly discuss their relevance in the process of hypnotic induction.

The main archetypes distinguished by Carl Jung are as follows:

1. The Mask Archetype
2. The Shadow Archetype
3. The Animus Archetype
4. The Anima Archetype
5. The Sage Archetype
6. The Self Archetype

Let's refer to them as the foundational archetypes for convenience.

Mask Archetype represents a form of group projection of socially significant aspects of the personality. It is the image of the self that is adopted to please and be accepted by others, rather than being created for one's own sake.

Let's introduce a hypnotic pattern utilizing the Mask archetype.

Exercise: "Awareness of the Mask Archetype"

1. Pair work.
2. The first participant induces a hypnotic trance in the second participant.
3. A comfortable trance motif is induced.
4. As the motif of the trance develops, the patient encounters a literal

mask image, suggesting that this mask represents the Mask archetype for the patient.

5. The process of putting on the mask is induced.
6. For a certain period of time, the patient becomes aware of their own changes.
7. From this state, the patient is invited to observe their social life, activities, and everyday goals while remaining in this state.
8. Subsequently, the patient is guided to exit the self-image in the trance and observe themselves from the outside, clothed in the social mask.
9. In this state, the patient gains a certain level of awareness regarding how they perceive this state from the outside, whether they can embrace this image, or if something requires transformation.
10. After some time, the patient is brought out of the trance.
11. Feedback is provided regarding the changes experienced by the patient during the trance state.

This exercise can serve as an excellent form of hypnotic introspection, gathering analytical material during the process of psychotherapeutic work.

Shadow Archetype is a product of group repression and suppression. It encompasses all aspects of the personality that are deemed unacceptable, unwanted, devalued, or disregarded by society. The Shadow is neither good nor evil but rather a collection of personality images that, for various reasons, are not needed or relevant during a particular period of life.

Here is a hypnotic pattern incorporating the Shadow archetype:

Exercise: "Integration of the Shadow"

1. Pair work.
2. The second participant identifies a current life task that needs to be addressed.
3. The first participant induces a hypnotic trance in the second participant.
4. A comfortable trance motif is established.

5. The process of searching for one's Shadow is initiated, aiming to gain awareness of an aspect that can contribute to more effective problem-solving.

6. For a period of time, the second participant explores an inner movie related to the search for their Shadow within the trance state.

7. The process of finding the Shadow can be linked to the phenomenon of motor analog signaling described earlier. For example, the unconscious patient may be instructed to raise their index finger when the Shadow is found and repeat this action when awareness of its content arises.

8. If necessary, the patient can be allowed to speak from the trance state to provide more detailed commentary on their experiences. It may also be possible to redirect the trance if the experiences are particularly significant and require further exploration within the trance state.

9. Subsequently, the participants are guided out of the trance state. Feedback is collected regarding the experiences during the hypnotic session.

The aspect of the Shadow can be varied depending on the need, as it is multidimensional and multifaceted. Simply confronting one's Shadow without specifying a particular aspect that requires conscious awareness may not lead to the desired therapeutic effects. However, working with any aspect of the Shadow activates the psychodynamics of the individual. Some aspects of the Shadow that can be addressed in both hypnotic and general psychotherapeutic work include:

- The Shadow that conceals creative potential.
- The Shadow that hides aspects of wisdom.
- The shadow is associated with significant life goals.
- The Shadow related to a sense of humor in life.
- The Shadow connected to spirituality.
- And numerous other aspects of the Shadow.

Animus Archetype encompasses collective projections of ideas about male behavior, the image of a man, and what it means to be one. C.G. Jung believed that as a boy grows up, he gradually associates himself with this archetypal structure, which shapes his behavior at a high abstract level. Women experience this archetype through its projection onto significant men in their lives.

Here is a hypnotic pattern using the Animus and Anima archetypes. This pattern will differ when working with patients of different genders. It can be performed with both male and female patients, but in the case of male patients, the process of association will occur with the Animus archetype, while in the case of female patients, it will involve the Anima archetype.

Exercise: "Animus and Anima"

1. Pair work.
2. Induce a trance state.
3. Establish a comfortable trance motif.
4. Create a suggestion of encountering two figures representing the Animus and Anima archetypes within the motif.
5. For a period of time, the patient observes the two figures in a trance state. Then, if the patient is male, he associates himself with the Animus archetype and vividly relives the feelings associated with this identification.
6. The patient then observes the figure representing the Anima archetype and, after some time, approaches it, touching its hands with his own. Subsequently, additional time is dedicated to integrating the flow of emotional data.
7. Suggest a sense of unity between the masculine and feminine aspects of the patient's consciousness.
8. Guide the patient out of the trance state.
9. Collect feedback regarding the trance process.

Anima Archetype is the counterpart to the Animus archetype and represents a collective image of feminine behavioral patterns and what it means to be a woman. As a girl grows up, she gradually associates herself with this archetypal structure. Men experience this archetype through its projection onto significant women in their lives.

(The hypnotic pattern for working with the Anima archetype is described in the section on the Animus archetype.)

Sage Archetype represents a collective projection of ideas about wise, righteous, and moral behavior. This image holds the answers to what, how, and when to do things in order to achieve desirable outcomes. In social groups, certain individuals assume facets of this archetype's projection, such as scholars, mystics, educators, and others.

The hypnotic algorithm utilizing the Sage archetype is as follows:

Exercise: "The Sage in the Forest"

1. Pair work.
2. The second participant identifies the problem they will work on.
3. The first participant induces a hypnotic state in the second participant.
4. The motif of the forest is induced, followed by a search for a cottage with a sage within it.
5. The participant is guided to enter the cottage and engage in a conversation with the sage, presenting their existing problem.
6. The sage then begins to prepare a medicine that can help the patient solve their problem. The patient observes the process of preparation.
7. Subsequently, the sage hands the medicine to the patient, who drinks it and experiences some changes for a period of time. The world, visually, audibly, kinesthetically, and at the level of meaning, may undergo transformations.
8. Afterward, the patient expresses gratitude to the sage, exits the cottage, and continues their journey.
9. The patient is guided out of the trance state.
10. Feedback is obtained regarding the changes that occurred during the

hypnotic work.

If desired, the motif of the forest can be replaced with an alternative motif.

The image of the sage can also vary, such as by taking on the form of a shaman, scientist, sorcerer, magician, healer, and so on.

Self Archetype, as defined by Carl Jung, represents the union of opposites. It signifies the image of natural balance that can be achieved by an individual on their life journey. Other words describing this archetype include experiential integration, consciousness wholeness, the ability to maintain equilibrium, and so on. According to Jung, the life path is the actualization of the archetypal Hero's Journey script, with the aim of understanding the balance of the Self as the primary abstract goal of the individual.

The hypnotic pattern for working with the Self archetype is as follows:

Exercise: "The Self and the Hero's Journey"

1. The first participant induces a trance state in the second participant.
2. A comfortable motif of trance is induced, envisioning a journey along a road in this motif.
3. Along the way, the patient encounters various forms of archetypes, both in their light and dark aspects.
4. Initially, the encounter takes place with the archetype of the Self as projected by the patient themselves. Some time is spent interacting with this archetype and integrating it. The form of interaction can be varied depending on the needs.
5. Then, the road leads the patient to a different motif of trance, where they encounter the archetype of the Warrior. Interaction with this archetype is actualized.
6. Next, there is a shift in the motif again, and the patient encounters the archetype of the Trickster and interacts with it.
7. In the final motif, there is a meeting with the archetype of the Prince

and the construction of some form of communication with it.

8. Some time is spent integrating the acquired experience.
9. Subsequently, the patient is guided out of the trance state.
10. Feedback is obtained regarding the experience gained.

Host Archetype encompasses the collective image of a person who possesses the ability to manage and holds high social and financial status. The dark masculine aspect of the Host archetype is the Cannibal. The bright feminine aspect is the Hostess. The dark feminine aspect is the Terrible Mother. The main energies associated with this archetype are power, status, and money.

Warrior Archetype includes collective projections related to warrior-like behavior, personal qualities, values, and beliefs associated with it. The dark masculine aspect of the Warrior archetype is called the Killer, the bright feminine aspect is the Huntress, and the dark feminine aspect is the Amazon. The primary energies of this archetype are physical strength and warrior-like courage.

Trickster Archetype integrates the collective projections of the wise wizard and the jester. The dark masculine aspect of the Trickster archetype is the Dark Magician. The bright feminine aspect is the Priestess. The dark feminine aspect is the Witch. The main energies of this archetype are intellect, wisdom, thinking, unconventional problem-solving, and humor.

Prince Archetype combines collective projections of aristocracy, external attractiveness, and the associated sexual aspects. The dark masculine aspect of the Prince archetype is the Wanderer. The bright feminine aspect is the Princess. The dark feminine aspect is the Naughty Girl. The main energies of this archetype are aristocracy, beauty, and sexuality.

We will not provide a detailed description of the archetypal structures in our work, as this information goes beyond the scope of our work and is associated with the theoretical and practical foundations of Jungian psychology.

Working with the transpersonal vector can also include the creation of the phenomenon of hypnotic regression into past incarnations, which we have already discussed earlier in the section on trance phenomena.

Cognitive Vector

This vector is based on the use of specific words and rules and their combinations in the context of trance work to enhance its quality and depth. Richard Bandler and John Grinder, the creators of Neuro-Linguistic Programming, played a significant role in the development of the cognitive vector in hypnotic work.

Initially, they simply modeled the semantics of effective psychotherapeutic statements that could lead to constructive mental changes in patients' consciousness. The initial models were based on Frederick Perls, the founder of Gestalt therapy; Virginia Satir, the "mother" of family therapy; and Milton Erickson, the pioneer of nondirective psychotherapy and hypnotic suggestion.

The first product of their modeling was a list of question categories that a psychotherapist could ask a patient to make the therapy session more effective. This list of question categories was named the "Meta Model." The goal of the Meta Model was to gradually "unpack" various abstract statements made by the patient in order to bring them closer to the information about their deep experience.

Bandler and Grinder considered what we say about our experience as the surface layer of experience. For example, phrases like "They don't love me," "The world is a lousy place," "All people are the same," and so on. The surface level of communication is always a truncated and compressed form of real experience, which often distorts the true meaning for the listener.

Behind the statement "They don't love me" could lie the fact that the child's parents did not indulge their whims. "The world is a lousy place" may mean that I don't get things for free just because I don't want to work hard.

Behind the phrase "All people are the same" may be the understanding that the person has discovered the greed of some of their friends. The meanings can be diverse.

Such statements are trance-related, as they create individual interpretations in the consciousness of different people. Initially, the meta-model patterns were used exclusively for conscious verbal "unpacking" of the patient's speech. A significant amount of information on this topic is covered in the books "Structure of Magic," volumes 1 and 2, authored by Richard Bandler and John Grinder.

Subsequently, these patterns began to be applied in NLP directly for the "packaging" of information with the purpose of hypnotic suggestion, as practiced by Milton Erickson, the pioneer of indirect hypnosis. However, he did not attempt to meticulously structure the cognitive semantics of his work.

Bandler and D. Grinder observed that M. Erickson utilizes specific combinations of words and their arrangements that enhance the hypnotic effect by completely bypassing resistance from the conscious sphere. Let's outline the main ones identified by Richard and John that are most adaptable to the process of hypnotic suggestion.

Meta Model patterns

Nominalizations
Abstract words that cannot be specifically perceived through any representational system. Examples include freedom, love, equality, brotherhood, and so on. Each of these words is interpreted differently in the consciousness of different individuals. The frequent use of such words in speech makes it more hypnotic, as they provide the freedom to choose unconscious interpretations. Many nominalizations can be effectively used in the process of hypnotic suggestion, such as trance, conscious, unconscious, exploration, understanding, transformation, change, and others.

Mind Reading

Phrases like "I know you can enter a trance state," "You are capable of doing great things", and "I believe you are a good person." On a conscious level, individuals rarely express resistance to such affirmative assumptions without formal justification of the preceding experience, making them easily penetrate our unconscious mind.

Causal relationships

Words like "when-then," "if-then," "often," "as," "throughout," "during." The language of cause and effect provides tools for forming non-directive suggestions in the process of hypnotic work. Examples: "When I touch your hand and slightly lift it, then you will begin to enter a trance state of consciousness," "If your hand lowers down, then the level of trance will increase," "Often, people are ready to enter a trance right now," "As I tell you something, you begin to change," "Throughout the hypnosis session, you can find answers to your questions," "During the next few minutes, you will discover a source of joy within yourself."

Complex equivalents

Phrases that equate the meanings of two different words, often two nominalizations. For example, "trance is relaxation," "friendship is understanding," "love is happiness," "the world is a set of possibilities," and so on. Due to the high level of abstract information presented, such equivalences cannot be interpreted unambiguously, thus encountering minimal conscious resistance in the individual's mind.

Universal quantifiers

Words like all, always, nobody, never, etc. The use of these words creates hypergeneralizations that make speech more hypnotic. Examples: "Hypnosis is always capable of healing," "All sensations have meaning," "Nobody can deprive you of the ability to change," and so on.

Modal operators

Words like can, possible, able. Using these words creates a sense of freedom of choice and the absence of coercion, which contributes to increasing the level of suggestiveness in speech. Examples: "You can enter a state of hypnotic trance," "Anything is possible when you are relaxed," "Can you imagine your future?" and so on.

Lost performatives

Words like they, these, people, someone, somebody, something. In this case, we also observe the generalization of certain elements into an indefinite category of experience. Examples: "These sensations can help," "Something wants to awaken," "Someone knows the answer."

Fuzzy comparisons

Phrases in which a comparison is made that is difficult or impossible to determine based on criteria. Words like more, less, stronger, weaker, kinder, crueler, etc. For example, "The strongest sensations await you ahead," "You are capable of understanding more," "Your unconscious is kinder than you think."

Lost referential index

Every belief statement has a source of formation. For example, if we hear the phrase "complex equivalent, 'trance is learning'," the intensity of our acceptance or rejection is directly related to whether we trust the source that is conveying this phrase to us. If the source is not indicated, our unconscious projections about the image that created the phrase begin, which can create a so-called meta-trance effect in relation to the existing trance effect of the current phrase. This hypnotic pattern can be transformed into its trance alternative, the antipode, with a specified referential index. In the process of hypnotic work, we either indicate an abstract referential index to reduce the level of conscious resistance in the patient or specify a specific referential index that, in our assumption, can be perceived as a hypnotic suggestion with minimal resistance. For example, "As Milton Erickson said, we are all capable of changing rapidly in a hypnotic trance."

Separately and distinctly, there is the trance language of presuppositions. Let's examine them in more detail.

Presuppositions

Presuppositional phrases are those that have a secondary meaning that is not literally reflected in them. R. Bandler and D. Grinder identified 29 types of presuppositions and described them in detail in their book "Patterns of Milton Erickson's Hypnotic Techniques." In our work, we will highlight some of them that are most adaptable to the process of trance induction.

Temporal subordinate clause
Words: "before," "after," "during," "when," "earlier," "while."
Example: "After you sit in the chair, you will enter a hypnotic trance."
Presupposition: You are not sitting in the chair now.

Pseudo-split sentence
Identified by the form: "that/what/that.../sentence/, so it.../sentence/."
Example: "What the unconscious wants is change."
Presupposition: The unconscious wants something.

Sentence with vocal emphasis
Example: "If you hear the voice of your WISDOM in a trance, you are lucky."
Presupposition: You heard something in a trance.

Complex adjectives
Words: new, old, early, present, previous, etc.
Example: "Your old experience can teach you a lot."
Presupposition: You have had a new experience.

Ordinal numbers
Words: first, second, third, fourth, next.
Example: "In the next trance, we will go deeper."

Presupposition: There was a previous trance.

Comparisons

Words: -er, -er, more, less.

Example: "A deeper level of trance will soon be achieved."

Presupposition: A certain level of trance has already been achieved.

Words of repeated action

Words: also, too, either, still, again, etc.

Example: "Again, the unconscious wants to manifest."

Presupposition: The unconscious has already manifested.

Verbs and adverbs of spatial and temporal movement

Words: come, go, leave, arrive, depart, abandon, etc.

Example: "Your consciousness has become confused."

Presupposition: Consciousness was in balance.

Verbs and adverbs of temporal change

Words: start, continue, finish, stop, complete, already, still, so far, etc.

Example: "You can continue to immerse yourself in a state of hypnotic trance."

Presupposition: You have already been in a trance.

Verbs of state change

Words: change, transform, become.

Example: "Soon, the mood will change."

Presupposition: The mood is currently unchanged.

Fictional verbs and adverbs

Words: strangely, inform, know, regret, etc.

Example: "It's very strange that you are diving into trance."

Presupposition: You are diving into a trance.

Phrase and adverbial commentaries

Words: happily, successfully, far, out of sight, gloomily, innocently, without a doubt, definitely.

Example: "Luckily, you showed up."

Presupposition: You showed up.

Reverse expectation

Words: happen, still, after all.

Example: "If you still want to stay awake, let me know."

Presupposition: You don't want to stay awake.

Questions

Example: "Who in a trance raised their hand?"

Presupposition: Someone raised their hand in a trance.

Negated questions

Example: "Wouldn't you like to enter a trance?"

Presupposition: You want to enter a trance.

Rhetorical questions

Example: "How much longer can one live without deep relaxation?"

Presupposition: One needs to relax.

The literal meaning of a phrase is perceived by our conscious mind.

Presuppositions that underlie the main meaning, most often remain unconscious and enter our subconscious. And the most important thing is that a person usually doesn't offer any conscious resistance to the semantics of presuppositions, which makes them an excellent non-directive tool for trance induction.

In our psychotherapeutic and laboratory experimental practice, we have significantly expanded the variety of cognitive structural patterns that can be applied in the process of hypnotic suggestion. Let's provide some examples.

Cognitive structural elements of trance induction

Non-specific, simple identification

Examples: psychologist, doctor, chemist, programmer, hypnotherapist, client, patient, suggester.

Trance phrases: programmer of destiny, client of the unconscious, doctor of the soul.

Unpacking question: What specific activity do you mean when you say that this person is a psychologist?

Non-specific qualitative identification

Examples: original, snob, revolutionary, rebel.

Trance phrases: the original in the way of healing oneself, rebel on the ship of symptoms.

Unpacking question: What exactly does the person do that allows you to give them the identity of a "rebel"?

Non-specific adjective

Evaluation examples: big, small, smart, foolish.

Trance phrases: the smart unconscious knows what to do; great wisdom can sleep deep inside.

Unpacking question: What exactly do you mean when you say that he is smart?

Sensory Examples: bright, loud, warm, agile, fragrant, delicious, balanced.

Trance phrases: vivid dream, warm trance, agile unconscious, delicious meaning.

Unpacking question: What exactly do you mean when you say that he is balanced?

Indefinite category of nouns

Examples: mechanism, automaton, apparatus.

Trance phrases: the apparatus of the unconscious functions steadily; complex mechanism of the soul.

Unpacking question: What specific apparatus do you mean? What are its functions?

Indefinite category of verbs

Examples: transforms, converts, emotes, reacts.

Trance phrases: the unconscious transforms personality, something in you reacts to my question.

Unpacking question: What exactly does he do when he emotes?

Unspecified time

Examples: today, yesterday, tomorrow, later, sometime, in the morning, during the day, in the evening, at night, in the near future, a long time ago.

Trance phrases: today is a good day for trance; we will delve deeper a little later; you will have a chance in the near future; not long ago, you were not swept away by the flow of changes.

Unpacking question: When exactly is "tomorrow"?

Unspecified place

Examples: here, there, in this city, in the country, in the world.

Trance phrases: here and now, everywhere, and always.

Unpacking question: Where exactly do you mean when you say "there"?

Unspecified expression

Examples: super, cool, wow, awesome.

Trance phrases: this is a super trance; when you reach the depths, something inside you will say "wow."

Unpacking question: What exactly do you mean when you describe something as "super"?

Indefinite "-ism"

Example: hypnotism, mesmerism, snobism, feminism, Marxism, sexism.

Trance phrase: You can feel the influence of hypnotism on yourself right now.

Unpacking question: What does the word snobism mean to you specifically?

Unspecified synesthesia

Examples: bright speech, warm image, sweet sound.

Trance phrase: The bright sound of my voice penetrates deep into your consciousness.

Unpacking question: What exactly do you mean when you describe your speech as bright?

Vague quantifier

Examples: some, sometimes, partially, not completely, not fully, not entirely, not absolutely, close to zero, almost to the maximum.

Trance phrase: some sensations provide understanding; partially, you know what a hypnotic trance is, the unconscious can engage your brain to the maximum. (some-NOT ALL-none) (always-SOMETIMES-never)

Unpacking question: What exact quantity does "some" refer to?

Unspecified representational system

Examples: realize, understand, contemplate, perceive, know.

Trance phrase: In trance, I realize something new.

Unpacking questions: When you say you realize, what specific sensations do you experience? How do you understand that you realize something?

Unspecified qualitative description

Examples: bright, intelligent, fast, funny.

Trance phrase: It's funny that you can unexpectedly immerse yourself in a trance.

Unpacking question: When you say it's funny, what exactly do you mean?

Unspecified motivation

Examples: I want to engage in sports; we need to immerse ourselves in a trance; change is necessary.

Trance phrase: the unconscious is compelled to immerse you into a hypnotic trance.

Unpacking questions: Due to what? For what reason? For what purpose?

Unspecified numeral

Examples: next time, previous conversation, initial stage, final step, few, many, a little, some, some amount, some.

Trance phrases: we will get more next time, the initial stage of immersion has been completed; we can invest a lot of effort for the better.

Unpacking questions: When you mention "next time," when and where will it happen? When you refer to the previous conversation, which exact conversation do you mean? When you talk about the initial stage, which specific stage do you mean? When you mention the final step, which particular step do you mean?

Unspecified value hierarchy

Examples: important, significant, priority.

Trance phrase: Everything that resides in the depths is significant.

Unpacking questions: What exactly do you mean when you say it's significant? How significant is it?

Omitted noun or nominalization

Examples: Take the kettle and put it (on the stove). Please open (the door) for me. Dive deeper (into trance).

Trance phrase: Close the windows of the unconscious (with your hand), now you will start to immerse yourself (into trance).

Unpacking questions: What should be used to close it? Where exactly should one immerse themselves?

Reverse meaning in an ironic statement

Example: Oh yes, he's the strongest.

Trance phrase: (after the patient enters a somnambulistic state), you now feel a tiny particle of trance intensity.

Unpacking questions: Do you mean he's actually the weakest? Do you mean the trance is very intense?

Noun as metaphorical identification

Examples: dynamite, fire, horse, burdock.

Trance phrase: You are the real fire; feel it.

Unpacking questions: What do you specifically mean when you say he's a burdock? What exactly do you mean by comparing me to fire?

Adjective as metaphorical identification

Examples: he's green (member of the Green Party), bright, dark.

Trance phrase: The sage you see is the true "bright" of your consciousness.

Unpacking questions: What do you specifically mean when you say he's green? What qualities exactly do you attribute to this identification? Based on what qualities do you classify him as bright?

Expressive identification

Examples: Superman, superhuman.

Trance phrase: deep within your unconscious sleeps the superhuman.

Unpacking question: What specific meanings do you attribute to the term "superhuman"?

Nominalization as a universal quantifier

Examples: world, universe, absolute, cosmos.

Trance phrase: A whole universe of meaning can unfold for you right now.

Unpacking questions: What exact meaning do you assign to the word "world"? What quantity of meanings can unfold for me?

Nominalization as identification

Examples: He is a true mystery; for him, it is joy.

Trance phrase: You can become a ray of serenity in the depths of the unconscious.

Unpacking questions: When you say it's a true mystery, what exactly do you mean? What qualities do you attribute to it? What meaning do you assign to the term "ray of serenity"?

Unidentified gender marker

Examples: child, person, creature, animal.

Trance phrase: The child of transformation is ready to grow in the depths.

Unpacking questions: What gender does the "creature" have? Child? Animal?

Exaggeration or diminishment of identities, nouns, or nominalizations

Examples: giant human, little human, boredom, giant, dwarf, giant.

Trance phrase: the giant of wisdom in your unconscious partially reveals its knowledge to you.

Unpacking questions: What specific meaning do you attribute to the word "giant human"? Giant? Dwarf?

Unspecified metaphorical submodal adverbs

Examples: purple, parallel.

Trance phrase: Let everything that has lived its course become purple.

Unpacking question: What exactly do you mean when you say "it's purple"?

Specific metaphorical numeral

Examples: I'll divide you by zero, you've completed the task at a five; do the job at a hundred percent.

Trance phrase: in contact with the resources of the unconscious, you will be able to perform your task at a "five"

Unpacking question: What exactly do you mean when you say the task is completed at "five"?

There may be more cognitive structural elements than we have described, but for now, let's focus on these 27 elements as the most fundamental.

Understanding the cognitive and linguistic structure of trance induction allows us to make hypnotic speech more rich, vivid, and diverse. And the diversity of speech can sometimes be one of the aspects that not only increases the level of hypnotizability but also turns trance speech into a form of art, where both the process and the result matter.

Regarding meta-model patterns, presuppositions, and cognitive structural elements of trance, in order to gradually learn to use them, we can recommend an exercise of selecting 2-3 elements from each category and attempting to compose a hypnotic induction using them. Then, repeat the same exercise with new elements. It is not necessary to memorize all 9 described meta-model patterns, 17 presuppositions, and 27 cognitive structural elements literally. However, going through these models several times in practice is essential to increasing mastery in this field.

Somatic Vector

Somatic vector provides us with the opportunity to create hypnotic work with minimal verbal suggestion. This vector demonstrates the visual representation of the relative nature of existing beliefs, where hypnosis is associated with suggestion and the heart of trance resides in the sound of the hypnotist's voice. Conversely, it shows how the semantics of verbal suggestion and skillful voice manipulation can be conveyed through touch and movement.

Observing the hypnotic work of Alexander Danilov, we repeatedly witnessed how he induced deep hypnotic states in his patients with minimal verbal interventions. Often, he employed some form of pattern interruption. For instance, he would engage in a slow, relaxed conversation with the patient, and just as the patient was about to respond to his next question, he abruptly placed one hand on the patient's occiput and the other on the forehead, swiftly tilting the head backward. Typically, at that moment, the patient transitioned into an altered state of consciousness. He could then sharply raise the patient's hand, demonstrating the phenomenon of catalepsy, or create vibrating hand passes near the patient, eliciting a trance-like dynamic of consciousness. Afterwards, he often brought the patient back as abruptly as he had induced the trance.

Based on these observations, we have noted that the three main stages of trance work—induction into trance, dynamic influence within trance, and emergence from the trance state—can effectively be accomplished without relying on verbal techniques.

Another intriguing aspect related to the embodiment of trance induction was observed in the work of Betty Alice Erickson. She demonstrated a technique for non-verbally inducing catalepsy in the hand, where the hypnotherapist lightly touched the patient's hand, resting on their knee, with their index and thumb fingers, and slowly began raising it in the air, incrementally, by a single millimeter, while making subtle micro-tremors from side to side and then up and down. Sooner or later, when executed correctly, the hand would enter a state of catalepsy. In some cases, we witnessed how this seemingly innocent technique led not only to catalepsy but to a complete hypnotic paralysis of the hand, wherein the subject openly commented that they were unable to move it with their conscious effort. Continuing to manipulate hands in a cataleptic state, we discovered that their movement could induce certain changes in the patient's states. Interestingly, these changes occurred when body manipulations were performed either very slowly or extremely abruptly, significantly surpassing the natural speed of human consciousness.

Over time, we found that, with a high probability, any manipulation of the subject's body would be perceived by their unconscious mind as a specific symbol and would be interpreted in a particular manner. Similar processes would occur if we began manipulating the patient's head or legs, which were equally effective for inducing catalepsy. Any other possible manipulations of the patient's body could also be interpreted as symbols and metaphors by their unconscious mind.

Thus, the patient's body can become a tool for communication with their unconscious mind. The main challenge lies in the fact that we cannot be completely certain about how our manipulations will be interpreted by the unconscious mind and what specific effects they may lead to.

As we have observed in the practice of somatic hypnosis, the overall framework of the goal of inducing a hypnotic state holds significant importance.

It will determine how various bodily manipulations are interpreted.

To begin, let us highlight a list of the main bodily manipulations that can be created during a hypnosis session without the use of verbal inductions. All manipulations are performed on the patient while they are sitting in a comfortable position on a chair with a backrest:

1. **Hand manipulations**

   Upward, downward, leftward, and rightward movements. Sideward and outward movement of the hand. Raising the hand as high as possible above the head. Placing the hand on the opposite shoulder, face, forehead, crown, or nape. Overlaying one hand on top of the other from above or below. Interlacing the fingers.

2. **Foot manipulations**

   Bending, straightening, lifting, and lowering (touching behind the knee and/or calf muscles).

3. **Head manipulations**

   Forward, backward, rightward, and leftward tilts. Right and left turns (grasping from behind or in front on the sides with both hands).

4. **Trunk manipulations**

   Forward, backward, leftward, and rightward tilts (grasping from behind and in front by the shoulders).

5. **Manipulations based on touch**

   After the touch, pressing, massaging, or vibrating movements are possible:
   - Fingertip touch between the eyebrows.
   - Fingertip touch to the temples on both sides.
   - Fingertip touch to the trapezius muscles.
   - Fingertip touch to the deltoid muscles on the sides.
   - Fist touch to the center of the sternum.

- Fist touch to the solar plexus center.

6. **Manipulations based on fingertip touch** to specific areas of the body and their movements:
   - Fingers touching the atlas vertebra, then moving toward the eyebrow and stopping there.
   - Touching the shoulders and moving the fingers along the trapezius, neck, head, and toward the temples.
   - Side touch to the neck and movement toward the deltoid muscle.
   - Touching the deltoid muscle and moving toward the elbow.
   - Touching the elbow and moving toward the wrist.

In our understanding, there is no need to involve other body parts in the process of somatic hypnotic work.

Now we can present a basic algorithm for somatic hypnosis work that focuses on the process of resolution. Once again, let's emphasize that the movements to be performed are symbols and metaphors for the patient's unconscious, so it is natural to vary them depending on the patient's request. The majority of the work should be done on an intuitive level. The hypnotherapist needs to maintain the meanings attributed to specific manipulations in their consciousness.

One possible algorithm for working with somatically-oriented hypnosis is as follows:

1. Work in pairs.
2. The second person determines the request they will work on.
3. The first person places one hand on the second person's occiput and the other hand on their forehead. Slowly tilts the head backward and continues to gently support it by holding the occiput.
4. The hypnotherapist takes the patient's right hand and gradually lifts it to shoulder level. They test whether catalepsy is present or not. The same is done with the left hand.

5. Next, the hypnotherapist stands behind the patient and holds **their** head on the sides. Slowly rotates it to the right to its maximum extent and holds it there for a while. Then the same action is repeated in the opposite direction. Finally, the head is centered.

6. After that, the catalepsy of both hands is recreated (if they dropped during the previous manipulations). The right hand is positioned horizontally at shoulder level, straight, and extended to the right. Similarly, the left hand is positioned to the left.

7. The fingers perform several tapping touches on the patient's brow region while slightly tilting their head backward.

8. Subsequently, the fingers exert gentle pressure on the patient's clavicle muscles.

9. The hypnotherapist stands in front of the patient, touches their hands with their own, extends the patient's hands in front of them, and makes a sudden, light pull towards themselves. This is done to bring the patient out of the altered state.

10. Feedback is obtained from the patient regarding the states they experienced during the hypnosis session.

Thus, the hypnotherapist provides the patient with a set of bodily metaphors that, within the context of the patient's request, exert a specific influence on their consciousness.

Particularly interesting and beautiful work can be done with individuals who have at least a slight predisposition to hysteroid accentuation and whose experiences may be overwhelming.

Formally, this work, in its structure, resembles the therapeutic philosophy of New Code NLP, developed by John Grinder in the early 1980s. He based his therapeutic algorithm on the following steps:

1. Identify the state that needs to be worked on.
2. Associate with it.
3. Dissociate from it.
4. Activate the New Code game and play it for 10−20 minutes.

5. Re-associate with the problematic state.
6. Observe how the states created by the game transform the problematic state.

In the context of somatic hypnosis, this algorithm can be adapted and integrated into the work with patients. The process involves identifying the specific state or issue that requires resolution, creating a sensory and kinesthetic experience associated with it, and then dissociating from it. The hypnotherapist guides the patient to engage in somatic manipulations and movements that represent the desired transformation or resolution. This engages the patient's unconscious mind and allows for the exploration and reshaping of their experiences.

Somatic hypnosis, combined with the principles of New Code NLP, offers a powerful and creative approach to working with patients, tapping into the potential of the body-mind connection and facilitating transformative experiences.

8

Structural Elements of Hypnotic Work

"Hypnosis is a court jester in the palaces of academia."
   Paul Watzlawick

The structural content of hypnotic induction can be divided into interventions intended for:

1. **Induction and suggestion of trance are used to simply shift a person into an altered state of consciousness**.
   At this stage, we will encounter resistance from the client to varying degrees, with rare exceptions. Resistance can be microscopic, requiring several hypnotic interventions to activate the trance process. It can be moderate, requiring 1-2 minutes of specific interventions to induce a trance. It can also be macroscopic, requiring 5 minutes or more for the initial signs of trance to appear in the client's consciousness. Naturally, there may be cases of unsuccessful attempts where success can be achieved through multiple hypnosis sessions.

2. **Inductions of the instrumental part of trance.**
   These inductions aim to guide the person through the trance process towards a specific transformational goal.   This may involve a

245

psychotherapeutic algorithm, a sequence of steps designed to achieve a therapeutic effect, specific algorithms guiding the client towards self-discovery processes, or algorithms creating the phenomenology of trance (e.g., hand catalepsy, hand levitation, and so on).

3. **Inductions are intended to bring the person out of the trance state**. These can be individual phrases (e.g., "Now you're beginning to come out of the trance state") or small algorithms gradually reducing the trance process, step by step, and transitioning the person into a waking state (e.g., "And now I will count from 10 to 1, and you will gradually emerge from the trance state"). We will discuss possible variations later on.

Before starting a trance induction (if we are specifically talking about the psychotherapeutic process), it is necessary to have a preliminary conversation that touches upon topics that help us create a trance process and prepare the patient for hypnotic induction. The questions that can be asked may include:

- Have you ever been in a state of hypnosis (trance)?
- Have you ever experienced altered states of consciousness (non-clinical forms of hypnosis, such as meditation, self-hypnosis, chanting mantras, or breathing techniques)?
- How do you envision the state of hypnosis?
- What do you expect from the state of hypnosis?
- Do you have any concerns or fears regarding the trance process?
- Have you ever observed someone else being induced into a state of hypnosis?
- What associations arise for you regarding the terms hypnosis and trance?
- What would you like to achieve from hypnosis?

Engaging in this preliminary conversation allows the hypnotherapist to gather important information about the client's previous experiences, expectations, concerns, and associations related to hypnosis. It helps establish rapport, address any misconceptions, and create a supportive therapeutic environment. Furthermore, it enables the hypnotherapist to tailor the hypnotic induction and subsequent interventions to the individual's unique needs and preferences, maximizing the effectiveness of the therapeutic process.

By addressing these questions, the hypnotherapist gains insights into the client's subjective experience, psychological disposition, and motivations, facilitating a more personalized and targeted approach to the hypnotic induction.

The next important topic for discussion is the direct positioning of the hypnotherapist in relation to the patient before and during hypnosis. There are three most popular positions: directly sitting in front of the patient, sitting to the right of the patient, and sitting to the left of the patient. Alternatively, if the client is standing, the positions can be standing in front of, standing to the right of, or standing to the left of the client. During the process of hypnosis, positional changes are possible, such as moving behind the client. However, the detailed meaning and significance of each spatial position will be discussed in the topic of psychogeography, where we will delve into the eight basic psychogeographic directions in relation to the patient. In this initial stage, we will focus on three basic foundations.

The position directly in front is perceived as a mirror or a confrontation, depending on the client's personality profile and gender. The position to the right and in front activates a paternal transference, while the position to the left and in front activates a maternal transference. This means that for the unconscious mind, the front position is interpreted as a reflection of certain qualities, often obvious ones. If there is trust (rapport) between the therapist and the client, the unconscious mind is more likely to perceive the suggestions emanating from this position favorably. In cases where "face-to-face" confrontation occurs between a male therapist and a female patient (or vice versa), there is a possibility of eroticized projections, which often hinder the therapeutic process. If a face-to-face position occurs between a male therapist and a male patient, aggressive projections may arise. Aggressive and eroticized projections are less likely to occur between a female therapist and a female patient.

To begin with, the positions to the right and in front and to the left and in front are more advantageous. The position to the right and in front of the client activates paternal transference, which means a higher likelihood of projections that the client will transfer onto the image of the hypnotherapist, connected with emotions related to the father figure. In which cases would this position be favorable or not? It all depends on the patient's relationship with the father figure. If the image of the father evokes predominantly positive associations in the patient, then this position would be preferable. If not, it is worth trying the mirror position, the left-front position, or the maternal position. The same rule applies to the left-front position, in which a person is more likely to transmit emotions associated with the mother figure.

It is worth adding that the paternal position is often more suitable for a directive style of delivery during hypnosis, while the maternal position is more suitable for a nondirective style. However, this rule is not obligatory to follow and is relative. In other words, it is possible to vary the positioning on an intuitive level.

The client's position on the chair should be maximally comfortable but not slouching. The back should be supported against the chair backrest, and the arms and legs should not be crossed. The hands rest on the knees. The fingers on the hands can be intertwined, but if we intend to reproduce any hypnotic phenomenon that requires the use of the client's hands, intertwined fingers may hinder us, so it is better to avoid any interlocking.

The possible structure of hypnotic work can vary in different ways. Some points may be entirely optional, while other methods may include points that are more characteristic of the classical form of work.

The **structure of hypnotic work** can vary, and here are some possible main variations:

1. **Preliminary conversation.**
   Questioning based on the aforementioned questions.

2. **Proper psychogeographical positioning.**

   For example, positioning oneself in front and to the right.

3. **Pattern interruption.**

   Techniques for creating confusion. Instrumental techniques for gradually inducing a hypnotic state.

4. **Creating trance phenomenology** and using it for simple demonstration, deepening trance work, and applying phenomenology for therapeutic purposes (will be described later).

5. **Instrumental psychotherapeutic patterns.**

   Direct algorithms leading to therapeutic effects.

6. **Techniques for bringing the patient out of trance.**

7. **Post-conversation.**

9

Psychogeographical Direction in Hypnotic Work

In psychology and psychotherapy books, we have found limited information about the projections our unconscious creates in relation to different directions from the perspective of the viewer. Most often, discussions revolve around four main directions. For example, in philosophical, spiritual, Christian, and Muslim literature, we come across mentions of the right side of the human body as being good, righteous, and masculine. The left side is interpreted as bad, dark, and feminine. Interestingly, the Latin word "*dexter*," which directly translates to "right," is also interpreted as "correct" or even "godly," while "*sinister*," meaning "left," has its root in the word "sin." Naturally, a question arises as to where such a specific division could have originated. If we turn to the neurophysiology of the brain, we can discover several intriguing answers.

Our left hemisphere controls the entire right side of the body, and it contains crucial brain centers that, according to many neurophysiologists, distinguish us from animals. One of these centers is the left prefrontal cortex, which allows us to exert voluntary effort, engage in purposeful planning, and take actions with delayed gratification. It enables us to exercise self-control and self-discipline. Any dysfunction in this brain region can rapidly reduce our behavior to an animal-like state.

In neurology, when discussing impairments in the functioning of the left prefrontal cortex, one often mentions the case of a patient named Phineas Gage. In 1840, while working as a miner in the southern United States, Gage suffered a severe injury to his left prefrontal cortex. A metal rod entered through his left eye and exited through the left side of his temporal-parietal lobe. Despite the horrific injury, Gage managed to reach a doctor who documented the partial destruction of his left prefrontal cortex. Gage survived but underwent significant behavioral changes. Prior to the injury, he was a devout family man who upheld moral values and laws, and did not exhibit strong aggression towards others. After the injury, a new personality emerged. He began drinking heavily, stopped attending church, engaged in fights, used profanity, cheated on his wife, and disregarded workplace rules. This case illustrates the potential consequences of left prefrontal cortex trauma. However, it is worth noting that individuals do not necessarily need to fracture their skull to exhibit severe behavioral disturbances. In some people, insufficient development of this brain region can result from genetic and environmental factors, which also influence their behavior.

Naturally, in ancient times, such individuals were interpreted as being possessed by demons when, in reality, they had problems with the correct formation of the left prefrontal cortex or suffered significant brain trauma. Additionally, in the left temporal lobe, in the majority of cases, speech centers are formed. These centers govern our ability to express ourselves and formulate speech with proper syntax.

One hemisphere of the brain will always dominate, and if it is the right hemisphere, which is more visual, irrational, and chaotic, our behavior rarely conforms to the minimum social norms. Our right hemisphere controls the entire left side of our body. I believe it is now clear why, in religious philosophy, the left side was often perceived as bad and even equated with sin. In our consciousness, the left side is also often associated with femininity due to the stereotype of perceiving masculine and feminine as dominant and subordinate, respectively.

Fascinating practical observations can be made regarding our preferences for holding a conversation, depending on whether it feels more comfortable to have the person on our right or left side. Similarly, which side do we tend to choose when walking alongside someone on the street? These preferences can reveal interesting insights.

Individuals who lack a masculine figure in their family often position themselves on the left side, effectively transforming the interlocutor into a paternal figure. This positioning aligns with a more paternal role. On the other hand, when the interlocutor is placed on the left side, it indicates the opposite—insufficient contact with the feminine figure and a symbolic attempt to restore that connection. Thus, we are dealing with two key psychogeographical transfers. The right side signifies the masculine and paternal, while the left side represents the feminine and maternal.

However, in practice, when we conducted social experiments to identify role functions and placed individuals in various spatial segments to the right and left of the interlocutor, we received diverse feedback.

The experimental format was as follows: we positioned the interlocutor in the center of the room and delineated the surrounding space into eight basic sectors, as follows:

Front-left sector	Front sector	Front-right sector
Left sector	Subject (the individual being observed)	Right sector
Back-left sector	Back sector	Back-right sector

Overall, nine individuals participated in the experiment. Each person stood around the subject, facing them, and then experienced a new state depending on the transfer sector. Initially, the central subject provided feedback regarding the intuitive role assigned to each person standing beside them. We then asked each subject from the surrounding group how they perceived themselves in relation to the person they were facing. Thus, throughout the nine-step experiment, each participant took on the central role and provided feedback from that position.

This experiment was then repeated with other groups of nine individuals, following the same procedure. Ultimately, we discovered that the role qualities attributed to each psychogeographical transfer by the participants may vary in detail but have a common underlying meaning and distinct social roles. The right-front position consistently represented the image of a paternal figure, while the left-front position conveyed a maternal image.

After some time conducting this experiment, we came across intriguing material while studying various Buddhist and Hindu meditation techniques. These techniques consistently placed the fatherly figure in the imagination front-right and the motherly figure front-left. This type of psychogeography had been known long before our laboratory findings.

Another interesting psychogeographical stereotype caught our attention during the study of various psychiatry books describing the symptomatology of auditory hallucinations in paranoid schizophrenics, particularly those patients who divided the hallucinated voices into approving voices, praising voices, condemning voices, and mocking voices. We were surprised to find that the overwhelming majority of patients heard approving voices from the right-rear and condemning voices from the left and rear.

In this case, two key rear sectors of personal psychogeography were involved: right-rear and left-rear. The right-rear position was perceived as the domain from which righteous moral wisdom emanated, while the left-rear position was associated with dark, egocentric, psychopathic wisdom leading to harm. Individuals occupying these psychogeographical sectors experienced corresponding states. We provisionally named these transfers the "bright mentor" and the "dark mentor" transfers, or transfers of the bright and dark archetypes. The content of the transfers could vary depending on the central subject's personality, but the overall cognitive and emotional vectors almost always coincided. Naturally, emotional reactions varied from subject to subject regarding each psychogeographical vector. Each person projected their own experience, and the vector organized it into a specific pattern.

At the beginning of the experiment, we presumed that different subjects would have their own roles in each vector, but that turned out not to be the case. The role-based psychogeographical vectors were nearly identical among the various participants.

We had the sense that we had delved into a very interesting and seemingly unexplored topic that had not been thoroughly described before—revealing the structure of psychogeographical conditioning of personal projections.

The next two fundamental psychogeographical transfers that intrigued us were the ones in front of and behind the research subject. The person positioned in front of the subject often elicited diametrically opposite reactions, either strong sympathy or aggression. What the subject projected onto the front sector represented their own core qualities. In our work, this transfer was termed the mirror transfer. Depending on the specific qualities of self-awareness projected by the subject, the reactions varied. For instance, if the subject harbored hostility within, it would be vividly projected onto the object of transfer, resulting in hostile reactions towards the object. Conversely, if an individual was inherently friendly, the mirror also reflected friendliness.

One noteworthy detail is that if individuals occupying a particular psycho-geographical sector were of the same gender as the central subject, their reactions were consistent. However, if the gender of the person in the transfer sector changed, the reactions could be entirely different.

For example, if the central subject was a daughter who held great love and respect for her father, any man standing to her right and in front would elicit similar reactions. However, if a woman occupied that specific sector, a range of negative emotions and strong resistance would be directed towards her. Similar processes occurred in the maternal transfer. The right-rear and left-rear transfers did not exhibit such clear gender conditioning, but changing the gender of the subject occupying a specific sector altered cognitive and emotional reactions towards them.

When the person in the front sector shared the same gender as the central subject, reactions were either simple sympathy or aggression. However, if the recipient was a person of the opposite gender, simple sympathy often transitioned into an erotic feeling.

The transfer behind it triggered the manifestation and actualization of repressed and suppressed elements. In other words, we project onto the figure behind us what we do not want or cannot consciously hold within ourselves for various reasons.

Naturally, a similar experiment can occur in everyday situations, such as when we hear someone walking behind us on the street. For a significant number of women, the image of a person walking behind them triggers aggressive or sexual projections, or sometimes a peculiar combination of both. For men, aggressive and antisocial figures are more commonly projected. Again, this varies depending on what the person carries within themselves but consciously tries to conceal. If the gender of the person behind is undifferentiated, the projections can be diverse. However, if we know that the person behind us is of the opposite gender, we often hear feedback regarding various sexual associations.

We specifically heard such feedback from the central subjects concerning the participants occupying the rear psychogeographical sector. Sex, aggression, betrayal, fear, and so on. However, some participants found what was behind them appealing. Naturally, this vividly described their strategies for engaging with the world and their personal preferences. Here, individuals can be loosely divided into two key profiles: those who chase their shadow and those who flee from it. This finding is also quite interesting.

The last two sectors that we analyzed were the right and left sectors of the central subject. Here, everything was relatively straightforward. These transfers did not possess a strongly hierarchical structure and were often perceived as equal entities. Furthermore, the figure on the right was perceived as a friend or colleague, while the figure on the left was seen as a rival or competitor. Emotional reactions to psychogeographical images also varied. For example, a person who had strong friendly relationships consistently exhibited positive reactions to the friendly transfer. Individuals who had experienced betrayals in their personal history perceived the friendly transfer as hypocritical and deceitful. Representatives of such a profile often empathized with the figure on the left, stating that they could trust someone more if there was some competition or rivalry between them. Reactions to the opposite gender from one's own also varied according to one's life experiences with other people. A man perceiving another man in a friendly transfer could experience highly positive and warm emotions, but when a woman occupied that position, reactions could change significantly.

In this way, we have mapped out eight fundamental psychogeographical transfers, the information of which can be effectively utilized in psychotherapeutic practice and any communicative context.

Let's once again enumerate all eight basic psychogeographical transfers:

1. Front-right. Paternal transfer
2. Front-center. Mirror transfer
3. Front-left. Maternal transfer
4. Right. Friendly transfer
5. Left. Competitive transfer
6. Back-right. Transfer of a bright mentor
7. Back. Shadow transfer
8. Back-left. Transfer of a dark mentor

We have found a very interesting application of this model in the practice of hypnotic suggestion.

Naturally, by varying the psychogeographical transfers during trance induction, we can achieve significantly different states in the hypnotic subject. Initially, the preferred basic transfers for hypnotic work will be the paternal and maternal transfers, as each person is primarily influenced by one or the other parental figure. This imprinting occurs in our consciousness during early childhood. We are accustomed to following commands from parental figures.

The paternal transfer will be more beneficial for "daddy's girls," while the maternal transfer will be more beneficial for "mommy's boys." As we have already mentioned, not only the psychogeographical vector but also the gender of the person interacting with us from that vector can play a significant role. If a "daddy's girl" receives hypnotic suggestion from a woman through the paternal transfer, it can evoke strong resistance, and vice versa. In this transfer, a man can be the most suggestive object for her.

Since variations in reactions can be highly diverse, it doesn't make sense to list all possible scenarios. Each case requires an individual approach.

If we can perform a laboratory exercise with the patient to calibrate suggestibility for each possible transfer, let's propose the following exercise:

Exercise: "Psychogeographical Calibration of Suggestibility"

1. Assume the paternal transfer towards the client and ask them to close their eyes. For one minute, deliver hypnotic phrases such as "you are falling asleep," "your body is relaxing," "you begin to recall pleasant moments of your life."

2. After one minute, interview the patient about the impact of your suggestions and the emotional reactions they experienced towards you. Evaluate the level of hypnotic response to your phrases and the positivity of emotional reactions on a ten-point scale.

3. Repeat steps 1 and 2 with the remaining seven psychogeographical transfers.

4. Identify the most favorable transfer, and using it, conduct a five-minute hypnotic session.

If you don't have time to explore all the variations of transfers, you can simply inquire with the client before the hypnosis session about their relationships with their parents and whom they accept and respect more. The transfer to the more respected parent will be more preferable. Additionally, quite often, in the initial hypnotherapy session, adopting a friend transfer by the hypnotherapist would be an optimal choice. We do not recommend using mirror and competitor transfers in the first therapy session. However, there have been interesting cases where these transfers have yielded excellent results.

When it comes to the three posterior transfers, things can become somewhat more complex. Each of them taps into various shadow aspects of the human mind, both negative and less so. By hypnotizing a person using these transfers, you can easily evoke something important, creative, wise, or dark and gloomy. Particularly, this holds true for the central posterior transfer. We do not want to impose rigid rules, but we will provide a recommendation. If you wish to conduct a full-fledged hypnosis session using these transfers, perform a brief preliminary hypnosis test from this direction to record the patient's main emotional reactions towards you. After the test, if their reactions are positive enough, you can proceed to a complete hypnosis session.

During the hypnosis session, you can vary the psychogeographical sectors by moving between them and providing different inductions. There can be numerous options for movement, but let's provide some basic examples:

- Algorithm for working with psychogeographical transfers:
- Begin the induction with the paternal transfer and immerse the patient in a hypnotic trance within it.
- Transition to the friendly transfer and explore existing unconscious processes. For example, facilitate hypnotic regression.
- Transition to the transfer of the bright mentor and activate the resources of the unconscious from within it.
- Transition to the maternal transfer and provide emotional support to the patient during the changes occurring in the hypnotic state.

Or consider the following algorithm:

- Initiate the hypnotic induction from the mirror transfer and immerse the patient in a hypnotic trance.
- Transition to the maternal transfer and gradually induce deep relaxation.
- Move on to the transfer of the shadow and uncover the positive intention underlying the symptom.
- Transition to the transfer of the bright mentor and seek advice on how to act in the current situation.

- These are examples of two variations of algorithms that can be further modified and customized based on specific requirements and needs.

The selection of a specific psychogeographical transfer to conduct the entire session can be based on the patient's request. Here are examples of recommendations for each transfer:

1. The paternal transfer is preferable if the patient wants to receive clear suggestions and guidance from the hypnotherapist. For example, direct suggestions for recovery, getting rid of something, or achieving goals.
2. The maternal transfer is a good choice if we want to induce deep relaxation, provide emotional support to the person, and activate mechanisms of empathy and compassion.
3. The mirror transfer is optimal when working with the patient's future, setting goals, and exploring ways to achieve existing goals.
4. A friend transfer can be a good option when the person simply needs to feel supported by people who are equal to them and receive feedback from the world.
5. The competitor transfer may be the patient's choice if they want to gain an internal critical perspective on the current situation, shaking off rigid views on the situation.
6. The bright mentor transfer is excellent for establishing a connection with and contact with inner moral wisdom.
7. The dark mentor transfer can help tap into knowledge and wisdom of a more psychopathic nature, where empathy and compassion are not the key values.
8. Shadow transfer is the best choice for working through repressed aspects of everyday life during hypnosis.

Another significant aspect when working with psychogeographical transfers is the vertical vector of height. Naturally, each transfer will be emotionally differentiated accordingly. The key aspect of differentiation is the hierarchical level. For example, if we take the mirror transfer and raise the voice above the patient's own voice, we get the "hero" transfer, the ideal mirror—the "I" the person would like to be. If we go down in the mirror transfer, we get the "fallen hero," the aspect of the mirror that is difficult to accept. Therefore, in hypnotic work, trance induction should be done at the level of the patient's head or slightly above if possible. Based on our observations, if the hypnotherapist is positioned slightly below the patient, it is not beneficial for both hypnotherapy sessions and the overall psychotherapeutic session, if applicable.

In a similar way, each of the eight sectors is divided:

1. **Paternal transfer**:
   The perfect father - the ordinary father - the worst father.

2. **Maternal transfer**:
   The perfect mother - the ordinary mother - the worst mother.

3. **Mirror transfer**:
   The hero - the mirror - the fallen hero.

4. **Friend transfer**:
   The perfect friend - the ordinary friend - the worst friend.

5. **Competitor transfer**:
   The perfect competitor - the ordinary competitor - the worst competitor.

6. **Light mentor transfer**:
   The great light mentor - the ordinary light mentor - the small light mentor.

7. **Dark mentor transfer**:
   The great dark mentor - the ordinary dark mentor - the small dark mentor.

8. **Shadow transfer:**

The large shadow – the ordinary shadow – the small shadow.

For each sector, individuals can have different projections. Sometimes they have a strong psychospiritual flavor. Transition to a higher transfer or a lower one occurs through a significant upward or downward shift of the speaking subject. It is important to note that all lower transfers are not suitable for psychotherapy or hypnotherapy.

The psychogeographic transfer above the person's head was first used by Sigmund Freud, who liked to sit in a chair behind the head of the lying patient. When we attempted to hypnotize patients from this position, we obtained very interesting results. Most patients projected elements of their collective unconscious onto this psychogeographic vector, manifesting various psychospiritual images. Their emotional reactions were closely tied to their personal relationship with this theme. The information originating from this transfer was often perceived as supreme wisdom and ultimate knowledge.

On the contrary, the psychogeographic transfer below, at the feet, seems to have not been utilized in hypnotic practice until now. At least, we found no mention of such a psychogeographic vector in hypnotic work. In laboratory conditions, we recreated it and attempted to conduct a hypnotic session from this transfer. People's reactions varied greatly, ranging from complete acceptance to outright rejection. The associations evoked by the voice emanating from beneath the feet were most commonly linked to the "voice of the earth" and naturally touched upon specific realms of the unconscious that are typically not activated in ordinary social communication.

10

Opponents of the Existence of Hypnosis

> *"Mesmerism is too vulgar nonsense to be taken seriously. We consider its advocates charlatans and deceivers. They should be expelled from the community of professionals."*
> Thomas Wakley, the first editor of The Lancet

In this small section of the book, we would like to touch upon the beliefs of various scientists who, at the time, actively attempted to prove the nonexistence of a hypnotic state as such.

One such example is the personality of American psychotherapist Theodore Barber (b. 1927). Drawing on Albert Bandura's cognitive-behavioral approach, he provided a specific interpretation of hypnosis and began to assert that hypnosis is not a unique state and that it is based on everyday physiological, cognitive, emotional, and social processes. According to T. Barber, all phenomena that can be reproduced through hypnotic methods, such as age regression, hallucinations, and anesthesia, are the results of subjects' thinking and imagination and their own motivation to achieve specific outcomes and effects. It is also worth noting an interesting fact concerning T. Barber. His colleague, Ernest Hilgard, once spread rumors about Theodore Barber's high hypnotizability. Perhaps he was battling against something he could not comprehend and accept within himself.

According to American professor of psychiatry Martin Orne, what happens to a person in hypnosis primarily depends on the influence of the situation and their expectations regarding the hypnotic process. Their notions about what can occur and what cannot. He discovered that in a genuine hypnotic state, a person can tolerate pain more easily than when it is simulated. Although Martin Orne's ideas regarding the division of hypnosis into genuine and simulated states are more akin to philosophical contemplations, in this case, for us, they merely serve as indications of the depth of trance and criteria for the patient's alignment with specific psychopathological profiles.

Let's draw an interesting analogy related to alcohol intoxication that sheds light on different aspects of understanding the term "simulation" in reproducing a hypnotic state. On many islands in Polynesia, alcohol was introduced for the first time by various colonizing countries, such as England and France. The indigenous people living on these islands tried alcohol, specifically from the hands of their invaders. A logical question arose: how would this previously unknown beverage affect people's behavior? The answer is quite simple. Their behavior would be modeled and imitated. On the islands where the invaders were English, who tended to behave more aggressively after consuming alcohol, the indigenous people also started to exhibit aggression after consuming it. However, on the islands colonized by the French, the example for the indigenous people differed significantly. Under the influence of alcohol, the French became more amorous. It was these reactions that their disciples later took advantage of, organizing drunken sexual orgies.

It is unlikely that the behavior of the indigenous people can be called a simulation. It is rather a reflection of the learning process. We believe that similar processes occur in working with hypnotic suggestion. If you have seen or have a rough idea of how people can or should behave during hypnosis, most likely these behavioral reactions will be triggered automatically when you are being hypnotized or when you believe that you are being hypnotized. And naturally, we are dealing with role-playing here. Despite this, some reactions in hypnosis may be influenced by our preconceived notions of it as a role function, while another part will inevitably have an inherent physiological basis. For example, the model of natural falling asleep. It does not require any learning whatsoever. If our consciousness does not know how to respond in a new and unconventional situation, the choice falls on one of the existing role models of behavior. This applies not only to hypnosis but also to any other role that is new to us.

American psychologist Nicholas Spanos (1942–1994) dedicated a significant amount of time to finding evidence that hypnosis is not an altered state of consciousness but rather an induced behavior. He believed that in hypnosis, "social constructions are created, controlled by rules of behavior, legitimized, and sustained through social interaction." Based on 250 studies, Spanos attempted to demonstrate that actions under hypnosis are heavily influenced by the context in which they take place and the meanings we attribute to that context. Spanos worked on his theories for over thirty years and claimed that most hypnotic phenomena can be explained through social psychology. Indeed, he made interesting findings in one experiment where he proved that people behave in hypnosis according to what they think is expected of them. Two groups were taken, one of which was given a lecture stating that during hypnosis, the hands should remain motionless. The other group did not receive this lecture. Both groups were then subjected to hypnosis. At the end of the experiment, observers noted that the group that received the lecture indeed had much less movement in their hands compared to the other group.

Spanos, to a large extent, attempted to redefine the hypnotic state and provide it with a different understanding, but he rather expanded our perceptions of hypnosis through his experiments. He passed away in 1994, at a time when doctors were just beginning to experiment with neurovisualization of the human brain during a hypnotic trance and unfortunately did not have the data on brain activity scanning that we have today. At one of the seminars, Jean Becker told us that since then, more than 100,000 publications on hypnosis using neurovisualization methods have appeared in the scientific literature (as of 2013). Based on such observations, we can assert that hypnosis is not simply induced behavior but a full-fledged altered state of consciousness, which can be observed as the activation of different brain regions that are not typically active in the ordinary state.

It is also worth noting that attempting to separate behavior and state is absurd since they are two complementary processes.

Theodore Sarbin and Emil Coué held very similar views, asserting that hypnosis is a form of role-playing and a variety of suggestibility. They commented that the hypnotized subject wants to please the hypnotist, which leads them to provide what the hypnotist wants to see. And, in our opinion, they are partially correct. More precisely, the desire to please can sometimes serve as an excellent platform for hypnotic suggestion and create deep trust in the hypnotist. However, it is evident that Sarbin and Coué have not encountered street fortune-tellers who make a living by using street hypnosis on passersby. It is unlikely that people who give money to a fortune teller want to please her.

A significant portion of criticism directed at hypnotic suggestion has helped uncover its hidden and intriguing characteristics. Therefore, any confrontation in an attempt to prove or refute something only enhances our understanding of the subject matter.

11

Hypnosis and Self-hypnosis in Oncology

American radiation oncologist Carl Simonton conducted interesting research on the use of self-hypnosis, self-suggestion, and visualization with a group of cancer patients. Together with his colleague Stephanie Matthews, he presented the results of their studies with terminally ill cancer patients who had less than a year to live. Out of 159 patients, 19% experienced complete healing, and the progression of the disease was significantly diminished in 22% of cases. Simonton provided his patients with the following technique: first, the patient would learn the technique of deep relaxation, and then, while in that state, they were to imagine their blood cells and immune system as fearless warriors, while envisioning cancer cells as cowardly, helpless creatures that the warriors could easily defeat. This would be followed by visualizing the destruction of cancer cells.

The findings of Carl Simonton are not conclusive, and it is difficult to attribute the complete remission in 19% of patients solely to visualization. However, his work, along with the research conducted by other investigators exploring this approach to combating cancer, may shed light on one of the possible ways of constructively influencing the disease.

One similar example is the case of an 11-year-old boy who was diagnosed with a cancerous tumor. Chemotherapy was not providing him with significant improvement, so he embarked on a visualization experiment similar to Simonton's approach. For several months, he began to imagine every day that his immune system and cancer cells were spaceships in outer space. He controlled his spaceships and shot down the cancer cell ships. As far as we remember, after six months of such visualization efforts, the cancer completely disappeared or significantly reduced in size.

We have heard similar examples of therapeutic visualizations from practitioners of Ericksonian hypnosis, who have reported solid results in accelerating bone healing after fractures using this technique in conjunction with visualization activation. However, no research has been conducted on this specific topic, so for now, we will classify this information as myths and legends.

Nevertheless, the concept of creating a visual metaphor to combat illness aligns with Ericksonian therapy, and techniques based on it can be used as adjunctive measures in psychotherapy and physiotherapy. In this context, conventional targeted visualization and the application of hypnotic suggestion can be suitable approaches.

12

Stage Hypnosis

"Animal magnetism is the most significant discovery ever made, even though it has generated more mysteries than answers."
  Arthur Schopenhauer, "Collected Works," Vol. IV

This form of hypnosis practice primarily aims to entertain and amuse the audience. The hypnotic phenomena recreated by stage hypnotists are very peculiar and, in our opinion, not environmentally friendly. Although this practice does not touch upon the moral aspect.

As some of Mesmer's students turned to patient therapy in clinics, others began to present various shows for audience entertainment. Some created a mix of therapy and showmanship. For example, stage hypnotists often brought their somnambulists to performances to demonstrate various hypnotic phenomena. Therefore, by the end of the 19th century, the role of the somnambulist was quite profitable.

In the history of hypnosis, there is a case described by Leopold Löwenfeld, a Munich historian of hypnosis and professor of psychiatry. It involves Madame Madeleine G. and the hypnotist Magin, who began their performances together in February 1904. Magin induced her into a hypnotic state of somnambulism and suggested her abilities in various forms of art, including playing the piano, singing, and dancing, in which she had no talents in her normal state.

Madeleine's performances exceeded all expectations of the audience. Her ability to pour her soul into singing and dancing mesmerized the spectators. Moreover, she awakened a strong dramatic talent that evoked intense emotions in the audience. Artists who observed Madeleine's performances found a new source of inspiration.

The creator of the term "hypnosis," James Braid, occasionally experimented with unique hypnosis techniques. When the singer Jenny Lind performed in Manchester, he invited her to participate in his hypnotic public demonstration, where he was supposed to work with an illiterate girl. She had good vocal abilities but no musical education whatsoever. J. Braid induced the girl into a somnambulistic state and asked the accompanying singer to perform a short yet complex vocal exercise. The hypnotized girl effortlessly replicated it upon J. Braid's command, something she couldn't do in her normal state of consciousness.

The remarkable ability to express emotions and play roles in a state of somnambulistic trance was also noted by another French mesmerist, Baron Du Potet Jean De Sennevoy. In 1849, he began discussing the metamorphoses of personality that occur during magnetization.

The biography of a 19th-century stage hypnotist named Lafontaine is intriguing. As we mentioned before, he was the teacher of James Braid. Lafontaine was born into an aristocratic family in France in 1803. In his youth, he aspired to become an actor and went to Paris in search of happiness. However, he gained fame not through the theatrical arts, although he later applied those skills to the process of hypnosis.

It is difficult to say for certain, but most likely Lafontaine became acquainted with animal magnetism directly from A. Mesmer and then began independent experiments in this art. At a certain point in his practice, he encountered a woman who easily entered a somnambulistic state under his magnetic influence, which led him to believe that he possessed immense magnetic power. As soon as Lafontaine began his magnetic performances, his family and friends turned away from him, and he became an outcast. He decided to devote himself entirely to the art of magnetism. He held numerous public demonstrations where he magnetized various individuals. Some of his performances ended in mass disturbances, requiring police intervention. Of course, this only increased his fame. It is known that his popularity was so immense that he fearlessly entered the dirtiest taverns in London, where he was recognized and left unharmed by the bandits who were afraid of him. There are also legends that wherever he went, the blind gained sight, the mute began to speak, and the paralyzed started to walk. These abilities are undoubtedly remarkable, but it is important to remember that we are dealing with rumors circulating among the people, not clinically documented facts. However, it is quite possible that many things that reach us through historical accounts could be true.

The newspaper "Manchester Guardian" described one of Lafontaine's sessions on its pages. During a group demonstration, Sir G. P. Linnell, one of the directors of the Athenaeum Company and a well-known and respected figure in the city, volunteered for the session. He was known to be educated, intellectual, and truthful. Before the performance, Sir Linnell did not believe in the power of magnetic suggestion. Approximately 10 minutes into Lafontaine's work, some of his techniques did not work on Linnell initially. However, Lafontaine intentionally induced drowsiness and then complete catalepsy of the entire body by closing his eyes. The newspaper reported that G. P. Linnell was fully magnetized, feeling no pain from needle pricks, showing no reaction to gunshots fired near his ear, and remaining unresponsive to smelling salts held to his nose. When he woke up, he described his sensations: "I felt tingling all over my body and limbs, and then drowsiness. It was as if my body were submerged in the sea. I seemed dead to my surroundings but remained aware that something was happening nearby."

What was known in Europe as magnetism thanks to the work of A. Mesmer and as hypnosis due to J. Braid, in America at the end of the 19th and early 20th centuries, became known as "electrobiology." In the book "The Philosophy of Electrobiology" by J. B. Dodds, which consisted of 12 lectures he delivered before the U.S. Congress, the fundamental postulates of this science were described. One of the European doctors who immigrated to the United States, Joseph Pierre Durand (1826–1901), convinced of the importance of this science, returned to France, where he adopted the pseudonym Dr. Philips and began conducting electrobiological experiments with the public in public halls. Philips' experiments began in Brussels in 1853. During one presentation, Philips handed out zinc metal circles with a different colored metal in the center to 18 volunteers. He then asked everyone to stare at the center of the disk for 20 minutes without looking away. At the end of this period, Philips approached each volunteer and touched their heads. Half of them entered a hypnotic state. The rest were asked to return to the hall and sit down. From the remaining volunteers, he chose one man and began the hypnotic work with him. First, he suggested that the man couldn't open his eyes; then he gave him a stone and suggested that it was hot; and later, he suggested that he forget his name and individual letters of the alphabet. The subject responded to all of Philips' suggestions in complete accordance. Next, Philips induced paralysis in specific body parts that the subject could not stop voluntarily.

The newspaper "Revue de Geneve" on October 29, 1853, made the following comments about Philips' performances: "Under suggestion, a stick was mistaken for a snake, a handkerchief transformed into a crow, the audience hall turned into a landscape, and ordinary water was perceived as wine, causing intoxication. Various forms of aphonia, lameness, and paralysis were also induced."

Sigmund Freud described his introduction to hypnosis during his student years when he participated in a public performance by stage hypnotist Dan Carl Hansen (1833-1897). Freud observed D. N. Hansen reproducing various hypnotic phenomena on the audience participating in the hypnotic session.

In the early years of his life, D. N. Hansen was a simple wholesale merchant, but his passion for magnetism completely consumed him, leading him to leave his previous business and dedicate himself entirely to magnetic work. He became such a skilled magnetizer that the public bestowed upon him the title of "the priest of hypnosis." Like his colleagues Donato and Lafontaine, D. N. Hansen most often induced a hypnotic state by using a shiny object that completely captivated the attention of the person looking at it. Then he would place his hand on the forehead of the hypnotized individual and give various suggestions that were immediately carried out. He urged the audience under hypnosis to do the strangest things: eating potatoes while perceiving the taste of a pear, riding furniture around the room, shaving with wooden chips, and so on.

Neuropathologist and historian of hypnosis Wilhelm Wilhelmovich Bittner writes the following about D. N. Hansen: "We mainly owe the attention of the entire scientific world to hypnosis to Hansen's performances, which enjoyed great success with the public."

Impressive stories also revolve around the Belgian magnetizer, former poet and journalist Donato (A.E. d'Hont, 1845–1901), who repeatedly delivered lectures on the therapeutic benefits of magnetism without assuming a pretentious healer status.

On March 21, 1885, the newspaper "La Meuse" published an announcement in the city of Liege that Donato planned to magnetize a multitude of people. To achieve this, they were required to come to his house on Rue Pont-d'Île at the designated time.

Essentially, Donato created something akin to a modern-day flash mob. At the appointed time, over 5,000 people gathered in front of Donato's house and along Pont-d'Île street. Unexpectedly, several individuals magnetized by him started running through the crowd. Among them were a violinist, a barber, a butcher, and other individuals. The crowd witnessed more than 30 magnetized individuals.

Subsequently, reporters in the newspaper wrote that even the most skeptical people regarding magnetism would be convinced of its power and that the experience Donato provided and the spectacle witnessed by all would go down in history. Another newspaper, "Journal de Liege," reported on March 23 that Donato had planned a magnetic performance on the city streets.

At precisely 2 o'clock, around 15 young people who had previously been magnetized by Donato would go to the newspaper vendor D'Eru on Rue Pont-d'Île, take some newspapers, pretend they were sheet music, and then proceed to St. Paul's Square, humming and dancing along the way. A crowd of observers and policemen stood along all the streets indicated on the route.

At the appointed time, the magnetized subjects rushed through the crowd, knocking people over in the process. They often faced retaliation from the crowd. People who observed the "magnetic" runners commented that they exhibited a wandering gaze and a blank expression on their faces. They reached their destination, took the magazines, and continued to the square, humming and dancing. Some of the magnetized individuals particularly demonstratively acted upon Donato's suggestions, making them undoubtedly appear insane.

Everything came to a halt only when Donato gave the corresponding suggestions to all the magnetized individuals. In total, Donato hypnotized over 300 people in Liege. Articles about the events appeared in numerous Belgian newspapers and magazines, including "Eclair," "Wallon," "Foyer," "Justice," and many others.

In this case, we witness magnificent abilities for mass immersion into a hypnotic state. This is no longer a simple hypnotic state where hand catalepsy is induced; instead, it involves madness on the streets with hundreds of people.

Also worth considering for our examination are the hypnotic experiments of Monsieur Charles Richet. In his work with his 43-year-old patient, Annette, he sequentially induced her into various dissociative states of personality. He transformed her into a little girl, a man, an old woman, and other personalities.

As a little girl, she babbled and asked for sweets and doll play. In the male persona, her behavior became more masculine, and in the role of an old woman, she had difficulty hearing others and asked for snuff tobacco. Each personality that the patient assumed under the influence of hypnosis manifested vividly, demonstratively, and impressively, as if she had always been precisely the personality just suggested to her.

It is worth noting that the overwhelming majority of mesmerists in the 19th century performed with their somnambulists, with whom they worked in pairs. However, this rule did not apply to Donato and D.N. Hansen; they did not hesitate to work with various individuals from the audience.

In our experience working with hypnosis and a large number of students, we have found that only a few of them, who could easily enter a deep somnambulistic state, could be fully utilized for vivid stage demonstrations. They could resemble the masters of the hypnotic stage. We have mentioned some experiments with somnambulistic patients in our work. Let's provide another example in which we intentionally tried to reproduce a stage approach to hypnosis.

In one of the hypnotic laboratory sessions conducted with our students in an office space, we selected a young woman who had previously demonstrated her ability to enter a somnambulistic state on multiple occasions. Using a sharp directive hypnosis technique, we induced her into a hypnotic state and gradually deepened it to the maximum level achievable. We suggested to her that she transition into an alternate personality named Elvira Edelweiss.

Within the suggestion, we created the illusion that she was not in an office center but rather in a hotel where she had recently arrived. We instructed her to descend from the 10th floor to the first floor and demand the keys to her room. Without hesitation, she opened her eyes and immediately acted on the command. She disregarded the words of those around her and failed to recognize anyone. The facilitator and the group of students followed her down to the first floor to witness her interaction with the concierge stationed at the entrance.

Approaching the concierge, she demanded the keys as instructed. Initially perplexed, he eventually handed her the spare key to the office space. At that moment, the facilitator approached the hypnotized young woman, placed his hand on her forehead, and induced her into an unconscious state once again using sharp directive commands. This time, the suggestion was not for a specific personality but rather for a specific action. She was prompted to open her eyes and see the concierge, a sixty-year-old Georgian man, in front of her, instantly falling in love with him and desiring his phone number.

Following the command, she began to execute the suggestion, and within a few minutes, she held his phone number in her hand, displaying remarkably realistic flirting behavior. It is noteworthy that she convincingly engaged in the role. After this role was completed, the facilitator approached her again, guided her back into an unconscious state, and proposed a third role in which she would assume the identity of a fifty-year-old woman who had worked as a concierge at the building's entrance for over a decade.

Upon emerging from the hypnotic state, she opened her eyes and positioned herself behind the desk, where the familiar concierge was already seated. When members of the hypnotic group attempted to interact with her, she failed to comprehend their intentions or the reason for their presence. We observed distinct changes in her verbal and non-verbal communication patterns during this period. Eventually, the facilitator issued commands for her to exit the hypnotic state, remember all that had transpired, and find amusement in her actions. True to form, she flawlessly performed every aspect of the suggestions, just as she had done previously.

When we asked her in the group about what she remembered and why she followed certain commands, she replied that she was completely absorbed in the suggested role and acted as if in a dream.

This is a basic example from our practice that many group participants captured on video and still keep to this day. When we show this kind of video to other people, we often receive feedback that they feel like the girl is simply playing a role like an actor. And in many ways, they are right; it is indeed playing a role, but from a deep hypnotic state that accounts for the majority of behavioral reactions.

If we attempted similar things with people who had not previously demonstrated their ability to enter a somnambulistic trance, we would often not achieve the desired effect. And here we can fully understand the mesmerists of the old school who took their somnambulists for public performances.

13

Archetypal Sound Rhythms of Ancient Shamans and Protogypnosis

Based on our knowledge from anthropology, it is highly likely that ancient Cro-Magnon shamans employed techniques akin to hypnosis in rituals for healing the sick and severely wounded. We are confident that these early techniques relied predominantly on chanting and dancing rituals performed by the shaman in proximity to the afflicted individual.

We strongly doubt that ancient shamans utilized any verbal techniques that are characteristic of modern hypnosis. Furthermore, we argue that shamanic hypnotism yielded fruitful results in the healing of various ailments and the alleviation of pain from wounds. If a shaman had not been capable of demonstrating their healing power, it is highly unlikely that they would have been respected and their services regularly sought.

Some researchers may suggest that ancient shamans employed archaic forms of hypnosis. However, in our opinion, it is not entirely accurate to consider the process of entering an altered state through the listening of a shaman's chant as hypnosis. Moreover, the ingestion of narcotic substances should not be attributed to the process of hypnotization.

In our work, we will consider ancient archaic techniques of altering states of consciousness as protogypnotic, preceding the majority of other trance techniques that would be developed later on.

276

Shamans in Australia had similar rituals and ceremonies. They were capable of inducing altered states of consciousness within themselves and then transmitting them to the hunters of their tribe. A case is described in which a shaman, using a similar method, removed the speech paralysis from a woman named Totmittu and restored her ability to stand and walk. These psychosomatic symptoms manifested in the Aboriginal woman following the recent death of her husband. Similar rituals are described by M. Eliade, Basilov, and other researchers among the Chukchi, Buryats, Tungus, Kalmyks, and others. Protohypnotic techniques can vary significantly depending on the ethnic group and possess their own mythological foundations, but the essence of the process of inducing altered states of consciousness to address various issues remains unchanged.

Legends exist about a ritual conducted by priests in ancient Greece at the Asclepieion, near the ancient Greek city of Epidaurus. During this ritual, the priest employed a form of verbal suggestion, providing patients with verbal messages that instilled confidence in the healing powers of Asclepius. The patients were then sent to a chamber, where they experienced a "sacred sleep." After the ritual, the patients would recount their dreams to the priest. The dreams were subsequently interpreted, and based on their meaning, appropriate healing procedures were prescribed. If healing occurred, it was attributed to the manifestation of Asclepius' magical power.

Formally, shamanic chanting can be considered the utterance of prolonged sounds in a melodic manner, representing the earliest known form of inducing trance states. The sounds and their combinations do not have a literal meaning; they simply serve as conduits for altered states of consciousness. The range of sounds can be highly diverse, including Siberian throat singing, which produces vibrating sounds, and the chants of North American shamans with their variations of "heya," "haya," "hey," "hi," "ho," and others. In essence, the two key ingredients of shamanic chanting are vocal vibration and vowel sounds such as "a," "o," "u," and "i."

The vocal vibrations produced by our vocal cords depend on muscle tension throughout the body, resulting in a wide range of voice pitch, from a slow, vibrating tone to a high falsetto. We can identify four body levels at which we can emit vocal vibration:

1. **Abdominal level**: The voice is very low, deep, and vibrating, representing one of the most shamanic and hypnotic voices. If this voice is capable of sustaining the singing of any vowel sound, sooner or later we can achieve a trance effect.

2. **Chest level**: The voice is sufficiently low, deep, and vibrating, but to a lesser extent than the voice emitted at the abdominal level. Speech can be faster than at the previous level. Similar to the abdominal voice, the chest voice is suitable for shamanic chanting.

3. **Throat level**: At this level, the voice is relatively resonant and high-pitched. It is more suitable for public speaking or casual conversation than shamanic singing. However, some hypnotists have successfully induced hypnosis using this level of vocal intensity. The effectiveness of hypnotic suggestion at this level is often related to the semantics of speech.

4. **Nasal level**: In this case, the voice is high-pitched, often monotonous, and lifeless. Such a voice is commonly found in individuals with a schizoid psychopathological profile and is directly related to strong tension in almost all muscles of the body. It is difficult to imagine that such a voice could be hypnotic, but despite this, we have come across video recordings of old Soviet psychiatrists who could effectively hypnotize their patients using a monotonous, high-pitched, and droning voice.

It can be generalized that the lower and deeper the voice sounds, the more relaxed the body of the person producing it becomes. Stephen Gilligan gave a beautiful metaphor related to the depth of the voice during a seminar, stating that a man becomes a man and a woman becomes a woman when they are able to relax the muscles of the pelvis and produce sound from there. Stephen is right, as we intuitively perceive a deeper and lower voice as the voice of a more mature and grown individual. On the other hand, a squeaky falsetto is often associated with infantillism and immaturity.

In the hypnosis laboratory, we have repeatedly attempted to recreate the prototypical hypnotic phenomenon that arises from listening to shamanic chanting. To achieve this, we provided students with several basic physical and vocal exercises that relaxed the muscle corset and deepened the voice. Here are some of the exercises that can be effectively used to "open up" the voice. After completing the exercises, you can note the qualitative changes associated with their performance. Before starting the exercises, try to utter a hypnotic phrase several times in the deepest and lowest voice you are capable of. Then proceed with the exercises.

Exercises to open up the voice:

1. **Fold Exercise**: Stand with your legs shoulder-width apart. Place your hands on your calf muscles and slowly and gradually pull your torso towards your legs. While remaining in the same position, the participant should sharply and explosively shout the sound "ha" 3–4 times.

2. **Backbend Exercise**: Place your hands on your hips, then arch your body as far back as possible. The participant shouts the sound "ha" 3–4 times.

3. **Twist Exercise**: Place your hands on your hips. First, rotate your body as far as possible to the right and shout the sound "ha" 3–4 times. Then, repeat the same movement to the left.

4. **Side Bend Exercise**: Place your hands on your hips. First, tilt your body as far as possible to the right and shout the sound "ha" 3–4 times. Then, repeat the same movement to the left.

5. **Forward Arm Thrust**: Stand with your legs wider than shoulder-width apart. Clench your fists and position them at your sides, with your elbows behind you. Then, explosively thrust your arms forward with a sharp "ha" sound. Your palms should open as you do this. Repeat this movement and sound 2-3 more times.

After performing these exercises, try uttering a hypnotic phrase several times with the deepest and lowest voice you are capable of.

Afterward, you can attempt an exercise that simulates the trance effect of shamanic chanting.

Exercise "Prototrance and Chanting"

1. Pair work.
2. One participant sits comfortably and closes their eyes.
3. The other participant begins to pronounce the vowels "a," "o," "u," "e" consecutively and then randomly over the next 5 minutes, aiming to create a coherent stream of vibrating and low-pitched voice.
4. After the time elapses, the partners provide feedback to each other regarding the states that emerged during the exercise. Both participants share their impressions.
5. Then, the pair switches roles and performs the exercise in reverse.

The use of an effect resembling shamanic chanting has been observed in some hypnotic inductions by Stephen Gilligan, where he would emit a slightly hissing sound that closely resembled the sound of the wind. The sound was produced both on inhale and exhale, creating a continuous effect. This trance technique can significantly deepen the trance state and expand its dimensionality.

Similarly, we started incorporating a vibrating vowel into the hypnotic induction, adding the effect of shamanic chanting to it.

Before Stephen Gilligan began emitting the sound of the wind during the trance induction, he framed his action by mentioning the blowing wind. Similarly, when using shamanic chanting, it is advisable to proceed in a similar manner. For example, creating a motif of trance in which the patient visits a shaman in the forest who starts chanting, thereby healing the patient.

To understand the peculiarities of the rhythm of shamanic singing and chanting, we highly recommend listening to recordings or, if possible, witnessing and hearing the chanting of a shaman live. This will provide a certain reference point that will enable you to recreate the trance chanting more skillfully and accurately.

14

Neurotransmitters and Hypnotic Suggestion

During the process of hypnotic suggestion, the neurochemical component of the brain undergoes changes that have gradually unfolded for modern hypnosis researchers only in the last few decades. Even before the early 1990s, some scientists attempted to attribute the process of hypnotic suggestion solely to social factors, considering hypnosis a form of "playing along." However, they did not consider the possibility of specific neurochemical changes in the brain that may occur during hypnotic phenomena.

Nowadays, it can be confidently stated that hypnotic trance work is capable of profoundly altering the brain's chemistry and shifting the activity of various regions. Therefore, the pivotal factor that effectively determines the alteration of consciousness states at the physiological level is the neurotransmitters—chemical substances actively involved in the transmission of information from neuron to neuron in the brain.

Neurotransmitters: What Are They?

No matter what our brain is engaged in, whether it's working on a scientific problem, trying to memorize a phone number, or gazing at a pastry display while choosing a dessert, the fundamental process underlying it all is the timely release of neurotransmitters in the synapses between neurons and their binding to the corresponding receptors of other neurons. We cannot even embrace someone without one biomolecule in our brain connecting to another, fitting perfectly like puzzle pieces.

A "neurotransmitter" is the mediator between neurons. It is a biologically active chemical substance through which the transmission of electrochemical impulses from one nerve cell to another takes place, which is why it is also referred to as a "neurotransmitter."

Every millisecond in the human brain, a remarkable chain of events unfolds: billions of neurons send messages to each other through trillions of connections called synapses.

Each synapse consists of the terminals of two neurons separated by a microscopic synaptic gap, measured in nanometers, which is one billionth of a meter.

When a neuron receives new information, it generates an electrical impulse that triggers the release of a neurotransmitter from a specialized vesicle called a synaptic vesicle. The neurotransmitter molecule then crosses the synaptic gap and binds to a specific receptor molecule on the end of the second neuron.

For each specific neurotransmitter, there is its own unique receptor that perfectly matches it in shape, as if it were a key fitting into a lock. The signal is transmitted through the network of neurons in the brain as well as from neurons to muscle tissue or glandular cells, initiating the movement of body parts or a specific stage in the functioning of an organ.

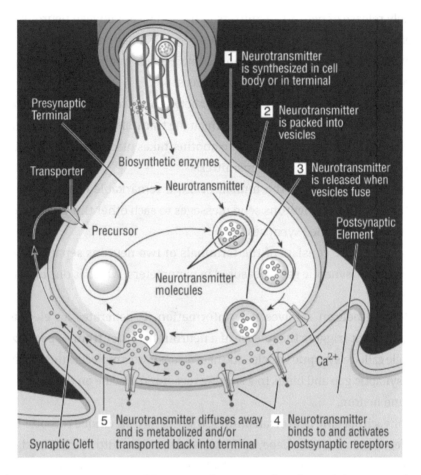

These processes occur with tremendous speed and precision, ensuring all brain functions, and any disruption in this finely tuned system leads to neurological and mental disorders, including autism, schizophrenia, Alzheimer's disease, and epilepsy.

Even a condition such as botulism (severe food poisoning) is related to a problem in signal transmission at the synapse. It is known that botulinum toxin attacks proteins that play a crucial role in the release of neurotransmitters, leading to muscle paralysis.

The function of synapses and the balance of neurotransmitters are extremely important for neurological and mental health and are areas of intense study by microbiologists, biochemists, and pharmacologists.

It is the balance of neurotransmitters in the human brain that determines an individual's ability to enter a hypnotic state and experience various specific effects during its occurrence. It is also worth noting that the act of entering a trance state itself may serve a balancing neurochemical function for the brain.

Several medications are aimed at correcting the imbalance of neurotransmitters in the brain in cases of mental disorders. For example, selective serotonin reuptake inhibitors (SSRIs) are commonly used in the treatment of depression. These medications block the reuptake of serotonin by the releasing neuron, thereby increasing its concentration in the synaptic gap and making it more available to the receiving neuron.

To date, about fifty neurotransmitters have been discovered. In our work, we will explore some of them, focusing on those that are more relevant to the processes occurring in human consciousness during hypnotic states.

Serotonin

This neurotransmitter helps regulate mood, appetite, pain, and sleep. Research shows that serotonin levels are reduced in depression, which is why pharmaceutical companies develop drugs aimed at increasing them.

An astonishing fact: 90% of serotonin is found in the gastrointestinal tract, and only 10% in the brain. Serotonin is involved in physiological processes such as digestion and blood clot formation. It belongs to the inhibitory, or calming, neurotransmitters, so a deficiency can lead to increased excitability and anxiety.

We are accustomed to hearing about it as the "happiness hormone," but serotonin is not a hormone, and its relationship to "happiness" is not as straightforward. Serotonin is a neurotransmitter that not only brings positive emotions but also reduces susceptibility to negative ones. It provides support for "adjacent" neurotransmitters such as norepinephrine and dopamine. Serotonin is involved in motor activity, reduces overall pain perception, and assists the body in fighting inflammation. Additionally, serotonin enhances the accuracy of active signal transmission in the brain and aids in concentration.

An excess of serotonin (e.g., with LSD use) amplifies the "volume" of secondary signals in the brain, leading to hallucinations. Serotonin deficiency and an imbalance between positive and negative emotions are the primary causes of depression.

The 5-HTTLPR gene encodes the serotonin transporter protein. The gene sequence contains a region of repeats, the number of which can vary. The longer the chain, the easier it is for a person to maintain a positive mood and switch from negative emotions. The shorter the chain, the higher the likelihood that negative experiences will be traumatic. The number of repeats is also associated with sudden infant death syndrome, aggressive behavior in Alzheimer's disease development, and susceptibility to depression.

During the hypnotic trance state, when a person's brain begins to produce theta waves, serotonin levels increase rapidly. This can lead to processes of decision-making and a sense of completion in consciousness.

Gamma-Aminobutyric Acid (GABA)

Another inhibitory neurotransmitter is GABA. Its release promotes re-laxation. Caffeine is a stimulant precisely because it suppresses GABA release, while many sedative medications, sleep aids, and tranquilizers act by facilitating the release of this neurotransmitter.

GABA plays an important role in vision and motor control. There are medications that work to increase GABA levels in the brain, assisting in seizures (epilepsy) and tremors (Huntington's disease).

GABA also regulates other neurotransmitters such as norepinephrine, dopamine, and serotonin.

A decrease in the normal level of GABA can lead to anxiety, impulsivity, an inability to cope with stress, restlessness, and irritability.

Even a single trance session lasting 15–25 minutes can significantly increase the synthesis of GABA neurotransmitters in the brain. This effect is particularly evident and pronounced when working with alcoholics using hypnotic suggestion. We have found that sometimes just one hypnosis session per week for several months can be sufficient to reduce alcohol intake by more than half. It is worth noting that the consumption of small amounts of alcohol stimulates the synthesis of the dopamine neurotransmitter in the brain. However, as the dosage begins to increase significantly, the GABA neurotransmitter comes into play in addition to dopamine. It is the sudden withdrawal from high doses of alcohol that can lead to delirium tremens, a severe withdrawal syndrome during which alcoholics may experience various hallucinations associated with the abrupt decrease in inhibitory GABA neurotransmitter synthesis.

Dopamine

This neurotransmitter performs a number of important roles in the brain, depending on its location. In the frontal cortex, dopamine controls the flow of information to other brain areas. It is also involved in functions such as attention, memory, problem-solving, and movement.

However, its most well-known role is as a pleasure mediator. When you take a bite of chocolate, dopamine is released in a specific area of your brain, motivating you to take another bite. Dopamine plays a crucial role in the development of addictions (alcohol, drugs, and gambling addiction). Addictions often arise when dopamine levels are lowered.

Reduced dopamine levels are common and manifest as decreased motivation, an impaired ability to concentrate on tasks, and difficulty retaining information.

Impairment in dopamine production can also lead to Parkinson's disease, which is characterized by a decrease in voluntary movement, tremors, muscle stiffness, and other symptoms.

On the other hand, a high level of this neurotransmitter, known as "dopamine storm," can lead to hallucinations, excitement, mania, and psychosis. Such cases require immediate medical intervention.

By activating neurons in different brain regions, dopamine plays multiple roles. Firstly, it is responsible for motor activity and provides a sense of joy in movement. Secondly, it evokes a sense of childlike wonder and the drive to explore something new. Thirdly, dopamine performs an important function in reward and reinforcement of motivation. Whenever we do something beneficial for human life, neurons reward us with a feeling of satisfaction (sometimes called pleasure). At a basic level, we are rewarded for simple human pleasures like food and sex, but overall, the ways to achieve satisfaction depend on individual preferences.

The reward system is connected to learning; as a person experiences pleasure, new cause-and-effect associations are formed in their brain. And then, when the pleasure fades and the question of how to experience it again arises, the solution is simple: do more.

Dopamine appears to be an excellent stimulant for work and study, as well as an ideal drug; most drugs (such as amphetamines and cocaine) are associated with the action of dopamine. However, there are serious side effects. "Overdosing" on dopamine can lead to schizophrenia (the brain becomes so hyperactive that it manifests as auditory and visual hallucinations), while a deficiency can result in depressive disorder or the development of Parkinson's disease.

Dopamine has five receptors, numbered from D1 to D5. The fourth receptor is responsible for novelty-seeking. It is encoded by the DRD4 gene, and the length of this gene determines the intensity of dopamine perception. The fewer repetitions, the easier it is for a person to reach the peak of pleasure. Such individuals are likely to be satisfied with a delicious dinner and a good movie.

The more repetitions there are—up to ten—the harder it is to experience pleasure. These individuals have to make an effort to obtain rewards: embark on a round-the-world trip, conquer a mountain peak, perform a motorcycle stunt, or bet their entire fortune on red in Las Vegas. This genotype is associated with the long-distance migration of ancient people from Africa to Eurasia. Unfortunately, there is also a sad statistic: the "unsatisfactory" variant of DRD4 is more common among prisoners convicted of serious crimes.

Transwork for a certain period of time increases dopamine synthesis in the

288

brain, and we hypothesize that during this process, the brain learns to bring dopamine to a more comfortable state for the individual. As a result, after a certain number of trance sessions, consciousness begins to independently produce trance states to slightly increase dopamine levels and balance the overall neurotransmitter background. At least, this is a phenomenon that we have observed repeatedly in some of our patients.

Acetylcholine (ACh)

This neurotransmitter plays a leading role in memory formation, verbal and logical thinking, and attentional concentration. ACh is also involved in synaptogenesis, the production of new healthy synapses in the brain. Acetylcholine itself is formed from a substance called choline, which is found in eggs, seafood, and nuts.

ACh plays a crucial role in movement. When it is released into the synaptic cleft between the muscle fiber and nerve cell, a series of mechanical and chemical reactions occur, leading to muscle contraction. When the level of ACh decreases, the reaction ceases, and the muscle relaxes.

Acetylcholine also carries out its activity in the autonomic parasympathetic nervous system, whose activity slows down heart function, improves digestive tract function, and is associated with erectile function in males.

In our opinion, it is precisely the neurotransmitter acetylcholine that is directly related to the skills of psychophysiological self-regulation, which can be acquired through the practice of ancient or modern methods of altering consciousness, such as yoga, meditation, or modern hypnotic induction.

Noradrenaline (Norepinephrine)

This is another excitatory neurotransmitter that helps activate the sympathetic nervous system, which is responsible for the "fight or flight" response to external stressors. Norepinephrine is important for attentional concentration, emotions, sleep, dreaming, and learning. When norepinephrine enters the bloodstream, it accelerates heart rhythm, releases glucose, and increases blood flow to the muscles.

A decrease in the normal level of this neurotransmitter leads to chronic fatigue, inattention, and weight problems. An increase in its level results in sleep problems, anxiety, and ADHD.

The autonomic sympathetic nervous system functions thanks to norepinephrine, which is associated with increased heart rate, slowed digestive tract function, and orgasm. This nervous system mobilizes the body's resources to solve tasks. The inability of the body to slow down its activity leads to a slowdown in the process of mental and physical recovery, thus predisposing to the development of various diseases.

Norepinephrine is a neurotransmitter associated with wakefulness and quick decision-making. It is activated during stress and in extreme situations, participating in the "fight or flight" response. Norepinephrine triggers an influx of energy, reduces the sense of fear, and increases the level of aggression. At the somatic level, under the influence of norepinephrine, the heart rate increases and blood pressure rises.

Norepinephrine is a beloved mediator among surfers, snowboarders, motorcyclists, and other enthusiasts of extreme sports, as well as their colleagues in casinos and gaming clubs. The brain does not distinguish between real and imagined events, so the risk of losing one's fortune in a card game is enough to activate norepinephrine.

A high level of norepinephrine leads to decreased vision and analytical abilities, while a deficiency results in boredom and apathy.

The SLC6A2 gene codes for the norepinephrine transporter protein. It facilitates the reuptake of norepinephrine into the presynaptic membrane. The duration of norepinephrine's action in the human body after successfully dealing with a dangerous situation depends on its function. Mutations in this gene can cause attention deficit hyperactivity disorder (ADHD).

Hypnotic trance at a natural level slows down the activity of the sympathetic nervous system and reduces the synthesis of the neurotransmitter norepinephrine, which greatly predisposes to the activation of natural processes of consciousness and body restoration.

Glutamate

This is one of the main excitatory neurotransmitters. Its release enhances the flow of electricity between neurons, which is necessary for the normal functioning of neural networks. Glutamate plays a crucial role in early brain development, as well as in memory and learning.

A deficiency in glutamate production leads to chronic fatigue and low brain activity. An elevated level of glutamate leads to the death of nerve cells. Imbalances in glutamate are associated with many neurodegenerative diseases, such as Alzheimer's disease, Parkinson's disease, Huntington's disease, and Tourette's syndrome.

Milton Erickson defined the state of trance as a process of effective learning. In a trance state, a person assimilates information much better and more deeply. In our opinion, this has a direct relationship to the increased synthesis of the neurotransmitter glutamate in the human brain during the process of hypnotic induction.

How Neurotransmitters Work

Nerve cells communicate with each other through their extensions, called axons and dendrites. There is a gap between them, called the synaptic cleft. It is in this space that the interaction between neurons takes place.

Neurotransmitters are synthesized within the cell and delivered to the end of the axon, at the presynaptic membrane. There, under the influence of electrical impulses, they enter the synaptic cleft and activate the receptors of the next neuron. After receptor activation, the neurotransmitter either returns back into the cell (a process called reuptake) or gets degraded.

Neurotransmitters themselves are not proteins, so there is no "dopamine gene" or "adrenaline gene." Proteins perform all the auxiliary work: enzyme proteins synthesize the neurotransmitter substance, transporter proteins are responsible for delivery, and receptor proteins activate the nerve cell. The proper functioning of a single neurotransmitter can depend on several proteins and, therefore, several different genes.

15

Afterword

In this work, I focused attention on the examination of personality profiling, hypnotic phenomena, psychogeography, the structure of hypnotic language, and many others. Our main goal was to provide readers with the most realistic understanding and representation of what hypnosis and trance are. What can be achieved with their help? What are the practical areas of their application? What are the sources of their formation, and how has hypnosis developed in different fields? Which notable figures in the history of science and art have influenced their development and establishment?

Part of the book discusses applied techniques for learning hypnotic suggestion, which can be used for its study. In our work, we have endeavored to present the maximum number of real examples of the application of hypnotic suggestion in educational and psychotherapeutic practice, accumulated over more than 10 years of work.

In the next volume of our publication on hypnotherapy, we intend to delve into numerous new topics in the realm of hypnotic suggestion. For example, we will explore the pathopsychological profile of a hypnotherapist and uncover potential and existing possibilities in various fields such as medicine, business, and everyday communication.

16

Bibliography

1. Nevsky, M.P. The Influence of Unconditioned Stimuli on Brain Electrical Activity in Hypnosis with the Suggestion of Insensitivity to Them. Neuropathology and Psychiatry (Collection of scientific works of the regional psychoneurological hospital and Chelyabinsk branch of the All-Union Scientific Society of Neuropathologists and Psychiatrists). Chelyabinsk, 1960. pp. 271-281.
2. Nevsky, M.P. The Influence of Conditioned (Verbal) Stimuli on Brain Electrical Activity in Hypnosis. Neuropathology and Psychiatry (Collection of scientific works of the regional psychoneurological hospital and Chelyabinsk branch of the All-Union Scientific Society of Neuropathologists and Psychiatrists). Chelyabinsk, 1960. pp. 263-269.
3. Platonov, K.I. Issues of Psychotherapy in Obstetrics. Kharkov, 1940.
4. Platonov, K.I. Psychotherapy. Kharkov: UPNI, 1930.
5. Platonov, K.I. Word as a Physiological and Therapeutic Factor. Second Edition. Moscow: Medgiz, 1957; Third Edition, 1961.
6. Platonov, K.I. On the Formation of the Combinative-Motor Reflex in Humans to Joint Sound and Light Stimuli: Dissertation for the Degree of Doctor of Medicine. Imperial Military Medical Academy, St. Petersburg. Typ. of the Main Directorate of Edicts, 1912.
7. Praykin, V. Healing with Words. Trud, 1985, 14-09, 3.

8. Preisman, A.B. Hypnosis in the Practice of a Gynecologist. Ural Medical Journal, 1930, No. 1, pp. 52-54.

9. Raikov, V.L. The Influence of Deep Hypnosis on Reserve Memory Capabilities and Registration of the Hypnotic State Level Using EEG. Psychological Research in the Practice of a Medical Expert: Collection of Scientific Papers of the TSEITIN MSO RSFSR. Moscow, 1969. pp. 128-136.

10. Raikov, V.L. Study of the Somnambulistic Stage of Hypnosis with the Phenomenon of Induced Role During the Active Activity of the Hypnotized Subject. Therapy of Mental Disorders. Moscow: Medgiz, 1968. pp. 463-469.

11. Raikov, V.L. On the Possibility of Improving Memory in Hypnosis. New Research in Psychology. Moscow, 1976, No. 1 (14), pp. 15-18.

12. Raikov, V.L. On the Development of Abilities for Visual Creativity Using Hypnosis. Scientific Notes of Moscow State Pedagogical Institute named after V.I. Lenin. Moscow, 1969, No. 331. Psychological Problems of Youth. pp. 140-142.

13. Raikov, V.L. Experience of Treating Neurosis of Obsessive States by Modifying the Higher School of AT according to Schultz with the Use of Hypnosis in the Conditions of a Psychoneurological Dispensary. Therapy of Mental Disorders. Moscow: Medgiz, 1968. pp. 392-398.

14. Raikov, V.L., Adamenko, V.G. On the Objective Study of the Hypnotic State. Therapy of Mental Disorders. Moscow: Medgiz, 1968. pp. 457-463.

15. Rozhnov, V.E., Rozhnova, M. Hypnosis from Antiquity to the Present Day. Moscow: Sovetskaya Rossiya, 1987. 304 p.

16. Rozenbach, P. Hypnotism. Brockhaus and Efron Encyclopedic Dictionary: in 86 volumes. St. Petersburg, 1893. Vol. VIIIa. pp. 726-734.

17. Rout, B. The Language of Hypnosis. Moscow: Eksmo, 2002. 320 p.

18. Sas, Yu.V. Application of Suggestion in Obstetrics and Gynecology. Questions of Psychotherapy (Abstracts of Reports at the All-Union Conference on Psychotherapy, Moscow, June 27-30, 1966). Moscow, 1966. p. 166.

19. Safin, V.F. Experimental Study of Suggestibility. Scientific Notes of Moscow State Pedagogical Institute named after V.I. Lenin. Moscow, 1969, No. 331. Psychological Problems of Youth. pp. 62-67.

20. Teaching Seminar with Milton H. Erickson, M.D. Edited and Commented by Jeffrey K. Zeig; Translated by T.K. Kruglova. Moscow: Klass, 2003.

21. Sukhorukov, V.I. Treatment of Hypochondriacal States of Neurotic Origin with Complex Psychotherapeutic Massage in Hypnosis.

22. Questions of Psychiatry and Psychotherapy. Tambov, 1977. pp. 411-414.

23. Sukhorukov, V.I. Application of Massage in Hypnosis for the Treatment of Thoracic Radiculitis. Theses of Reports at the VI Congress of Neurologists and Psychiatrists of the Ukrainian SSR. Kharkov, 1978. pp. 227-228.

24. Waterfield, R. Hypnosis. Hidden Depths: The story of Hypnosis. AST, 2006. 477 p.

25. Waterfield, R. Self-Hypnosis. Hypnosis. Hidden Depths: The story of Hypnosis. AST, 2006. pp. 442-444.

26. Fedunina, N.Yu. Franco-Russian Contacts in the Field of Hypnotism and Suggestion in the Late 19th and Early 20th Centuries. Methodology and History of Psychology. 2011. Vol. 6. Iss. 2. pp. 74-91.

27. Hayvens, R.A. The Wisdom of Milton Erickson: Textbook in the Specialty of Psychotherapy. Translated by A.S. Rigin; Edited by M.R. Ginzburg. Moscow: Klass, 1999.

28. Hailey, J. About Milton H. Erickson. Translated by V.M. Sarina, Yu.A. Khudokon. Moscow: Nezavisimaya firma Klass, 1998.

29. Hoke, R.R. Behavior in Hypnosis. Forty Studies that Changed Psychology. 5th International Edition. St. Petersburg: PRIME-EVROZNAK; Moscow: OLMA-Press, 2003. Ch. 2: Perception and Consciousness. pp. 82-91. (Psychology Best Project).

30. Sharko, Jean-Martin. Brockhaus and Efron Encyclopedic Dictionary: in 86 volumes. St. Petersburg, 1890-1907.

31. Shertok, L. Hypnosis. Translated from French. Moscow: Meditsina, 1992. 224 p.

32. Shertok, L. Hypnosis: Theory, Practice, and Technique. 1961.

33. Erickson, M. My Voice Will Stay with You: Milton Erickson's Teaching Stories. Translated from English by L. Hoffmann; edited and commented by S. Rozena. St. Petersburg: Peterburg-XXI vek, 1995.

34. Erickson, M. The Strategy of Psychotherapy: Selected Works. Authorized translation from English and edited by L.M. Shlionsky. St. Petersburg: Rech, 2002.

35. Erickson, M. Man from February: Hypnotherapy and Development of Self-Awareness. Translated from English by E.L. Dlugach. Moscow: Nezavisimaya firma Klass, 1995.

36. Erickson, M., Rossi, E., Rossi, S. Hypnotic Realities: Induction of Clinical Hypnosis and Forms of Indirect Suggestion. Translated from English by M.A. Yakushina; edited by M.R. Ginzburg. Moscow: Klass, 2000.

37. Yapko, M. Hypnosis for the Psychotherapy of Depression. Moscow: Marketing, 2002. 247 p.

38. Bernheim, H. New Studies in Hypnotism. Translated from French by Sandor R.S. International University's Press, New York, 1980.

39. Bernheim, H. Suggestive Therapeutics: A Treatise on the Nature and Uses of Hypnotism. Translated from French by C.A. Herter. G.P. Putnam's Sons, New York, 1889.

40. Bowers, K.S. "Hypnosis and Healing." Australian Journal of Clinical & Experimental Hypnosis, Vol. 7, No. 3, November 1979, pp. 261-277.

41. Cedercreutz, C. "Hypnosis in Surgery." International Journal of Clinical and Experimental Hypnosis, Vol. 9, No. 3, 1961, pp. 93-95.

42. Collyer, R.H., M.D. Mysteries of the Vital Element in Connection with Dreams, Somnambulism, Trance, Anesthesia, Nervous Congestion, and Creative Function. Modern Spiritualism Explained. 2nd ed. London: Savill, Edwards and Co, Printers, 1871.

43. Edgette, J.H., Edgette, J.S. Handbook of Hypnotic Phenomena in Psychotherapy. Brunner/Mazel, 1995. 318 p.

44. Fredericks, L.E., Evans, F.J. The Use of Hypnosis in Surgery and Anesthesiology: Psychological Preparation of the Surgical Patient.

Springfield, IL: Charles C Thomas, 2001.

45. Janet, P. L'Automatisme psychologique. 1889.

46. Jones, L., Othman, M., Dowswell, T., Alfirevic, Z., Gates, S., Newburn, M., Jordan, S., Lavender, T., Neilson, J.P. "Pain Management for Women in Labour: An Overview of Systematic Reviews." The Cochrane Library, Vol. 3, 2012.

47. Lockert, O. Hypnose: Évolution Humaine, Qualité de Vie, Santé. Paris: IFHE, 2013. 715 p.

48. Van Der Hart, O., Brown, P., Van Der Kolk, B.A. "Pierre Janet's Treatment of Post-traumatic Stress." Journal of Traumatic Stress, Vol. 2, No. 4, 1989.

49. Powell, R., Scott, N.W., Manyande, A., Bruce, J., Vögele, C., Byrne-Davis, L.M.T., Unsworth, M., Osmer, C., Johnston, M. "Psychological Preparation and Postoperative Outcomes for Adults Undergoing Surgery under General Anesthesia." Cochrane Database of Systematic Reviews, 2016.

50. Sampimon, R.L.H., Woodruff, M.F.A. "Some Observations Concerning the Use of Hypnosis as a Substitute for Anesthesia." The Medical Journal of Australia, 23 March 1946, pp. 393-395.

51. Wobst, A.H.K. "Hypnosis and Surgery: Past, Present, and Future." Anesthesia & Analgesia, Vol. 104, No. 5, May 2007, pp. 1199-1208.

52. Wolfart, K.C., Mesmer, F.A. Mesmerismus: Oder, System der Wechselwirkungen, Theorie und Anwendung des thierischen Magnetismus als die allgemeine Heilkunde zur Erhaltung des Menschen (in German, facsimile of the 1811 edition). Cambridge University Press, 2011. (Foreword.)

53. Yeates, L.B. "James Braid: Surgeon, Gentleman Scientist, and Hypnotist." Ph.D. Dissertation, School of History and Philosophy of Science, Faculty of Arts & Social Sciences, University of New South Wales, January 2013.

54. Abdullaev, G. I., et al. (1968). Experience of hypnotherapy in a thoracic surgery clinic. Surgery, 12, 21–24.

55. Abramova, G. I. (1968). On the issue of hypno-psycho-therapeutic effects during chronic intoxication in the period of abstinence. Ques-

tions of Psychotherapy in General Medicine and Psychoneurology: Conference Abstracts and Theses, 236-238.

56. Abramovich, G. B. (1951). On the projection of hallucinatory images in V. M. Bekhterev's mental images. Journal of Neurology and Psychiatry, 5, 58-60.

57. Arkhangelsky, G. V. (1965). The history of neurology from its origins to the 20th century. Moscow: Meditsina, 430 p.

58. Bekkio, J., & Rossi, E. (2003). Hypnosis of the 21st century. Moscow: Klass, 256 p.

59. Bekhterev, V. M. (1925). Memories of J.-M. Charcot. Modern Psychoneurology, 8, 14-17.

60. Boldyrev, A. I. (n.d.). Characteristics of hypnotic state in certain neuro-psychic disorders of infectious origin. Proceedings of the Fourth All-Union Congress of Neuropsychiatrists, 381-383.

61. Boltun, S. A. (2009). Modern self-hypnosis. Center for HYPNOLOG website.

62. Bul, P. I. (1958). Hypnosis and suggestion in the clinic of internal diseases. Leningrad: Medgiz.

63. Bul, P. I. (1975). Hypnosis and suggestion. Leningrad: Meditsina.

64. Bul, P. I. (1966). The magic of words. Techniques of the youth, 4, 23-24.

65. Bul, P. I. (1955). Techniques of medical hypnosis. Moscow: Meditsina, 68 p.

66. Burno, M. E. (1978). On one form of hypnotic somnambulism. Psychotherapy of alcoholism and neuroses, 11-16.

67. Burno, M. E., & Karavirt, K. A. (1960). On forms of hypnotic somnambulism according to clinical grounds. Journal of Neurology and Psychiatry, 8, 1187-1191.

68. Bandler, R., & Grinder, J. (2005). Patterns of hypnotic techniques of Milton Erickson. (S. Ryseva, Trans.). St. Petersburg; Moscow: Prime-Evroznak; OLMA-Press, 512 p.

69. Vaisblat, A. S. (1955). Pain syndrome relief in iridocyclitis and glaucoma by hypnotic suggestion. Proceedings of the Academy of Sciences of the Tajik SSR, 40, 169-173.

70. Vaisblat, A. S. (1955). Experience of hypnotic influence on color perception. Proceedings of the Academy of Sciences of the Tajik SSR, 40, 159-163.

71. Varshavsky, K. M. (1973). Hypnosuggestive therapy. Leningrad, 55 p.

72. Vish, I. M. (n.d.). Influence of verbal suggestion on vascular reactions. Questions of Neurotic and Mental Disorders and the Organization of Psychoneurological Assistance: Collection of Works of the Out-of-Town Scientific Session of the State Research Institute of Psychiatry and the Interdistrict Conference in Tambov, 259-272.

73. Vish, I. M. (1966). Suggestion and autogenic training as means of restoring nervous activity. Questions of Psychotherapy: Abstracts of Reports at the All-Union Conference on Psychotherapy, 37-38.

74. Vish, I. M. (1971). Suggestion and self-suggestion of states for restoring nervous activity. Proceedings of the II All-Union Congress of the Society of Psychologists of the USSR, 849.

75. Vish I. M. Hypnosis and suggestion in alcoholism.

76. Tambov, 1958.

77. Vish I. M. On the application of hypnotic suggestion in allergic urticaria. Issues of neurosurgery, neuropathology, and psychiatry: Collection of articles. Saratov, 1975. pp. 257-258.

78. Vish I. M. Experience of studying vegetative reflexes in patients with reactive states in connection with their psychotherapy treatment. Neuroses: Proceedings of the conference dedicated to the problems of neuroses, Leningrad, June 6-9, 1955. Petrozavodsk, 1956. pp. 84-90.

79. Vish I. M. Psychotherapy in hypnosis for sleep disorders in elderly and senile patients. Moscow, 1975. Vol. 3. pp. 461-462.

80. Vish I. M. Psychotherapy in the clinic of presenile psychoses. Issues of neuropsychiatric disorders and the organization of psychoneurological assistance: Collection of works of the out-of-town scientific session of the State Research Institute of Psychiatry and the interdistrict conference in Tambov, July 19-22, 1957. Tambov: NII of Psychiatry, Ministry of Health of the RSFSR, 1954. Vol. 20. pp. 247-258.

81. Vish I. M. Psychotherapy in the complex treatment of schizophrenia.

Psychotherapy of alcoholism and neuroses. Moscow, 1978. pp. 18-20.

82. Vish I. M. Psychotherapy in certain nervous, mental, and somatic disorders: Abstract for the degree of Doctor of Medical Sciences. Tambov, 1959.

83. Vish I. M. Psychotherapy in organic diseases of the nervous system. Issues of neuropsychiatric disorders and the organization of psychoneurological assistance. Tambov: NII of Psychiatry, Ministry of Health of the RSFSR, 1954. Vol. 20. pp. 234-246.

84. Vish I. M. The role of psychotherapy in the decompensation of patients with schizophrenia. Neuropathology and Psychiatry. Kiev: Zdorov'ya, 1978. Iss. 7. pp. 84-88.

85. Vish I. M., Melkumova M. A. On the application of psychotherapy in the comprehensive treatment of nonspecific ulcerative colitis: Theses of reports of the conference on psychotherapy (Moscow, March 1973). Moscow, 1973. pp. 158-160.

86. Vish I. M., Romanyuk V. K., Gorkovaya A. A. The place of psychotherapy in the rehabilitation of mentally ill patients: Theses of the International Symposium on Psychotherapy (October 18-19, 1979). Moscow, 1979. pp. 68-70.

87. Vish I. M. Hypnotherapy of sleep disorders in combat participants. Journal of Neurology and Psychiatry. 1946. No. 6. pp. 69.

88. Voropaeva M. S. Foreign studies of hypnosis: theories and experiments. Bulletin of Moscow University. Series 14. Psychology. 2009. No. 3. pp. 78-87.

89. Gartshteyn N. G. Some modifications of hypnosis treatment. Issues of psychotherapy in general medicine and psychoneurology (Theses and abstracts of the conference, December 23-27, 1968). Kharkov, 1968. pp. 80-81.

90. Gasul Ya. R. Autogenic training in combination with hypnotherapy and motivated self-suggestion in the treatment of patients with psychogenic diseases. Psychotherapy in resort medicine. Kiev, 1966. pp. 229-232.

91. Gasul Ya. R. Introduction of therapeutic information in the waking

state in combination with informational effects in hypnoid phases. pp. 248-249.

92. Gelmet K., Jennifer B. Hypnotherapy: A Practical Guide. Translated by R. Balyberdina, M. Gnevko, G. Shishko. Moscow: EKSMO-Press; St. Petersburg: Sova, 2002. 352 p.

93. Gilligan S. Therapeutic Trances: The Cooperation Principle in Ericksonian Hypnotherapy. Translated from English. Moscow: Klass, 1997. 416 p.

94. Godean, J. New Hypnosis: Glossary, Principles, and Method: Introduction to Ericksonian Hypnotherapy. (Translated from French by S. K. Chernetskogo). Moscow: Institute of Psychotherapy Publishing, 2003. 298 pages.

95. Goldberg, B. Hypnosis of the Third Millennium. (Translated from English by M. Sh. Khasanov). St. Petersburg: Future of the Earth, 2004. 208 pages.

96. Goltzman, E. Pierre Janet, Sigmund Freud, and Multiple Personalities. Science and Life. 2002. No. 6. pp. 77–82.

97. Grishin, A. Getting Acquainted with the Subconscious. Practice of Self-Hypnosis. Path to Self. No. 19, 1991.

98. Zharikov, N. M., Tyulpin, Yu. G. Psychiatry: Textbook. Moscow: Medicine, 2002. 544 pages.

99. Zharikov, N. M., Ursova, L. G., Khritinin, D. F. Psychiatry: Textbook. Moscow: Medicine, 1989. 496 pages. (Textbook for medical institute students. Sanitary and hygienic faculty.)

100. Zamotaev, I. P., Sultanova, A., Vorobyeva, Z. V. Influence of Hypnosuggestive Therapy in Bronchial Asthma. Soviet Medicine. 1983. No. 2. pp. 7–10.

101. Zakharov, A. I. Clinical-Experimental Study of Suggestion in Children and Adolescents. Problems of Psychological Influence. Collection of Scientific Works. Ivanovo, 1978, pp. 137–148.

102. Zdravomyslov, V. I. Hypnosis and Suggestion in Obstetrics. Moscow, 1938.

103. Zdravomyslov, V. I. Labor Analgesia by Suggestion. Moscow, 1956.

104. Iofee, A. Notes of a Hypnotist Doctor. Novosibirsk, 1972.

105. Isomiddinov, A. I. Hypnosis and Medicine. Dushanbe, 1975.

106. Kamenetsky, S. L., Slutsky, A. S. Implementation of Hypnotic Therapeutic Suggestion in the Clinic of Neuroses. Third All-Russian Congress of Neuropathologists and Psychiatrists, Kazan, June 27-30, 1979 (Thesis Reports). Volume II. Neuroses and Psychology. Moscow, 1979, pp. 258-268.

107. Kamenetsky, S. L. On the Hypnotizability of Patients with Hysterical Neurosis. Current Issues in the Organization of Psychiatric Care, Treatment, and Social Rehabilitation of Mentally Ill Patients (Thesis of the Scientific-Practical Conference of Psychoneurologists in Moscow Institutions). Moscow, 1978. pp. 297-298.

108. Kannabikh, Y. V. History of Psychiatry. Moscow: AST, Minsk: Harvest, 2002. 560 pages.

109. Katkov, E. S. Kinesthetic Technique of Hypnosuggestion. Questions of Psychotherapy (Abstracts of Reports at the All-Union Conference on Psychotherapy, June 27-30, 1966). Moscow, 1966. pp. 43–44.

110. Katkov, E. S. Technique of Constructing a Hypnosuggestive Session. Psychotherapy in Resortology. Kiev, 1966. pp. 194–207.

111. Kogan, B. S. Experience of Group Hypnosuggestive Therapy Application in the Clinic of Nervous Diseases. Collection of Scientific Student Works of Kursk Medical Institute. Kursk, 1954. pp. 14–16.

112. Korkina, M. V., Lakosina, N. D., Lichko, A. E., Sergeev, I. I. Psychiatry: Textbook. 3rd edition, revised and expanded. Moscow: MEDpress-inform, 2006. 576 pages.

113. Cue, Emil. School of Self-Control through Conscious (Intentional) Self-Suggestion. LKI Publishing House, 2007; 2015.

114. Marenina, A. I. Changes in Brain Potentials during Different Phases of Hypnosis in Humans. Proceedings of the I. P. Pavlov Institute of Physiology. Moscow, Leningrad, 1956. Vol. 5. pp. 299-306.

115. Marenina, A. I. Changes in Brain Potentials under the Influence of Stimuli During Different Stages of Hypnosis. Proceedings of the Institute of Physiology of the USSR Academy of Sciences. Moscow,

1957. Vol. 6. pp. 330–334.

116. Marenina, A. I. Study of the Somnambulistic Phase of Hypnosis by the EEG Method. Proceedings of the I. P. Pavlov Institute of Physiology. Moscow, Leningrad, 1952. Vol. 1. pp. 333–338.

117. Melnikov, I. Gypsy Hypnosis: The Technology of Deception. LitRes, 2000. 63 pages.

118. Munipov, V. M. V. M. Bekhterev, the Founder of Comprehensive Study of Human Beings. Questions of Psychology. 2007. No. 5. pp. 110.

119. Munipov, V. M. V. M. Bekhterev and His Place in the History of Russian Pedagogy and Educational Psychology: Abstract. 1968. 25 pages.

120. Narbutovich, I. O. Possibility of Inducing Hypnotic Sleep and Dehypnotization in Humans Using Indifferent Stimuli by the Method of Conditioned Reflexes. Archive of Biological Sciences. Moscow, 1934. pp. 1–14.

121. Narbutovich, I. O. Study of Rapport Selectivity in Hypnosis. Questions of Psychotherapy. Moscow, 1958. pp. 76-77.

About the Author

Dr. Artem Kudelia is a psychologist, therapist, and coach with extensive expertise in integrative approaches. He employs a wide range of therapeutic methods, including cognitive, behavioral, hypnotic, psychodynamic, transpersonal, systemic and other approaches.

By incorporating different perspectives and techniques, Artem aims to provide a holistic and personalized therapeutic experience. He understands that coaching, unlike therapy, focuses on supporting individuals without severe mental health issues in realizing their full potential and achieving success in various areas of life. His work is influenced by integral models of psychology, which encompass all quadrants and levels of human experience. Artem embraces a multidimensional view of human nature, considering biological, psychological, social, and spiritual aspects in his therapeutic interventions.

Subscribe to my newsletter:

✉   https://booksprout.co/reviewer/team/37195/psychology-by-artem-kudelia-phd

Also by Artem Kudelia PhD

This educational publication explores the fundamental approaches in psychotherapy. The **Psychology & Psychotherapy Theories & Practices Series** extensively covers the history of these approaches along with their theoretical and practical aspects. It can serve as a textbook for courses such as "Foundations of General Psychology", "Fundamentals of Psychological Counseling", and "Fundamentals of Psychotherapy". It is intended for psychologists, medical professionals, psychology students, and readers with a wide range of interests.

Psychotherapy
Introduction to Healing Vectors

Do you want to understand the variety of methods of psychotherapy and choose the one that is best for you?

In the vast world of psycho-technologies, there are numerous methods of psychotherapy that encompass a wide range of personality theories and concepts.

Drawing upon an integral framework, the book maps out the complex landscape of psychotherapy, encompassing vectors such as psychoanalytic, hypnotic, provocative, humanistic, behavioral, existential, transpersonal, cognitive, somatic, psychodramatic and psychedelic therapies, among many others.

This book will provide you with valuable knowledge that will allow you to choose the most suitable therapeutic path for specific circumstances and personality types.

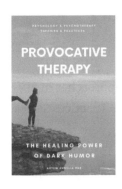

Provocative Therapy
The Healing Power of Dark Humor

Who said that psychotherapy can't be hilariously funny?

Explore innovative ideas about the power of humor in psychotherapy and coaching.

Uncover the archetypal foundation of Provocative Therapy inspired by the myths of the Trickster and the Holy Fool.

Delve into the transformational potential of **Group Provocative Psychotherapy** and the important rules that define successful group dynamics.

Explore the effectiveness of **Provocative Coaching** and its focus points.

Dive into the fascinating world of **Provocative Drama** and its role in therapeutic interventions.

Explore the **pathopsychological profiles**, including **hysteroid, paranoid, psychopathic, obsessive-compulsive, schizoid, epileptoid, schizophrenic,** and **manic-depressive** profiles.

Humanistic Therapy
From Crisis to Self-Actualization

Do you want to explore a world where people are seen as unique holistic systems with infinite potential waiting to be discovered?

Immerse yourself in the theories and practices of humanistic therapy and explore the **transformative path from crisis to self-actualization**.

Unlike psychoanalysis, which focuses on internal complexes and personal traumas, humanistic therapy emphasizes the **study and development of positive personality qualities**.

Humanistic philosophy has also influenced fields such as **education**, promoting **empathy** and **support** as the foundation of learning.

This holistic approach recognizes the **interconnectedness of mind, body, and spirit** and seeks to stimulate personal **growth** and **well-being**.

Take the first step towards self-awareness, personal growth, and a more fulfilling existence.

Somatic Therapy
The Wisdom of the Body

Would you like to establish a connection with your body and access the source of wisdom?

Unleash the transformative power of **somatic therapy** and embark on a journey of **self-discovery** and **healing**.

Explore the profound connection between the **mind and body**.

Discover the **seven levels of muscular armor** and their connection to specific emotions such as sadness, anger, and fear.

By exploring different body segments, you will unlock **powerful techniques** for releasing pent-up emotions and promoting harmony throughout the organism. From **eye movements** and **jaw exercises** to **deep breathing** and **body movements**, this book offers **practical methods** for **accessing the wisdom of the body** and **restoring emotional balance**.

Acquire unique knowledge about **healing after birth trauma and psychosomatic medicine.**

Existential Therapy
Journey to Authenticity

Do you want to know who you really are? What is your personal meaning of existence?

Embark on a **transformative journey** to uncover your **true essence** and embrace the **principles** of existential therapy.

Explore the rich philosophical roots of **existential psychotherapy** and find your path to **personal authenticity**.

Explore key themes such as **freedom, responsibility, meaning**, and **choice**, and learn to courageously and authentically navigate the complexities of existence.

This book provides **practical ideas and techniques** for **applying the principles of existential therapy** to your own life.

Gain a deep **understanding** of your **values, beliefs**, and **desires**, and learn to **embrace uncertainty** and **transform** life's **challenges** into **opportunities** for **growth** and **self-discovery**.

Drama Therapy
Potential of Psychodrama and Family Constellations

Explore the unique world of drama therapeutic approach!

Therapeutic model of intervention that encompasses **12 powerful speech patterns** capable of significantly **influencing conscious and unconscious processes**.

Through **psychodramatic techniques** and **family constellations**, you will **gain practical knowledge** to enhance your therapeutic practice.

Addressing a wide spectrum of **psychopathological profiles**, including **hysteria**, **paranoia**, and **obsessive-compulsive disorders**, this book equips you with effective dramatherapeutic activities and psychodynamic exercises.

It serves as a **comprehensive guide** to **crisis intervention**, **counseling theory**, and **strategies for addiction rehabilitation**.

Gain an understanding of the right hemisphere and the **neuroscience** underlying drama therapy, and learn to **navigate complex emotional situations** with **understanding** and **acceptance**.

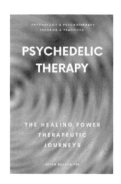

Psychedelic Therapy
The Healing Power Therapeutic Journeys

Embark on a transformative journey into the world of psychedelic therapy!

Explore the fascinating **history** of **psychedelic substances** and potential benefits of working with consciousness-altering substances in clinical practice.

Learn comprehensive information on various **psychedelic therapies**, including **ketamine therapy**, **psilocybin**-assisted psychotherapy, **MDMA**-assisted psychotherapy, and **ibogaine** psychotherapy.

Gain knowledge about **mental health** in the **perinatal period**, the **role of hypnosis**, and the transformative power of **holotropic breathwork**.

Understand the profound impact of **psychedelic medicine** and the potential of **psilocybin microdosing**.

Explore the therapeutic applications of **ketamine** in the **treatment of depression** and **psychosynthesis in coaching**.

311

Beyond Psychiatry
Exploring Anti-Psychiatry Method

Challenge traditional psychiatry and psychotherapy!

This book presents an **alternative to conventional** ideas of normalcy and offers a **fresh perspective on psychological disorders**, inviting readers to question existing paradigms.

Delve deeper into **psychopathological profiles** and **anti-psychiatric** forms of psychotherapy, examining various profiles including **hysteria, paranoia, psychopathy**, and more.

Gain an understanding of the intersection of psychotherapy and existential philosophy, **challenging the myth of mental illness** within families.

Explore the **treatment of psychosis, trauma**, and **emotional disorders from a holistic perspective**.

Integrative Therapy

Personal Transformation Guide

Discover the Power of Integrative Therapy and Embark on a Journey of Personal Transformation!

This book challenges traditional divisions in **therapeutic approaches** and explores the potential of **combining multiple vectors** to create a **comprehensive and integrated therapeutic system.**

Immerse yourself in the world of neuro-linguistic programming (NLP), **cognitive styles, neurological levels,** and **integral philosophy,** among other concepts.

Explore practical methodologies such as shifting negative thinking, **creating rapport,** and using linguistic patterns to facilitate positive change.

Unlock the transformative **power of anchors, changing personal history** and submodalities.

Gain an understanding of maps of the world and the **metamodel** for **effective communication.**

Psychotherapy Fundamentals

Complete Guide

Do you want to understand the variety of methods of psychotherapy and choose the one that is best for you?

In the book, you will be able to delve deeper into the vast world of psycho-technologies and discover dozens of different schools of psychotherapy.

This comprehensive guide offering a unique exploration of various psychotherapy vectors that span the spectrum of personality theories and physiological concepts.

Gain a profound understanding of provocative therapy, humanistic therapy, somatic therapy, existential therapy, drama therapy, psychedelic and post-psychedelic therapy, anti-psychiatric therapy, and integrative therapy. Each chapter provides insights into the key themes and approaches of these psychotherapy vectors, expanding the possibilities for both practicing specialists and enthusiasts to enrich their therapeutic toolkit.

Seize this opportunity to deepen your understanding of psychotherapy, expand the horizons of your therapeutic work, and embark on a path of personal and professional growth.

AUTISM

Family System

Autism Family System
Transformation Therapy Structure

How Do We Understand the <u>Hidden Causes</u> of <u>Autism</u> and <u>Possible Paths to Healing?</u>

Based on years of psychotherapeutic practice, the author presents a **unique perspective on Autism Spectrum Disorders** in this groundbreaking book.

Delve into the history and evolving **scientific** views on Autism, including Kanner and Asperger syndromes.

Gain valuable insights into the **psychological profile** of individuals with autism and learn how to **see the world through their eyes** by modeling their subjective experiences.

Discover the power of Integral Theory Quadrants and how they can form the foundation for effective **therapeutic approaches** for individuals on the autism spectrum.

Explore the **holistic** pathopsychological profiling of ASD, unraveling the fascinating world of savant syndrome.

Deepen your understanding of the **psychodynamics** of savant individuals with autism through **real-life clinical and practical examples**.

Unlock **alternative ways to communicate** and connect with individuals with autism, opening up new possibilities for interaction.

Investigate the interplay between **autism and evolutionary theories**, uncovering the evolutionary significance of autism and its relation to the unique strengths and challenges faced by individuals on the spectrum.

This comprehensive book goes further by offering an extensive **psychotherapeutic perspective**, focusing on the transformative power of **family therapy** (constellations therapy) and the **effective techniques** of Ericksonian therapy.

Authored by leading experts in the field, this invaluable resource provides reliable guidance for parents, psychologists, and therapists navigating the complexities of autism spectrum disorder.

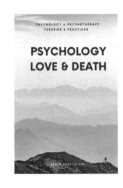

PSYCHOLOGY LOVE & DEATH

Psychology of Love & Death
Therapeutic Path to Fundamental Balance in Life and Relationships

How to Achieve Fundamental Balance in Life and Relationships?

Explore dualistic nature of human consciousness, along with the profound impact of seeking balance between fundamental continuums of **love and death, instinct and spirituality, masculinity and femininity** in shaping our experiences and relationships.

Explore the psychopathological profiles and manifestations of love and death, including profiles such as hysteria, paranoia, psychopathy, and others.

Uncover different types of love, from **eros** to **agape**, and study the **three-component Theory of Love**.

Familiarize yourself with **real-life psychotherapy cases** that illustrate the complexities of love, death, and therapy and gain **valuable insights** into the human experience and its challenges.

Breathwork Therapy Seminar
Holotropic Journey to Unconscious Mind Secrets

Tap Into the Wisdom of Transpersonal Psychology!

This book is the transcript of a seminar that addresses the profound questions of **subconsciousness**, offering a unique perspective on personal growth and healing.

Gain profound insights into the workings of your mind and explore the mysteries of human consciousness.

Access practical exercises and techniques to facilitate personal growth, healing, and self-awareness.

Written for seekers of self-awareness, psychology enthusiasts, and anyone curious about the depths of the human mind.

Explore the integration of spirituality and psychology, uncovering your inner potential.

Author Page
I would greatly appreciate it if you could take a moment to write a **review** and give a **5-star rating**.

Your feedback will not only support my work but also help others find happiness.

Thank you in advance for your kind assistance!

Artem

Made in United States
Troutdale, OR
12/23/2023

16391666R00186